Anchor
of Faith

Anchor of Faith

THE ENDURING SPIRIT OF THE
BLACK MEN'S GATHERING

Written and compiled by
Frederick Landry and Richard Thomas

BAHÁ'Í
PUBLISHING

WILMETTE, ILLINOIS

Bahá'í Publishing, Wilmette, Illinois
401 Greenleaf Ave, Wilmette, Illinois 60091
Copyright © 2022 by the National Spiritual Assembly of the Bahá'ís
   of the United States
All rights reserved. Published 2022
Printed in the United States of America ∞
25   24   23   22   1   2   3   4

Library of Congress Cataloging-in-Publication Data

Names: Landry, Frederick, author. | Thomas, Richard, 1939–author.
Title: Anchor of faith : the enduring spirit of the Black Men's Gathering / written and compiled by Frederick Landry and Richard Thomas.
Description: Wilmette, IL : Bahá'í Publishing, [2022] | Includes bibliographical references.
Identifiers: LCCN 2021051754 (print) | LCCN 2021051755 (ebook) | ISBN 9781618512093 (paperback) | ISBN 9781618512109 (epub)
Subjects: LCSH: African American Bahais. | African American men—Religion. | Bahai Black Men's Gathering. | Bahai Faith—United States—History—20th century.
Classification: LCC BP388.A35 L36 2022 (print) | LCC BP388.A35 (ebook) | DDC 297.9/30811—dc23/eng/20211213
LC record available at https://lccn.loc.gov/2021051754
LC ebook record available at https://lccn.loc.gov/2021051755

Cover design by Carlos Esparza
Book design by Patrick Falso

Dedicated to the loving memory
of the participants and supporters of the
Black Men's Gathering
who have passed on from this world.

CONTENTS

CONTENTS

ACKNOWLEDGMENTS

A debt of gratitude is owed to the participants of the Black Men's Gathering who, over the years, were instrumental forces of change and transformation in their own lives, in the lives of their families, and in their communities. In addition, a great deal of thanks is owed to those brothers, their family members, and the friends who assisted in the creation of this book by recounting their own transformational moments from the Gathering. Having access to these memories provided precious and reflective insights into the participants' unique spiritual experiences, without which this book would not have been possible. Especially helpful and illuminating were the heartfelt testimonies from wives, daughters, and mothers who witnessed the transformative influence of the Black Men's Gathering on their husbands, fathers, and sons.

ABOUT THE COVER

The cover image of *Anchor of Faith* was illustrated by Jihmye Collins (1939–2011). Titled *Men of the Gathering,* this illustration was contributed from the collection of Jihmye's wife, Susan Collins.

Jihmye was well known as an elder of the Black Men's Gathering, and his humble artistic contributions became a recurring tradition embraced by participants each year. His work demonstrated the uplifting properties of art at the Gathering, and many of the other participants drew inspiration from his example and added to the beauty of the Gathering with their own creations.

A prolific poet and artist from San Diego, California, Jihmye was honored as a City Heights community hero, and his image is displayed in the public square along with other significant community advocates. His influence lives on through programs of support for underserved youth in the San Diego community, such as the Jihmye Collins Memorial Tutoring Program of the Malcom X Library.

Among many dedications and tributes to Jihmye is a serene, colorful garden created and named in his honor by the San Diego Bahá'í Community. The garden surrounds the San Diego Bahá'í Center, symbolizes the oneness of humanity, and reflects the personal virtues and artistic beauty for which Jihmye will always be remembered.

NOTE ON SOURCES

Different sources were used to document the major events and communications during the history of the Black Men's Gathering between 1987 and 2012. Among them were letters between the institutions of the Bahá'í Faith and the participants of the Black Men's Gathering (BMG). These documents reflected both the love and devotion of the BMG toward various Bahá'í institutions and the constant love and guidance provided by these institutions to the BMG. The correspondence included letters both to and from local, regional, national, and international institutions of the Faith.

The personal narratives contained in this book have been adapted from written statements, journal entries, phone conversations, virtual and in-person interviews, and past correspondence, typically in the form of letters or emails.

Other sources include written testimonies from BMG participants, family members, friends, and observers of various BMG activities and experiences. These accounts were obtained from online survey responses. Because the responses from these are personal in nature, the names and references to individuals have been omitted.

PREFACE

2012 marked the formal conclusion of the Black Men's Gathering. But prior to the formal conclusion, during the previous year the first book on the BMG, *The Story of the Bahá'í Black Men's Gathering,* was published. That book attempted to share the history and personal stories of the Black men who participated in the Gathering during the twenty-five years of its existence. While *The Story of the Bahá'í Black Men's Gathering* covered key historical events during that period, it was far from an exhaustive account of the complex forces and threads that contributed to the spiritual transformation of the individual participants and the Gathering's influence on the culture of local Bahá'í communities. More time would need to pass before a more complete account of the BMG could be written.

The format of this book is different from the 2011 publication. While this book covers major events in the history of the Gathering, it is largely structured around chronological "moments" recounted by participants and those individuals who were spiritually connected with the Gathering. The purpose of this format, which captures the intimate spirit that the BMG offered, is to place the reader in the position, to the fullest extent possible, of a participant in the Gathering. While it is not possible to include every participant's recollection of the Gathering, those that are included attempt to illustrate the variety of treasured moments and personal exchanges that made the Gathering such a transformative experience over its twenty-five-year history.

This book also expands and builds on some of the undeveloped themes of the first book by including more voices of BMG participants and supporters of the Gathering. For example, the post-BMG section of the book is based on responses to survey questions—written several years after the conclusion of the BMG—from BMG participants, their friends, and their relatives. While personal transformation is a major focus of this book, the responses gathered from these surveys produced a rich harvest of information related to the influence of the BMG on the greater community. For example, the responses indicate that BMG-style devotional gatherings, with drumming and singing, have become more prevalent in the Bahá'í community. The answers given to survey questions regarding the impressions of first-time participants of the Gathering, their friends, and relatives also reveal unique insights into the dynamics of race within Bahá'í community life. Finally, other responses show that the Gathering helped increase participants' involvement in their local communities.

FOREWORD

You got a right, I got a right,
We all got a right to the tree of life;
Yes, you got a right, I got a right,
We all got a right to the tree of life.
The very time I thought I was los'
The dungeon shook an' the chain fell off.
You may hinder me here
But you cannot there
'Cause God in his heaven
Goin' to answer prayer.
O Brethren, You got a right, I got a right
We all got a right to the tree of life.

This was one of hundreds, perhaps thousands, of hymns created and sung by people held in bondage in the United States before the Civil War. These "spirituals" gave voice to the feelings of women and men who endured inconceivable humiliation, oppression, and abasement, who had no control over their lives or even their own bodies—yet whose faith sustained them and gave them the courage to endure. In spite of the attempts by their enslavers to rob them of their humanity, these people still knew in their hearts that there was a God who saw them, who loved them, who knew their true value, who understood their trials, and who would in time redeem their sufferings. Many of these songs affirmed the hope of a time to come when all of God's children would live in freedom.

As countless children of Africa intoned these verses amidst their unrelenting, unrewarded toil, the Tree of Life sprang up anew upon the soil of a faraway land, in the Person of Bahá'u'lláh, the Glory of God. Bahá'u'lláh, and the Cause He founded, were the fulfillment of the prophecies in ancient scripture that God's Kingdom would be made manifest on earth. At long last, humanity had now entered an era that would witness the establishment of universal peace and the advent of divine justice.

This book is the story of a small group of African American men, descendants of those slaves and our own contemporaries, whose hearts were enkindled by the vision proclaimed by Bahá'u'lláh of a world free from prejudice in all its forms and suffused with the spirit of divine love—a world in which all would be able to realize their full potential and make their contribution to "an ever-advancing civilization." Together, they gathered every year over the course of a quarter century to understand, and then to realize through active service, the part they were called upon by Bahá'u'lláh to play in what they understood to be the greatest spiritual enterprise in human history.

The first Black Men's Gathering (BMG) was convened in 1987 with twelve participants. Over the course of time, the numbers of participants at national, and later regional and local gatherings, grew into the hundreds. Using artistic forms that drew upon the traditions of their forebears, the gatherings were characterized first and foremost by intense prayer and devotion. In these settings, an atmosphere of loving intimacy, trust, and openness was created in which the participants studied the Bahá'í sacred texts and other guidance with the aim of charting the course of their services to the Cause of God.

The intent of the Black Men's Gatherings was not to create a segregated cadre of Bahá'ís pursuing their own lives in isolation from the rest of the believers. Rather, it arose out of recognition of the need for a space where people could come together who had borne, and continued to bear, the heaviest effects of America's omnipresent racial prejudice—an insidious and pervasive national derangement that even the Bahá'í community itself was struggling to come to grips with.

In these gatherings, the participants could speak frankly of their personal struggles against incessant indignities, find solace in each other's loving sympathy, and together reconnect with their inner nobility and the purpose for which God had created them. Upon remembering who they truly were in God's sight, they could, with renewed determination, enter into the arena of service alongside their follow Bahá'ís.

Perhaps no other statement from the Bahá'í writings was a greater source of strength and inspiration than these words of 'Abdu'l-Bahá: "Bahá'u'lláh once compared the colored people to the black pupil of the eye surrounded by the white. In this black pupil is seen the reflection of that which is before it, and through it the light of the spirit shineth forth."

In these words. an entirely new vision was revealed, at complete odds with the dismissive notions of Black people promoted and enforced in countless ways by the dominant culture in the United States. Bahá'u'lláh Himself had indicated that people of African descent had an essential contribution to make to the spiritual transformation of society. His statement implied that their sufferings had in some way prepared them for a noble and outstanding destiny. It meant that their trials had made them keenly aware of the need for justice, deeply appreciative of the nature of true freedom, and attuned to the special joy that comes from service to One Who also had trodden the path of sacrifice for the betterment of the world:

"The Ancient Beauty hath consented to be bound with chains that mankind may be released from its bondage, and hath accepted to be made a prisoner within this most mighty Stronghold that the whole world may attain unto true liberty. He hath drained to its dregs the cup of sorrow, that all the peoples of the earth may attain unto abiding joy, and be filled with gladness . . . We have accepted to be abased . . . that ye may be exalted, and have suffered manifold afflictions, that ye might prosper and flourish."

The fruits of the faith of these Black men are to be found in the services that unfolded over the years and manifested themselves in numerous teaching activities at the local, national, and international levels. The exploits chronicled here relate how a small but growing group of believers, with firmness of purpose and fidelity to the Covenant, achieved victories that added great luster to the annals of Bahá'í history. Certain characteristics stand out in the ample records of these services, such as an intense focus on prayer and reliance on divine assistance; deep study of the Word of God; a warm and loving relationship with all the institutions of the Faith; and a commitment to translate the teachings into reality in the field of action. Animating their service was a spirit of loving concern on the part of each participant for each of his brothers and a commitment from all to walk and grow together in the path of spiritual transformation.

Especially impressive is the close relationship that the BMG participants enjoyed with the Universal House of Justice,* as the reader will see in the messages that went back and forth in the wake of each annual gathering. In these messages one can see not only the unreserved love of these friends for the Supreme Institution of the Bahá'í world, but also the manner in which this love was fully recip-

---

* The Universal House of Justice is the supreme administrative body of the Bahá'í Faith. It is sometimes referred to as the House of Justice or Supreme Body.

rocated. Indeed, the unceasing streams of loving encouragement poured out to these friends by the House of Justice serve as a model worthy of emulation by all Bahá'í institutions. Take, for example, the following statement in 1996, where the House of Justice expressed its appreciation for the BMG and the services of its members to the Cause of God:

> The universal spirit conveyed from a group of individuals who are daily pressured by the myopic cultural vision of those among whom they live and work, the certitude of the participants' commitment to the Lord of Mankind, the clarity of their understanding of the essentials of the Four Year Plan in relation to the individual, the institutions and the community, the vibrancy of their fellowship—all evoke in us feelings of admiration and gratitude.
>
> This is an exemplary achievement at a time when so many other groups in the United States are gripped in the self-imposed strictures of cultural divisiveness. Would to God that news of this accomplishment be noised abroad as a lesson and inspiration to others.

For their part, the brothers of the BMG—seeing in this service the greatest means possible by which a new society, founded upon divine justice, would ultimately be established—became increasingly devoted and capable teachers of the Faith. They expressed their sentiments in these words: "The Plan of God is our answer no matter the question!" This clarity of vision, this ardent love, this devotion to the teaching work, had its effect upon countless souls with whom they came in contact, whether in the United States, the Americas, Africa, or elsewhere.

I cannot help but add my own expression of admiration for these men, with whom I frequently interacted over the course of time.

The most memorable occasion of all was when a BMG group met with the National Spiritual Assembly of the United States on the eve of their departure for an international teaching trip. To this day, this meeting remains one of my brightest memories of service on this institution. The Assembly received the friends in the national Ḥaẓíratu'l-Quds, where the discussion and ensuing devotions generated a sense of spiritual power that was unusual even in that rarefied setting. This power must have felt very similar to the experience of the Bahá'ís of another country, who described the teachers who had come to them on behalf of the BMG as "angels in our midst."

Over the course of time, the advancements brought by the series of Plans initiated by the Universal House of Justice yielded new opportunities. By the early years of the twenty-first century, African countries and other lands of the African diaspora had developed their own flourishing communities. The era of international travel-teaching and pioneering* was by then giving way to more localized needs, as the BMG participants themselves were beginning to see. The Universal House of Justice affirmed this view and eventually called upon the friends to focus their services on the fellow Americans among whom they lived. Rather than characterizing this as a diminishment of their work, the House of Justice called on the friends who had benefited from the Gatherings to "raise their sights to new horizons." The great work of transformation was now to be concentrated at home, in countless local communities throughout America. "Let the well-prepared army you have assembled," wrote the House of Justice, "advance from its secure fortress to conquer the hearts of your fellow citizens. What is needed is concerted,

---

* Any [Bahá'í] who arises and leaves his [or her] home to journey to another country for the purpose of teaching the Cause. (Momen, *A Basic Bahá'í Dictionary*, p. 179)

persistent, sacrificial action, cycle after cycle, in cluster after cluster, by an ever-swelling number of consecrated individuals." Thus, in view of the "new possibilities" described by the House of Justice, another important chapter in the lives of these men, and in the history of the Faith, was inaugurated. This story has only just begun and will surely be told in time.

It would be remiss not to mention the person whose vision and initiative were decisive in fostering these achievements. Dr. William (Billy) Roberts, whose services combined masterful encouragement of his brethren and an attitude of constant reference to the guidance of the institutions, was commended by the Universal House of Justice itself, having earned its "satisfaction, admiration and abiding love." His legions of friends and admirers feel the same way, as the reader will discover in these pages. But Billy would often remind the BMG brothers of the statement attributed to 'Abdu'l-Bahá, Who reportedly said to Louis Gregory, "Praise is wonderful so long as you don't inhale it!"

No reader should underestimate the meaning of what is described in this volume. In the ample testimonials contained within these pages, and even more clearly in the deeds of these precious souls, one can discern signs that the prayers of their ancestors for a new way of living are being answered. Beyond this, in the spread of the Bahá'í Faith across the globe and through the means in which it has given voice to peoples of virtually every background and description, we can see a movement possessing true transformative power and the signs of the fulfillment of Christ's prophecy that "the last shall be first," and the meek "shall inherit the earth." At long last, we can see in the emergence of such a community, wherein all of God's children take their rightful place, the promise entailed in these words: "Universal peace will raise its tent in the center of the earth, and the Blessed Tree of Life will grow and spread to such an extent that it will overshadow the East and the West."

In a memorable letter written to Pope Pius XII at the outset of World War II, President Franklin Delano Roosevelt seemed to have intuited the manner in which global justice and unity would finally be established—not by the great and famous, but through the humble faith of those who recognize and pursue God's purpose:

> . . . We remember that the Christmas Star was first seen by shepherds in the hills, long before the leaders knew of the Great Light which had entered the world.
>
> I believe that while statesmen are considering a new order of things, the new order may well be at hand. I believe that it is even now being built, silently but inevitably, in the hearts of masses whose voices are not heard, but whose common faith will write the final history of our time. They know that unless there is belief in some guiding principle and some trust in a divine plan, nations are without light, and peoples perish— They know that the civilization handed down to us by our fathers was built by men and women who knew in their hearts that all were brothers because they were children of God. They believe that by His will enmities can be healed; that in His mercy the weak can find deliverance, and the strong can find grace in helping the weak.
>
> In the grief and terror of the hour, these quiet voices, if they can be heard, may yet tell of the rebuilding of the world . . .

May the reader of this book hear these quiet voices as they embark on a journey, whose end has not yet been written, to rebuild and to bring their light into this world.

Kenneth E. Bowers
Wilmette, Illinois
September, 2021

INTRODUCTION

What was it like for Black men, who were accustomed to being part of a multiracial and multicultural religious community, to suddenly be exposed to and encouraged to participate in the Black Men's Gathering? It should be noted that some saw the Gathering as contradictory to the basic Bahá'í teachings of the oneness of humanity and the watchword of the Bahá'í Faith—unity in diversity.* Many participants, however, realized that the Gathering presented an opportunity to heal deep, emotional wounds—inflicted on them by the greater society—that perhaps their local Bahá'í communities and close friends and family either did not understand or know how best to address.

Of course, not all African American Bahá'í men experienced the same degree of emotional and spiritual despair from their experiences in wider society. Many had learned how to adapt and adjust to the racial hardships, slights, and insults that became part and parcel of their daily lives. In the midst of this toxic racial environment, they had raised families, had taught and served the Faith in a variety of ways, had pioneered to faraway places, had been called upon to serve in various appointed and elected roles within

---

* Shoghi Effendi, *The World Order of Bahá'u'lláh,* p. 42.

1

the Faith, and had succeeded in building a range of fulfilling and notable careers.

Yet despite their ability to adapt, adjust, and prevail, even these hardy souls still bore the wounds of living in a society often bent on breaking the spirits of Black males. Notwithstanding the great love and affection they no doubt received from their families and communities, they needed—often unbeknownst to even themselves—something more. Like many minority groups within any society, these Black men craved a genuine validation of their racial self-worth that could only be given to them in an environment of caring and loving Black men who shared relatable and quite often similar histories and journeys.

How did it feel to be in the company of these supportive men, who were working together to heal wounds and uplift spirits? The first section of this book attempts to convey this unique experience, and the comments that follow explore some of the participants' first impressions of the Black Men's Gathering. These impressions from participants' experiences ranged from the time of the 1987 meeting to the time of the last Gathering in 2012. These recollections also include the reflections and comments of relatives and friends of BMG participants.

As previously mentioned, some individuals approached the Gathering with a certain degree of skepticism. However, once these individuals found themselves either at the Gathering or in the presence of a participant of the Gathering, they were able to witness its power and significance. They were also able to grasp the value and importance of the Gathering through the guidance of local, national, and international Bahá'í institutions, and they were able to see the unity present in the BMG. Armed with this understanding, their concerns regarding the BMG quickly vanished.

From the comments below, one can see the differences in the various experiences of those who had the bounty of being connected in some way to the Gathering. However different their experiences, the love, joy, and commitment to being a better Bahá'í and serving mankind is embedded in each of these reflections. This first comment speaks volumes to what could be described as an unfortunate sense of racial alienation that existed among some Black men who did not feel spiritually or emotionally connected to their Bahá'í community and who had resigned themselves to the status quo: "My first impression was that I had never thought [I would witness] something like this in the Bahá'í Faith, and I was delighted."

A non-participant but supporter of the BMG shared this impression: "Wow, this is amazing, what a blessing for those long-suffering brothers, how dear they must be to the heart of the Blessed Beauty."

The first impressions of most of the participants in the BMG were often deeply influenced by the powerful spiritual and emotional energy that pervaded the Gathering. Even longtime Bahá'ís expressed wonder and awe at how the Gathering, with its intensive prayer sessions, singing, hugging, drumming, fellowship, and study of the guidance, had affected their spirits in ways that they could never have imagined. One of the original twelve BMG members who met in 1987 wrote, "though I had been a Bahá'í for quite a while, my first BMG experience can be summarized as an unprecedented conversion experience."

One must ask why the BMG made such an impression on a longtime Black Bahá'í that he would consider it an "unprecedented conversion experience." What was it about a gathering of Black men that would create such a transformative experience, amounting to a feeling of conversion? Other BMG participants shared similar comments:

"It was a very spiritually moving experience. The camaraderie among the Black men is a feeling that I've never had before. Genuine love and fellowship. I totally miss the BMG experience."

"Earth shattering, transformative, personal recreation."

"I was enthralled."

"Excellent and very uplifting experience."

"Complex and eye- and heart-opening experiences."

"Fantastic. It has been my anchor with the Faith."

There was an urgent need for a spiritually and emotionally secure space to heal wounded souls. The Black Men's Gathering provided that space for participants to address concerns unique to the experiences of Black males in a society that marginalizes them. As the following reflections suggest, some BMG participants also sought spaces within the Gathering to understand and contextualize their racial and cultural identities:

"I found the freedom to worship in an African American male setting, and I realized that I could give unrestricted testimony about my feeling for race within our faith."

"A welcoming and familiar atmosphere in the presence of a diverse group of African American men."

While there was obvious joy among BMG participants for the unprecedented opportunity to gather and bond in fellowship, the first impressions of their wives, daughters, and female friends offer additional and valuable insight into how they perceived the BMG.

An African American Bahá'í woman shared this comment: "It was wonderful. Very powerful and spiritually uplifting. I thought it was a brilliant idea whose time had come; there was an urgent need in the American Bahá'í community to have this."

Several wives of BMG members made similar comments:

"Completely and utterly moved!"

"Something so needed, water in the desert, light in the darkness. . . . support for the wounded, restoring them to grow stronger and more confident and to feel less alone."

"[I]t was an interesting way to support a group that has been marginalized."

"Wonderful excitement! Very much needed in the U.S. Bahá'í community."

"I was very happy that African American men had come together under the banner of the Greatest Name."

After reading reports of the BMG in *The American Bahá'í*, the wife of a future BMG member decided to act on his behalf. She was so enthusiastic and explained, "I urged my husband to participate. I thought it would uplift him."

A daughter of a BMG member wrote:

I thought it was a great idea and very necessary. I feel that the BMG positively influenced my dad and made him a much stronger and devoted Bahá'í. He became very involved with

BMG activities all around the country, and he even traveled to Africa because of it.

They were some of the most moral, upright, and caring men I have ever met. They embraced me when I first became a Bahá'í and made me feel like it was a Faith I could belong to because others with my shared experiences as an African American were in the Faith. They also let me drum with them often, and they even asked me to travel places with them to drum with them—even though I am a woman—because they recognized my talent, and this made me get a real sense of what unity could be.

1987

In 1982, Dr. William (Billy) Roberts was appointed to serve as Auxiliary Board member* for Propagation serving Mississippi, Georgia, North Carolina, and Bermuda. Later, as a member of the Board for Protection, he served the states of Maine, New Hampshire, Vermont, Massachusetts, Connecticut, Rhode Island, New York, New Jersey, Pennsylvania, Washington, D.C., Virginia, West Virginia, and Bermuda. He observed that in the early to mid-1980s, many news media outlets featured headlines referring to Black men as "an endangered species." In newspapers, magazines, and television, there were growing conversations throughout the world about the challenge of being Black and male in the United States. In fact, in Harlem, a Black person was very likely to die before the age of fifteen. In Harlem, which was 96% Black, only 40% of men would live to sixty-five years of age due to cirrhosis, homicide, heart disease, drug dependency, and alcohol.[1] In the entire United States, a Black male was nearly seven times more likely to die of homicide than a white person.[2] In 1987, the chance of being a homicide victim for a

---

* A Bahá'í who is appointed to serve under the direction of the Continental Boards of Counselors to promote and protect the Bahá'í Faith. An Auxiliary Board member is sometimes abbreviated as ABM.

Black young adult male age 18–24 was 96.4 per 100,000, whereas for a white male it was 12.3—indicating that a Black young adult male was eight times more likely to be a victim of a homicide than his white counterpart. In addition, Black females had a 19.6 per 100,000 chance of being such a victim, while white females had a 4.6 per 100,000 chance—indicating that a Black woman was approximately 4 times more likely to be a victim of a homicide than a white woman. A Black male was most likely to be the victim of a homicide committed by another Black man,[3] and there were statistics showing that the percentage of Black men incarcerated in jail or prison was virtually the same[4] as the percentage of Black men to complete a college degree or higher.[5] While these tragic figures from the wider community were troubling, they reflected the reality that many men of African descent faced in the United States. The Bahá'í community, too, had its own challenges that required the transformative power that the Gathering would provide in years to come. In the 1960s and 70s, thousands of people of African descent—both men and women—had entered the Cause in the United States.[6] However, by the mid-80s, many of these individuals were not active participants in Bahá'í community life. Moreover, attendance at many regional and national Bahá'í events included fewer and fewer men of African descent. When they were present, they gave only passing acknowledgment to each other—as if it were taboo for them to be seen with one another for too long. An internal conflict appeared to exist for these Black men. On the one hand, they had accepted Bahá'u'lláh and believed in the oneness of mankind. On the other hand, they felt pressured to not associate with others who were of African descent. Instead, many felt obligated to be the "integrators" of the Bahá'í community and to associate with other races. They felt that if they were seen together with other African American men, others would see them as not being "true believers."

An unspoken rule seemed to exist where no more than one of each of them had to be in a group, and with so few of them, they had to spread themselves around.

Another phenomenon Billy Roberts considered was the societal conditions with which men of African descent had to contend. He saw that regardless of the goodness of their hearts, Black men were constantly being forced to grapple with the image that the media and a historically racist society imposed on them. According to this image, Black men were to be feared, were lawless, unpredictable in their behavior, and most likely to be criminals of some sort. In other words, being a Black male meant always being dehumanized as being the potential suspect of a crime. Additionally, Billy observed that while a number of women of African descent were serving as role models in the Bahá'í community, very few Black men were visibly serving the Faith, either regionally or nationally.

With that, Billy asked himself, what can I do about this situation? How can I help change the lack of and the waning presence of Black men in the Bahá'í community? What does Bahá'u'lláh have in mind for us, and what does Bahá'u'lláh expect from Black men in this community? Essentially, who are we in the eyes of God, and what part are we to play in the development of a new world civilization? As an Auxiliary Board member, Billy thought that perhaps he had the type of regional recognition and responsibility to assist Black men in the Bahá'í community to discover the role Bahá'u'lláh had given them. As he reflected on these questions, Billy realized that the answer surely was not to continue in the same vein and face the same challenges without doing anything.

What Billy did next may have seemed sensible in hindsight, but at the time, it was audacious and courageous, and it was precisely what was needed. He decided that he would call together various men of African descent whom he knew, and he did so completely independently. He made phone calls to these men in September and October to invite them to meet together over a weekend and discuss the many challenges facing Black men in the Bahá'í community.

One of those invited was Jack Guillebeaux of Montgomery, Alabama. Jack's initial feeling was that the idea was interesting and made sense. He immediately embraced the concept and was excited to be involved in this kind of a meeting, particularly in a Bahá'í context. For Jack, it was an exciting and interesting opportunity, and for some reason, he felt that being part of the meeting was the right thing to do. He certainly did not feel any fear or confusion about attending, nor did he have any apprehension about alienating anyone in his community. He actually felt in his heart that this new idea was compatible and in harmony with the ultimate aims of the Faith, and he felt honored to be invited. He looked forward to joining others and participating in the weekend.

Ed Peace of Williamsville, New York, was also one of those invited. Ed first learned about the Bahá'í Faith in 1960 but formally declared years later in 1967, and he knew Billy from his service in the Northeast. When Billy called him to invite him to Greensboro, North Carolina, Ed knew something momentous was about to occur, and he was honored to be of those invited.

Another who received an invitation was Van Gilmer. Van, who had joined the Faith in 1964, was actually from Greensboro—it was his hometown. He had been born in and grown up in Greensboro during the time of segregation, and he had attended segregated schools and had graduated from an historically Black institution of higher learning—North Carolina A&T State University. Fighting for racial equality, Van had begun "sitting in" with a few Greensboro locals in the summer of 1962 and had assisted in continuing the historic demonstrations begun by the "Greensboro Four" in 1960.

Van was part of the formation of the Greensboro Chapter of the Congress of Racial Equality (CORE). Van and his wife, Cookie,

Pictured at the far right of the lunch counter: Van Gilmer

had actually met Billy and his wife Bette Roberts at the Green Acre Bahá'í School in the early 1970s, and at the time, Van was simply excited to see another Black couple in the Faith. Both Van and Cookie had come from a strong Black community and church environment. While he and his wife were in love with the Faith, they also were in that adjustment stage of having left in some ways an indelible piece of their culture and families for a new way of life—and they felt that they were doing it practically alone. Both of them knew single Black Bahá'ís, but to discover a Black couple who mirrored so many of their own experiences? That was truly hard to find among the young people of the Faith during those years. They talked about their encounter with Billy and Bette all the way back from Maine to Maryland. It helped reassure them that they had done the right thing by becoming Bahá'ís and that they were not all alone in the Faith. Notwithstanding the exciting chance encounter with Billy, Van had some concerns about attending a meeting of only Black men. Although he had committed to going, he nevertheless felt the invitation was, at least initially, just a little strange in that it was the first time he had heard of only African Americans getting together, particularly Black males.

Gene Andrews of Peekskill, New York also received an invitation from Billy. Gene had been compelled to investigate the Bahá'í Faith in 1971 in an attempt to "save" his younger brother Kevin, who had become a Bahá'í. Gene was worried that Kevin had joined a cult and felt he needed to intervene by attending firesides.* One fireside led to another, however, and in 1973, Gene declared as a Bahá'í.

Gene's love, knowledge, and commitment to the Faith were quite sincere. In time, he was appointed to the National Teaching Committee, and he was serving in this capacity when he received his phone call and invitation from Billy. Unlike some of the other men who attended the Greensboro meeting because they knew Billy so well or because of his role as an African American ABM, Gene immediately saw the value of attending such a meeting with other African American Bahá'ís, and he would have attended whether the invitation had come from Billy or any other Bahá'í of African descent.

Three longtime friends from Detroit, Michigan—John Mangum, Richard Thomas, and Marvin Hughes—were three more African American who were invited to attend the meeting in Greensboro. Marvin, the oldest of the trio, had become a Bahá'í in the late 1950s, while Richard and John had embraced the Faith in 1962 and 1964, respectively. Richard and John had first met in Greenville, South Carolina, in the summer of 1964 during a Bahá'í summer youth program. At the time of the invitation, John was a police officer in Detroit, Michigan, Richard was a professor at Michigan State University, and Marvin was a social worker. Of the three, John and Richard were the most radical, as they had been involved in Black

---

* A meeting or gathering often held in one's home for the purpose of teaching the Bahá'í Faith. (Momen, *A Basic Bahá'í Dictionary*, p. 84)

Power Movements during the 1960s. They were also part of a larger group of young African Americans invited by the National Spiritual Assembly (NSA) in the late 1960s to discuss racial issues with representatives from that body. While Marvin knew Billy well, John and Richard did not. Because of his radical background both before and after joining the Faith, and because he had gone through a period when he had felt alienated from the Faith, Richard was a bit uneasy about an invitation to an all-Black meeting, particularly since he did not know Billy all that well.

A group from the meeting with the National Spiritual Assembly of the Bahá'ís of the United States, fall 1969. Pictured left to right: Ernestine Mehtzun, Gwen Clayborne, Firuz Kazemzadeh, Richard Thomas, Bruce Settles, unknown, unknown, Robert Henderson, William Smith, Steve Moore, John Mangum, Glenford Mitchell.

Roy Jones of Hemingway, South Carolina joined the Bahá'í Faith in 1970 when he was an undergraduate student at the University of Massachusetts in Amherst. His first contact with the Faith occurred two years earlier during his freshman year. During his years at the University of Massachusetts, Roy met other young African American Bahá'ís who would go on to serve the Bahá'í Faith in various capacities. Roy was serving as the director of the Louis Gregory Bahá'í Institute (LGBI)—a Bahá'í education and retreat center in Hemingway, South Carolina—and as chairman of the Race Unity Committee when he received the call from Billy inviting him to attend the Greensboro meeting. During the call, Roy realized that Billy was exercising caution because of the potential of the meeting to be misunderstood and misread. He surmised that Billy was fully mindful and aware of the possible negative reactions from the people he initially contacted and that Billy hoped that no one would overreact and report his invitation as some kind of covert, subversive activity. He knew that Billy wanted people with whom he was in tune— people he trusted, people who trusted him, and people who realized that there was a conversation that needed to happen regarding the spiritual destiny of African American men in the Bahá'í community.

William Varner became a Bahá'í in 1967. When Billy contacted him to invite him to Greensboro he, like several of the other invitees, was very apprehensive about attending an all-Black meeting. Despite being apprehensive, William respected Billy and was willing to participate due to his high regard for him. William Varner, like many of the participants of the Greensboro meeting, brought certain expectations with him. Mainly, he wanted to get grievances off his mind. Although he had a sincere love for the Faith, he also had had some very disappointing experiences in the Bahá'í community. These grievances, however, would be eclipsed by the spiritual unity he would feel that weekend. The level of respect the men had for one another and the spiritual dynamism that existed once they were in the hotel conference room—praying, singing, laughing, crying, and simply enjoying each other's company and friendship—opened William's heart and soul to Bahá'u'lláh.

The meeting in Greensboro was a transformative experience for the twelve Black men. Each man came to the meeting with unique experiences and accomplishments from his past, and over the course of the weekend, the men became friends on a deep and spiritual level. As a result, they felt a unifying sense of equality among themselves. Over the course of the weekend, some shed tears, but they all felt the spiritual power of the meeting on their lives and its potential influence on the lives of other Black men. It was clear to each that they had taken part in something special, and they vowed to reconvene the following summer at the Louis Gregory Bahá'í Institute.

The twelve Black men who ultimately gathered in Greensboro were Gene Andrews, Van Gilmer, Jack Guillebeaux, Marvin Hughes, Roy Jones, John Mangum, Ed Peace, Billy Roberts, Len Smith, Richard Thomas, William Varner, and James Williams. The following is a reaction by James Williams as he returned home from that significant meeting.

November 1, 1987
[James Williams, en route to Roanoke, Virginia]

While driving home, I realized that I was emotionally stirred to my very core. I was drifting through a cascade of mental and emotional implications, each one new and life-changing. What happened to me this past weekend? One thing is that I found new brothers. But what made me hug them as if I had never hugged Black men before? I wasn't quite sure, but I realized that I would never perceive my people, especially other Black men, the same way ever again. And I pondered what I just learned about them . . . about myself. If we always had this great spiritual capacity for seeing the reflection of God within each other, especially to the extent I had just experienced, then why did such deep perceptions of self-hatred exist among my people?

I wept many times on my journey home. As I drew closer, I thought of my deceased father. He died suddenly (twelve years before) at the young age of fifty. His body was buried less than ten miles from my home. I didn't process why, but I found myself yearning to be with him. So, I drove to his gravesite and stood, respectfully, gazing down at the grassy plot. Having spent many moments of self-reflection this past weekend, I couldn't help but do the same with him. We were never really close. His legacy was that he died a Baptist preacher like his father and grandfather. The church pews overflowed with other preachers at his funeral. Standing there at his grave, I couldn't help but reflect on how he left this world not knowing the transforming spiritual power that descended upon the Black men at our meeting. Ours was a spiritual reality that had been denied men of his generation and that of his forefathers. Thus, it had been impossible for him to even dream that one day Black men—each one like him, inwardly weary from bearing the chains of oppression and social abuse—could be healed from self-hatred through the words and prayers of a new Revelation. For that reason alone, there was no need to forgive him like sons must often do. While standing there, I completely understood why there had been a hole in his heart for as long as I had consciously known him. He died, like his ancestors before him, while still imprisoned by slavery's legacy. I simply had to tell him that I, his eldest son, had been set free.

Following the meeting in Greensboro, Billy wrote to the Universal House of Justice, the International Teaching Center, and also to the National Spiritual Assembly of the Bahá'ís of the United States. In those letters, Billy described the circumstances of the weekend and what had taken place. He also shared the plans of the participants and their decision to continue to meet. He soon received encouragement from the Universal House of Justice and also from the International Teaching Center to continue the meetings.

Billy also wrote to the brothers present at the meeting in Greensboro. The words he wrote were telling of the powerful and spiritual bonds the meeting had helped create, and they foreshadowed the influence that this first meeting and future such gatherings would have on the participants.

November 1, 1987
My Dearly Loved Brothers,

What a time we've shared together! I can't tell you how indebted I am to each one of you for the powerful experience of this past weekend. It was a healing experience. It was an identity-building experience. It was a spiritually renewing experience.

Our time together was indeed epoch-making, demonstrating the new level of maturity which exists in the Bahá'í community.

The bonds which tie us have been strengthened and reinforced and will serve as a springboard, catapulting each of us into the arena of far greater service than we had as yet visualized.

I thank Bahá'u'lláh for the inestimable privilege of His gift.

Enclosed please find the list of names and addresses which I promised to send to you. I encourage you to use it often as we continue to nurture the relationships that have been established.

I will look forward to seeing your impressions as soon as possible since the longer we wait to commit them to paper the greater the possibility of losing them. For those who wish, I would be happy to receive them on tape, in song, as an artistic or pictorial rendition or in any way you see fit.

Please know my love runs deep for each of you and I long to join you again in the near future. My soul basks in your brilliance!

In His service,

Billy Roberts

As the letter mentions, to encourage the ongoing connections formed in Greensboro, Billy sent the participants the contact information of the other brothers. In addition, he made copies of the reflection piece by Gene Andrews below and shared it with the brothers in attendance.

Greensboro Reflections

As I reflect on that special meeting of 12 Black Bahá'í men in Greensboro, there is but one word that can best describe the experience . . . love. Love for Bahá'u'lláh, love for all of mankind, and love for each other. Because of this very special love for each other, we were able to engage in a level of sharing uncommon among men. Sharing that was informative, but more importantly, intimate and nurturing. Sharing conducted on a very spiritual and prayerful plane.

As a result of that meeting, I am sincerely grateful for having had the opportunity to be reminded of the special obligation Black Bahá'í men have to the Black community, especially in serving the needs of Black youth who daily struggle with the cancerous process of denigration and denial. These are youth who very often are faced with role models that represent the ills of society rather than the hope of humanity.

As I prepare to leave the American Bahá'í community for service at the World Center, it saddens me to think that I will not have the benefit of being a part of what lies ahead for a group of men that have so tenderly touched my heart, a group so dedicated to building the World Order of Bahá'u'lláh. Each in his own way inspired by the memory of Louis Gregory and the example of 'Abdu'l-Bahá. The meeting in Greensboro was an historic one, and I am convinced that we will reflect in years to come with wonderment at its fruits.

In closing, I'm reminded of a comment made at the meeting by William Varner: "Listening to every soul in here is helping my soul." Thank you one and all for helping my soul. I will remember you in my prayers at the Holy Shrines.

Warmest Bahá'í love to my brothers,

Gene Andrews

November, 1987

It would not take long before news of the Greensboro meeting made the rounds of the African American Bahá'í men. The returning participants shared their enthusiasm with both their Bahá'í and non-Bahá'í friends. While many Bahá'ís shared their enthusiasm, some were skeptical. For them, an exclusively Bahá'í Black male gathering violated the core teaching of the Bahá'í Faith: the unity of humankind. Many well-intentional Bahá'ís shared their concerned views, but they did not understand or were unwilling to face the fact that Black males both within and outside the American Bahá'í community faced special challenges. If anything was learned during the Greensboro meeting, it was that some, if not most, longtime African American Bahá'ís were experiencing a sense of spiritual, cultural, and racial alienation in their local communities. If they were going to remain active and productive Bahá'ís, they needed emotional, cultural, and spiritual affirmation. Most importantly, they needed a safe place to bare and share their deepest wounds with others who had undergone similar experiences, and this safe place could only be found in the company of other wounded African American Bahá'í men. This was the gift that the BMG could and would offer partici-pants—from the Greensboro meeting to years into the future.

1988

Roy Jones, one of those courageous men that met in Greensboro, was serving as the school administrator of the Louis Gregory Bahá'í Institute, and he was thrilled at the prospect of having a second meeting, which was termed a "retreat" at the time. Therefore, after the scheduling took place, the twelve men who gathered in Greensboro, along with other Black men they thought would want to attend, were invited to LGBI. The following is one of the invitations sent out.

June 12, 1988
Dear Van:

There is clear evidence of enthusiasm, excitement and anticipation for the upcoming retreat planned for Black men. According to most of the responses we have received thus far, we are now able to confirm the retreat dates for July 14–17, 1988. Although confirmation cards are still trickling in and more names are being added to the list, we needed ample lead time to notify you about the dates. At this point the number attending will fall somewhere between 15 and 50.

Bahá'u'lláh, 'Abdu'l-Bahá, and Shoghi Effendi will be present to determine the agenda. You may come armed with the "fire of the love of GOD" and the qualities attributed to the "pupil of the eye." Together, we will pray, consult, laugh, cry, and go forth with a renewed sense of what it means to be a Bahá'í.

We will have accommodations available in our dorms (limited) and the Coachman Inn (Hemingway). The Coachman is $35.00 a night for double occupancy. You may reserve a room by calling the motel directly at (803) 558-2576. Please tell them you are attending a meeting at the Louis G. Gregory Bahá'í Institute. If you want to reserve a bunk on campus, please let me know immediately by writing or calling. A dorm bunk is $10.00 per person. Meals will be served regularly at a cost of $2.50 breakfast, $3.00 lunch, and $3.50 dinner. We ask that you be prepared to have all meals on campus to make planning convenient.

We look forward to seeing each of you. If we may be of any service to you, do not hesitate to contact me.

In His service,

Roy I. Jones

One of the signature features of the BMG shared by the participants was the magical moment in their lives when they were first touched by the spiritual power of the Gathering. Such an encounter would eventually lead to various instances of emotional and spiritual transformation. Participants other than those present in Greensboro were invited to the retreat in South Carolina. If the life-changing experiences gained by those brothers meeting in Greensboro were indicative of the experience that a new participant would have, Bruce Reynolds of Marietta, Georgia would soon attest to his own transformative experience. In the following account Bruce recalls his first encounter with the Gathering.

July 15, 1988
[Bruce Reynolds, Hemingway, South Carolina]

I'm not quite sure what to think about this gathering. Yesterday, upon arriving I got out of the car and greeted a few brothers out on the porch. Then fast forward to this morning when I experienced an elevated level of prayer . . . something I had never experienced in the Faith before (and I've been a Bahá'í since 1969). Prayer led to tears; tears led to joy . . . it opened up a whole new phase of my life. This was transformative for me. It was enlightening. It took a burden off my soul, so to speak. Prior to this weekend, I wasn't sure I was in the right place with the Bahá'í Faith. Me and my wife had always lived in places where we were always the only Black folks in our community. I didn't know if this was a place I wanted to be. This first morning sealed the envelope for me. This was something I needed to have.

Later that weekend, there was a special call for funds to be raised, and I told a story about why I felt so dedicated to the Bahá'í Fund. When I was a kid, my parents would send me and my brother to church on Sundays. They'd give us money to put in the basket at church. We detested it, because the same preacher that we were contributing funds to would frequent our home and take our food, specifically our chicken dinners! And to a young child who understood that we had limited means, that was upsetting. My brother and I just stopped putting money in the basket. But when I became a Bahá'í, and I realized where the funds were going and how they were being spent, I became very supportive of and was enthusiastic about raising money for the Fund.

So with the fundraiser that was going on, after there was a general announcement or appeal for funds, I notice Dan McCoy leave and only later did I learn that he went to his house nearby. Later that afternoon, Dan comes back with this bag full of coins as his contribution to the fundraiser. It was very moving to me as Dan wasn't a person of means of wealth. For him to do that was very moving, and it choked me up pretty bad. It opened up another light for me about the Fund.

It was at this Gathering and after Bruce shared his experience that Billy pulled Bruce aside and asked him if he would serve as the treasurer of the Gathering. Bruce was honored to be asked and he accepted. Bruce would serve faithfully in this capacity for the next twenty-four years until the formal conclusion of the Gathering. The trust that Billy and the rest of the participants of the Gathering placed in him greatly enhanced Bruce's spiritual connection to the Faith and no doubt further contributed to his personal and spiritual transformation as well as his overall connection to the Faith.

1989

One of the important parts of the Gathering was the time reserved for personal introductions. One by one, the brothers would stand up and introduce themselves. The steps were easy—each brother said his name, where he was from, and why he was there. Although the pattern was simple, it led to a very profound atmosphere—both for the brother introducing himself and also for the rest of the Gathering. There was something particularly powerful as a participant reflected on *why* he was at the Gathering. It might seem like a minor question to answer, but deep and meaningful responses were very common.

1989 was the second year that the BMG would be held in South Carolina at the Louis Gregory Bahá'í Institute, but it was Martin Varner's first Gathering. Martin watched as brother after brother stood up and gave his introduction. When it was time for Martin to give his, he talked about why he was there and what being there meant to him. He reflected back to the days when he was a young boy playing with his friends in the schoolyard. He recalled how he and many of his friends often did not have enough clothes to stay warm in the wintertime. If he or another child were too cold, their friends would shout out, "Pile on!" and all of them would surround the cold child to warm him up. Martin shared that his experience at the Gathering was similar to those days on the schoolyard. In his introduction, Martin explained how he often felt very alone and, figuratively speaking, "cold" in the world—but here at the Gathering, he concluded that he felt that the brothers were surrounding him with love that warmed his heart. At this point, the brothers present there in the room immediately surrounded Martin. They recreated the experience that Martin had as a young boy, but instead of physically adding warmth, they showered him with love and affection. Someone uttered the phrase "Alláh-u-Abhá,"* and others soon joined in.

Over the years, the practice evolved to where the surrounding brothers would place their hands on the head or shoulders of the brother being "piled on." As the Gathering grew in size, so too did the "pile on," with its concentric circles of love and warmth. Hence the "pile on," Black Men's Gathering style, was born. It became a type of spontaneous prayer that was really a visceral expression of love. The situations that led to a "pile on" would vary. Sometimes a brother was having a difficult time and was in need of support. Other times, a brother's actions deserved praise and warranted encouragement. At other times, a brother might be getting ready to embark on a new experience or area of service. Regardless of the reason, the moments were always special and spiritually significant.

---

* "Alláh-u-Abhá" is a Bahá'í greeting that in Arabic means "God is All-Glorious." (Momen, *A Basic Bahá'í Dictionary*, p. 15)

1990

In 1990, the brothers at the Gathering reached an important conclusion and communicated it in their message to the Universal House of Justice. Quoting scripture, the brothers made reference to Christ's words: "How is it that ye sought me? wist ye not that I must be about my Father's business?"[1] The following e-mail from Billy to the Universal House of Justice, with the attached letter from the brothers to the House of Justice, illustrates how this scripture expresses how the participants at the Gathering were determined to redouble their commitment and effort to the work of the Faith:

Dearly Loved Friends,

The following letter was prepared and approved by a gathering of the believers to be sent to you. I consented to send it via electronic mail so that you could receive it as soon as possible. As you will note it was an exceptional meeting filled with love and ending with great resolve and action. I happily share it with you. Loving greetings to you all.

July 29, 1990

The Universal House of Justice

Dear Friends,

The participants of the Black Men's Gathering initiated by Counsellor William Roberts would like to extend its sincere love to you. It is with joyous Bahá'í greetings that we relate to you a few of the highlights of this year's Gathering.

The first day of the Gathering was spent deepening and consulting on the 1990 Riḍván Message. As we discussed the message, everyone realized that the time for timidity had passed, and it is truly the hour for us to get on with "our Father's business."

During the second day of the gathering we discussed various methods for teaching Black people in America. Focusing on our special bounty as the "pupil of the eye" of humanity and our responsibility as spiritual descendants of the Dawn-breakers,* we experienced a rare level of unity through consultation that concentrated our resolve to advance Bahá'u'lláh's Cause among Americans of African descent.

Consultation on the need to sacrifice more to the Bahá'í Fund increased our commitment to the economic security of our beloved Faith. Our privilege and obligation to the construction of the Arc was not overlooked. Therefore, in the spirit of love and sacrifice we humbly offer a contribution of $10,251.73 to be used to help complete the building of the Arc on God's Holy Mountain. We will forward this contribution through the National Spiritual Assembly.

---

* The heroes and martyrs of the earliest days of the Bábí-Bahá'í Dispensation. (Momen, *A Basic Bahá'í Dictionary*, p. 64)

Finally, we humbly request your prayers, that we may become steadfast lions, roaring Bahá'u'lláh's teachings throughout the inner cities, suburbs, and rural communities of this nation.

Sincerely,

Black Men's Gathering 1990

Cc National Spiritual Assembly United States

   Counsellor Magdalene Carney, International Teaching Centre

1991

Bernie Streets was perhaps one of the few participants in the BMG who had met Hand of the Cause* Louis Gregory and his wife Louisa. As a youth visiting Green Acre Bahá'í School, Bernie was fortunate to make the acquaintance of the Gregorys. He would in time regale the Gathering with stories of visiting Mr. and Mrs. Gregory, in their later years, at their home in Eliot, Maine. Bernie's parents met Mr. Gregory and had joined the Faith in the 1940s.

Bernie Streets was an example of how some veteran African American Bahá'í men became aware of the BMG and fully embraced its purpose. He said:

> In December, 1990, I had heard that a number of African American Bahá'ís had been called together by Dr. Billy Roberts; however, I knew very little about it except that its formation had been brought about to create a forum for Bahá'í men of African descent to consult on how they might significantly

---

* Individuals appointed first by Bahá'u'lláh, posthumously by 'Abdu'l-Bahá, and later by Shoghi Effendi, for the purpose of protecting and propagating the Faith.

increase their efforts to serve the Faith. Central to this endeavor was the energetic sharing of the message of Bahá'u'lláh with others, particularly with people of African descent, no matter where they resided. As my wife Diane and I were preparing to depart for Costa Rica on a pioneering trip, I reflected that although I had heard of the BMG, I had not attended any BMG-related events. However, I was determined that, upon my return to the States, I would definitely become involved in the BMG and its activities. I recognized that my pioneering journey would likely be a spiritual segue and connection to my hopeful future journey to the Gathering.

The overall participation and involvement in the Gathering by men of African descent was growing year by year. Not only was the Gathering expanding in size, but the maturation of the brothers was increasing through their continued and dedicated study of the divine guidance and their ensuing consultation and reflections. In addition, as Billy mentions in the following invitation letter for the annual Gathering, the brothers were being challenged to offer and increase their service to the Faith by stepping outside the American Bahá'í community to other communities throughout the world.

May 21, 1991
Beloved Friends,

The year has passed with great speed and it is now time for us to gather again to pray, consult and to review the commitments we made to one another and to the Blessed Perfection.

I anxiously look forward to seeing you together again and to welcome a number of newcomers to this potent occasion.

This year the Gathering will consider the call of the Supreme Body to publish far and wide the Mission and Personage of Bahá'u'lláh in preparation for the Holy Year, the completion of the Six Year Plan, and the newly released statement of the National Assembly, "America's Most Challenging Issue—The Vision of Race Unity." Our three days will be chock full so please come prepared to be totally involved.

We have seen over the past several years how the Gathering has impacted the American Bahá'í community, and now we will see how you will impact other National communities as well.

Please make your travel arrangements now to arrive at the Louis Gregory Institute on Thursday, July 25, 1991. We will end on Sunday July 28, 1991 about noon as is our practice.

This year promises to be another magnificent demonstration of the spiritual power available to each of His believers.

". . . Witness how the Beloved One has answered our entreaties. See how He has enriched our lives with new brethren and new institutions in lands hitherto closed to His healing Word. Consider with what potency His divine prescriptions are being affirmed as guidelines for the behaviour of nations large and small. Surely such abounding benedictions have imbued you with indomitable courage and with confidence to face a challenging but brilliant future." (Universal House of Justice, Riḍván 1991)

Truitt White and Jennie Greene at the Institute will gladly receive your reservation. Please make contact soon since this year we anticipate an overflowing crowd. If you would like to suggest other individuals to participate, please let me know since the Gathering is not an open meeting but invitational.

You are in my prayers, each and every one of you.

Love, Billy

In 1988, one of the principal outcomes of the second Gathering was the creation of an Education Fund under the trust of the LGBI. Over the past few years, the participants of the Gathering had donated substantial sums of money to that fund to support local students and their educational aspirations. The following letter from Truitt White, director of LGBI, echoed Billy's invitation to the brothers but also added a request to them to increase their dedicated contributions to the Education Fund.

May 24, 1991

Dear brothers:

On behalf of the Louis G. Gregory Bahá'í Institute I warmly welcome you to the Gathering which is being sponsored by our dear Counsellor, Billy Roberts. We look forward to welcoming you home for a spiritually intense weekend experience.

Enclosed you will find information about the Gathering. It is essential that you return the enclosed registration card, since a large number of people is expected.

Counsellor Roberts has urged us to, once again, present a case for the Louis Gregory Bahá'í Institute "Education Fund" which helps support qualified South Carolinian Bahá'ís to continue their higher education. The "Education Fund" was created at the second Black Men's Gathering in 1988 to respond to the urgent needs of these students. This is your Fund!

Over this past year the Education Fund supported eight students, through the sacrificial but limited offerings collected at last year's Gathering. The funds were depleted so rapidly, however, that one of the students who was starting his third year was unable to attend his first semester. After working for three and a half months he returned for the second semester and is completing the academic year in summer school.

Unfortunately, the L.G.I. "Education Fund" is often the only supplemental assistance students receive to help defray admission fees, textbooks, dormitory rooms, meal tickets, and / or transportation to and from school, so this assistance is essential.

Counsellor Roberts has asked that we try to arrange a small reception, so that you can meet some of these special youth, on Friday during the Gathering.

We recognize the financial commitments that each of you is undoubtedly facing to support yourself / your family, and the various Bahá'í funds, with the clear understanding that any financial contribution that you make to the "Education Fund" would be over and beyond these commitments. We humbly place this situation before you, for your prayerful consideration and action.

You may wish to consider a one-time offering, or regular monthly contributions. Then again, you may want to consider financially adopting a student for a year or more. We are currently assisting five students and two others have asked us for assistance beginning September 1991.

We anxiously look forward to your growing and continued support of this important development project, which you created several years ago.

I look forward to seeing you in July.

Yours In His Service,

Truitt A. White

Executive Director

Louis G. Gregory Bahá'í Institute

At the conclusion of the 1991 Gathering, the letter written to the Universal House of Justice spoke, among other things, to the response that the brothers had given to one of the major points of focus of the weekend—the Education Fund. The participants' commitment to that fund, as well as to the National Bahá'í Fund, was touching and inspiring, as every single one of the brothers in attendance contributed in some way toward both funds.

28 July 1991
The Universal House of Justice
Dearly Loved Friends,

This marks the fifth anniversary of the Black Men's Gathering held this year at the Louis G. Gregory Bahá'í Institute. We take this opportunity to express our thanks and gratitude to the Universal House of Justice and to our National Spiritual Assembly for their prayers and support. Twelve men attended the first gathering in Greensboro, North Carolina. This year fifty-eight men attended from sixteen states.

We began by deepening and consulting on the compilation "Creating a Vision of our Future" compiled by Shapoor Monadjem. We explored the writings on the power of the Covenant and understanding the station of Bahá'u'lláh. We discussed the importance of obedience to the institutions of our Faith. We studied, deepened, and consulted on the 1991 Riḍván message. We felt hopefully toward the beginning of the Holy Year and the coming World Congress.

Through song and prayerful fellowship, we removed the "veils" from the "pupil of the eye" that 'Abdu'l-Bahá envisioned. We saw how the culture and heritage of African Americans has enhanced this Cause. We renewed our commitment to "ferociously" teaching the Cause of Bahá'u'lláh. We have rededicated ourselves to teaching and sharing the station of Bahá'u'lláh wherever we move. We recognized that we have a responsibility, individually and collectively, as African American Bahá'ís, to be positive role models for Black youth and children, using the dynamic force of example.

Within this diverse group of Black males, there were those among us who had never experienced a gathering of this type. They brought joy as well as pain, anger as well as hope to this assemblage. By the consuming power of this Cause, we were transformed into a unified spirit.

The gathering was addressed by two young Bahá'í students, one male and one female. These youth have benefited from the Education Fund established by the Black Men's Gathering four years ago. We were moved as they told of their experiences and expressed appreciation for the love and support shown by the Black Men's Group and the Bahá'í community in general. These young people described how the financial support they received had literally changed their lives and brightened their vision of their future. As a result, the gathering resolved to establish a permanent endowment to provide financial support for South Carolina Bahá'í students now and in the future.

A year ago, we were encouraged by Counsellor Roberts to expand our teaching efforts to the international arena. Two of our number responded to that call. This year more of us are endeavoring to commit ourselves to this important activity.

Our consultation also included the need to understand that giving to the Fund is a spiritual act, and is a personal statement from the individual to His God. We then joyfully contributed a total of $4818.42 to the National Bahá'í Fund with 100% participation.

Finally, we wish to express our heartfelt gratitude to Counsellor Roberts for his commitment and dedication to the continuation of this regenerating occasion.

Sincerely in service to His Cause,
The Black Men's Gathering

The Universal House of Justice's response succinctly yet beautifully applauded the efforts of the gathering's conveyed aspirations:

6 August 1991
Dr. William Roberts
c/o National Spiritual Assembly of the Bahá'ís of the United States

Kindly convey to the participants in the Black Men's Gathering 1991 our deep appreciation for the information and sentiments conveyed in their message of 28 July 1991, and the assurance of our ardent prayers at the Holy Threshold for the realization of their laudable aspirations in service to the Cause of God.

Universal House of Justice

1992

Alfred Fox, would-be longtime participant of the BMG, grew up in a Christian family in Roanoke, Virginia. Although he was a relatively good student, Alfred lived a somewhat disillusioned childhood. During his elementary school years he first learned about slavery, but much of what he learned was a sanitized version of the history of racism in the United States. As a result, he did not realize the extent to which he and African Americans continued to suffer the harsh consequences of slavery. Alfred gradually learned the value of asking questions to reach deeper meanings that would increase his understanding. For example, upon learning that Abraham Lincoln "freed" the slaves, young Alfred considered the historical significance of 1863 but pondered, if slavery was so wrong, why other presidents before Lincoln had not ended it.

Many years later, Alfred found himself asking more deep questions about his life and his spiritual journey. In the 1970s, Alfred moved to Washington, D.C., to be with his father. One of Alfred's aunts began to develop an interest in Buddhism. Neither Alfred nor his aunt really understood, at first, what joining Buddhism entailed. After some months of learning, however, Alfred developed a strong attraction to the teachings and became a practicing Buddhist.

After becoming Buddhist, Alfred was encouraged to pray to the Buddha, and he was told that if he prayed to the Buddha, he could have anything he wanted. Instead of wishing for anything for himself, Alfred prayed for world peace because the desire for world peace, after all, had been what attracted him to the teachings of Buddhism. After months and months of praying and dutifully observing the practices of Buddhism, a deep sense of peace came over Alfred. Of course, world peace had not been reached; instead, he felt *inner* peace and tranquility within his own heart. Despite his prayers not resulting in peace throughout the world, Alfred was still amazed.

After experiencing the inner peace from observing the practices of Buddhism, years later Alfred found himself attracted to Christianity and its message of love, and he soon began attending church. However, a feeling of clarity came over him during a discussion with his minister. During this conversation, the minister made negative comments about Judaism, Islam, and Buddhism. Alfred responded to the minister's remarks and developed an unshakable belief that there was only one God and that the adherents of *all* religions, including Buddhism and Christianity, worshipped this one God. He was realizing that there was unity and true harmony between the religions.

In 1989, Alfred and his wife Sharon moved next door to a woman named Claudia Whitworth, who was a Bahá'í. Claudia, who owned a Black newspaper— *The Roanoke Tribune*—soon befriended Alfred and Sharon, and they all became close friends and would spend extensive periods of time together playing cards and socializing until the late hours of the night. On one occasion, Claudia asked Alfred how he felt about religion, and he told her that he knew that there was only one God and that somehow the members of all religions worshipped that same God. Claudia told Alfred that she believed he was right, and they conversed deeply about religion, but after this initial conversation, they never really talked about religion again. Instead, it was Sharon, Alfred's wife, who was initially drawn to the Faith. Specifically, she was intrigued when she learned that many people from different races were Bahá'í. Over time, she would learn more and more about the Bahá'í Faith and would share what she was learning with Alfred.

On May 1, 1992, at 11:30pm, Sharon asked Alfred to invite Claudia over to play cards and to tell them about her religion. Alfred did as Sharon had asked, and Claudia said she would be right over. After Claudia walked through the door, Alfred left the room and went to the back of his house to play music. Not long had passed when he walked back into the room to witness his wife signing her Bahá'í declaration card. She told Alfred, "I'm going to sign this card and learn all about Bahá'u'lláh." After hearing Sharon's words, Alfred stopped and said, "Well, if you're going to do it, I'm going to do it, too!"

The next day, Alfred and Sharon's Bahá'í community was observing the celebration of the twelfth day of Riḍván, and Claudia asked Alfred and Sharon if they wanted to go. They said yes, and they had a wonderful time meeting many of their fellow Bahá'ís. As Alfred learned more and more about the Faith, he realized that he was thirsty for knowledge about the Faith and that he was facing a challenge—the Faith had no clergy. Therefore, he decided that, in the absence of a minister, he would learn how to do something his childhood educators had failed to teach him—to read. Alfred sought out volunteers and friends in the Bahá'í community who would help him learn to read. As Alfred immersed himself in the Bahá'í writings, reading book after book, over time he would achieve the goal he set for himself. Two years later in 1994, Alfred learned about and attended his first Gathering.

The Gathering would meet that summer as usual at LGBI. Year after year, participants of the Gathering would find strength in such a prayerful atmosphere, and this year was no exception. That recommitment to being better Bahá'ís and to teaching the Faith of Bahá'u'lláh, was noticed by the brothers' communities as well as the institutions of the Faith.

The Universal House of Justice received the customary letter of the brothers after their meeting, and its response was yet another sign of the institution's growing love and support of the Gathering. The Universal House of Justice commented on the Gathering's recommitment to Bahá'u'lláh, which was becoming a known hallmark of the BMG.

3 August 1992

COUNSELLOR WILLIAM ROBERTS

OUR HEARTS WERE TOUCHED BY THE SPIRIT OF RECOMMITMENT TO BAHÁ'U'LLÁH WHICH ANIMATED THE BLACK MEN'S GATHERING 1992. KINDLY CONVEY TO THE PARTICIPANTS THE ASSURANCE OF OUR PRAYERS THAT THEY MAY BE DIVINELY AIDED TO FULFILL THEIR ASPIRATIONS IN SERVICE TO THE BLESSED BEAUTY.

UNIVERSAL HOUSE OF JUSTICE

Van Gilmer, Marvin Hughes, John Mangum, Moses Richardson, William Varner, James Williams, Bruce Reynolds, Ed Peace, and Billy Roberts at the 1992 Black Men's Gathering (Photo Courtesy of Bob James)

Black Men's Gathering, 1992, Louis Gregory Bahá'í Institute, Hemingway, South Carolina
(Photo Courtesy of Bob James)

1993

Service in the name of Bahá'u'lláh was one of the ongoing fruits of the Gathering. In Billy Roberts' invitation letter to the brothers, he focused on the contributions made by the participants of the Gathering. With the recently held World Congress in New York City forming an energizing backdrop to the Gathering, the brothers looked forward to considering, as Billy's letter below stated, "the greatness of [the] Cause and the necessary part [they were to] play in its advancement."

April 18, 1993

My dear brothers,

Reflection on the Holy Year will yield multiple and varied stories which challenge our ability to foresee the potency and enormity of this experience.

Imagine those future Bahá'ís and interested historians who will examine this period and celebrate the events both exhilarating and exasperating which occurred during these brief few months. They will see each of you and will explore the role you played in the realization of the new world civilization during a time filled with unique potentialities.

I suggest that contributions made by each of you, some great and some small have enhanced the development of the Bahá'í community in ways undetectable but so very essential. Service at the Bahá'í World Congress, travel teaching in the international field as well as on the homefront, service in the various Institutions of the Cause—local, regional, national and international—expansion of the appreciation of music and the arts, written articles and commentaries for the public as well as the Bahá'í community, speeches whether in small fireside gatherings or in great assemblies, conversations with individual believers, and certainly the ingathering of new souls who have entered the Faith shepherded by resilient and gallant followers of the Blessed Perfection, are but a few of the extraordinary demonstrations of faith and devotion you have made.

The time has come for us to gather again to consider the greatness of this Cause and the necessary part we must play in its advancement. I look forward to those joy-filled days when we can be with one another and share, with an intimacy and calmness which propels the spirit of Bahá, connecting and melding our hearts together, the thinking which will guide our actions in fulfilling the goals of the coming Three Year Global Plan.

The Gathering will be held at the Louis Gregory Institute in Hemingway South Carolina beginning 22 July through 25 July 1993. I hope to see all of you there. If there are others who you think should be invited please forward their names and addresses to me. The limitations of space will not allow all to be invited so please do not invite them lest they be disappointed if we cannot accommodate them. Jennie Greene of the Institute staff will be ready to receive your reservations for the program. Please make hotel reservations on your own.

I promise to remember each of you in the Holy Shrines at the World Centre and anxiously await the time when I can greet you face-to-face.

With loving Bahá'í greetings,
William Roberts

1994

The Black Men's Gathering was certainly a place where men of African descent were experiencing spiritual transformation, both collectively and individually. Although a group of Bahá'í men had started the Gathering, participation in the Gathering was not reserved exclusively for registered Bahá'ís. Non-Bahá'í participants of the Gathering would attend and would be just as engaged in the uplifting experience as those who were registered Bahá'ís. The Gathering embodied a unique spiritual energy that galvanized the souls of African American males, whether they were Bahá'ís or friends of the Faith. For example, Eric Dozier of Nashville, Tennessee first attended the Gathering as a friend of the Faith, and soon after participating in the Gathering, he declared as a Bahá'í.

Eric grew up in a small town—Bakewell, Tennessee. His family went to a local Baptist Church, and he would always watch his mother direct the church choir while his father played the piano. His grandparents, aunts, uncles, and cousins were members of the choir, and they would all sing their hearts out at church. As a young boy, Eric learned that Black folks do more than just recite their theology—they sing it! Hearing the joyful singing in his church left a lasting impression on him, and he would later reveal that he learned more about the true spirit of Christianity from his immersion in

African American sacred music than he did during the years he would later spend in the seminary. Eric credited not only his mother and father but also his entire community with providing him with a solid theological and creative education. They taught him to sing, to pray, to worship, to seek justice, and to serve humanity, and they thoroughly prepared him for what was to come.

Eric's first encounter with the Bahá'í Faith occurred when he was working at a community center in Durham, North Carolina. He and his director had gone to a socioeconomic development conference in South Carolina. At the time, Eric was serving as the community development program coordinator in a "high risk community." He sat down at the table for lunch next to a gentleman whom he had not met before. He asked the gentleman his name and what he did for a living, and the man introduced himself as Truitt White. Since the lunch groups rotated, Truitt was actually on his way out of the lunch area when Eric was just getting settled in. Still, Truitt was able to explain to Eric that he worked for a community center in Hemingway, South Carolina, and he left Eric with a Bahá'í pamphlet containing a picture of Louis Gregory. It showed one of the most radiant faces Eric had ever seen.

Eric did not think much more about his encounter with Truitt afterward. He went home, back to his job, and continued to serve his community while awaiting acceptance into Duke University Divinity School. The following summer, two gentlemen who wanted to do a spiritually based literacy project in his neighborhood approached Eric. The following day, one of the men asked Eric to lunch and took him to meet some of his friends who were Bahá'ís living in Chapel Hill, North Carolina. As they were driving, a pamphlet that was apparently placed between the seats slid onto the floor. It was the same pamphlet with the radiant face of Louis Gregory on it that Eric had been given months prior. The gentleman saw the pamphlet as it slid to the floor and, right on cue, said, "that's my religion; let me tell you about it."

In the coming days and weeks, Eric began to attend several Bahá'í events and activities. At one point, he was asked if he would like to go visit the Louis Gregory Bahá'í Institute. Eric accepted the invitation.

When they arrived at LGBI, Eric was greeted at the door by a familiar face. It was Truitt White, the gentleman who had given him the pamphlet at the socioeconomic development conference. He welcomed Eric inside to the program—which happened to be the Black Men's Gathering—and what Eric witnessed set his heart on fire. He observed brothers praying, crying, singing, and calling to their Lord. He was deeply moved by the intimacy and the spiritual fervor of the Gathering, and he felt as if he were back in Bakewell, Tennessee with his family, friends, and community. All of the songs started flooding into his spirit: "In That Great Gettin' Up Morning" and "I Know I've Been Changed." Although Eric was a newcomer, the brothers embraced him as a son who had returned home. Immediately, Eric returned to his car, grabbed a declaration card he had been given a few weeks before, and enthusiastically signed it.

Participants at the 1994 Black Men's Gathering
(Photo Courtesy of Bob James)

Participants at the 1994 Black Men's Gathering
(Photo Courtesy of Bob James)

1994

Black Men's Gathering, 1994, Louis Gregory Bahá'í Institute, Hemingway, South Carolina
(Photo Courtesy of Pierre Johnson)

1995

As the yearly Gathering continued to take place at LGBI in the summers, brothers of the Gathering developed an understanding that it was beneficial to hold smaller, more localized Gatherings. In February, members of the BMG decided to hold their first local Gathering on the west coast in Oakland, California. One of the defining moments of the Oakland Gathering was the richness and spirited consultation that took place. The following letters written from the Oakland Gathering to the Universal House of Justice and the National Spiritual Assembly of the Bahá'ís of the United States attempted to convey the spirit that permeated the Gathering over the weekend.

February 19, 1995
Universal House of Justice
Bahá'í World Centre
Dearly loved Friends,

The first Black Men's Gathering to be held on the west coast of the United States of America was convened on 17 February 1995 at 6:30pm in Oakland, California.

This special meeting was attended by twenty-five of the believers from all over the west coast and as far away as

Canada. For two days we turned our hearts completely toward Bahá'u'lláh in search of His desire for us.

Joining Counsellor William Roberts at this session were several believers who attended the first such meeting held some eight years ago in Greensboro, North Carolina. The presence of these original participants, who traveled great distances to share their love and experience with us, helped to generate a spiritual environment that galvanized those present to become one.

Extended periods of prayer and song preceded each consultation. This provided us with a radiant spirit of unity, enabled us to consult with a powerful love and affection about difficult and complex issues which inhibit us as individuals in responding to your calls.

The consultation endowed individuals with a new spiritual energy and a personal commitment to the growth of the Cause of God. Frank and unfettered discussion clarified our responsibility to the Faith, ourselves and mankind.

The systematic deepening, skillfully led by Counsellor Roberts, enabled us to re-evaluate and gather a deeper and more spiritually profound understanding of the Riḍván 151 message, the 7 December 1994 message, excerpts from the Compilation *Promoting Entry by Troops*, and two letters dated 31 October 1993 and 4 January 1994, each a gift to us from your Mighty Institution. This potent process raised our sights and has led us to anticipate the receipt of future correspondence from the Universal House of Justice as a personal letter from your hearts to ours.

A great deal of consultation was centered on the building of the Arc and Mount Carmel projects and our responsibility to it and concluded with our eyes opened by the realization that building the Arc is also that opportunity to remove from ourselves a poverty mentality and the fear of lack of security which has prevented us from achieving that nobility identified for us by the Manifestation Himself. With love and humility we contributed a token of three thousand seven hundred fifty dollars ($3750.00). This action will be followed by contributions in the communities in which we reside to assist in the achievement of this special goal.

With grateful hearts we anticipate your next message.

We beg you for the favor of your continued prayers in the Holy Shrines that our efforts and the tears emptied out here will become emblems of our action in response to the Three Year Plan.

With Bahá'í love,
Black Men's Gathering—West
Oakland, California
February 19, 1995

February 19, 1995
National Spiritual Assembly of the Bahá'ís of the United States
c/o Dr. Robert Henderson, Secretary-General
Dear Bahá'í Friends,

We, the twenty-five participants of the first Black Men's Gathering to be held on the west coast, are pleased to report an astounding success thanks to your prayers and the blessing of our Supreme Institution, the Universal House of Justice.

For two spirit-filled days we turned an upper room of Motel 6 into a sanctuary where crying, praying and praises to the Blessed Perfection penetrated every soul in that spot. Our beloved Counsellor, Dr. William Roberts, skillfully led our consultation which helped us to raise our level of awareness to degrees of service which we pray will make us yet another jewel in the crown of Bahá'u'lláh. The consultation also moved our hearts to lovingly contribute three thousand seven hundred fifty dollars ($3750.00) for the vineyard of our Lord, a small token of love, to assist our beloved Universal House of Justice in the completion of the Mount Carmel Projects.

We humbly submit ourselves to your service. We pray for you and we love you from the innermost depths of our hearts. We thank you for your prayers and support and we beseech that Bahá'u'lláh continue to guard your sacred unity.

We are yours in loving service,

Black Men's Gathering—West

Oakland, California

February 19, 1995

The Universal House of Justice responded to the letter the brothers wrote with encouraging and uplifting words. Most notably, the Supreme Body focused on the Gathering's "resolution in upholding the Divine Standard" and its efforts to promote the Cause of God. Below is the letter to the Gathering from the Universal House of Justice.

8 March 1995

We have read with keen interest and warm appreciation the expressions of hopeful endeavour in the path of service to the Blessed Beauty conveyed in the message of 19 February 1995 from the Black Men's Gathering—West. Aware as we are of the difficult background and discouraging atmosphere against which Black people in America struggle, we were deeply touched by the participants' resolution in upholding the Divine Standard and in promoting the Cause of God, for only thus can they contribute genuinely to removing the barriers that prevent all those who suffer injustice from attaining progress and happiness. We are also grateful for their generous offering to the Arc Projects Fund.

These brethren may rest assured of our love and best wishes and of our ardent supplication at the Holy Threshold that their devoted efforts may attract abundant divine confirmations.

The Universal House of Justice
cc: International Teaching Centre
   National Assembly of the United States

Upon receiving this response from the Universal House of Justice, Billy personally wrote to the Supreme Body, and that same day, he also wrote a letter to the brothers who had gathered in Oakland the previous month. As part of that letter, Billy shared his personal response to the Universal House of Justice and also included its response to the Gathering's message. Below are Billy's letters to the Gathering and to the Universal House of Justice.

March 8, 1995
To each of the participants in the Black Men's Gathering—
West held in Oakland, California on 17–19 February 1995
My dearest brothers,

I am still moved by the spirit generated at the Gathering held recently on the west coast. Surely we experienced a taste of the call of the Beloved Master when he urged us to "become as one soul in many bodies."

How amazing it is to become catapulted into a new consciousness. The realization of what we can become and the development of a deeper understanding of the mission which has been given to us by the Manifestation of God Himself is humbling.

I enclose here with great joy the messages prepared and sent to the Universal House of Justice and to the National Spiritual

Assembly of the US from the Gathering. How thrilled we all were to hear and ratify them.

Now, I am pleased to share with you the response of the Supreme Body. The melodic tone with which they address us makes me ever more aware of the majesty resident within our Faith. So moved was I by this message of love to us that I could not help but send an immediate letter of thanks. I have included this as well.

I thank you for the many notes and telephone calls which I have received since we were together. Joy for me are the shining spirits which I detect within your voices and will see acted out in the services you are rendering.

Please know you are each held very close to my heart in a spiritually loving embrace.

I love you my brothers!

With a joy filled heart I greet each one of you,

Billy Roberts

March 8, 1995
Universal House of Justice
Bahá'í World Centre
Beloved Friends,

I cannot help but express my gratitude for the loving and spirit-filled message you have sent to those souls who participated in the Black Men's Gathering—West. The depth of your love and sincere interest in the efforts which they are exerting can only instill a potency within each thought and action which is made in service to the Cause of God.

These souls who have historically been isolated and unsure of their place in this world have found a home in the Cause and have arisen to do their part in reinforcing its foundation with a vigor and an undaunted enthusiasm which can only result in joyous victory.

Your gratitude for the offering to the Arc Projects Fund while undeserved is embraced and celebrated with a determination to multiply this contribution many times over.

Please know that our prayers co-mingle with yours as we strive to achieve the vision you have outlined.

May Bahá'u'lláh increase His affection for the Supreme Body and each one of His servants who work to serve it.

With loving admiration,

William Roberts

Black Men's Gathering, 1995, Louis Gregory Bahá'í Institute, Hemingway, South Carolina (Photo Courtesy of Bernard Johnson)

In July, the brothers met at LGBI for their annual plenary BMG. The following BMG letter—written after the Gathering had taken place—to the NSA was remarkable for two reasons. First, it reported that "one hundred and eleven black men" had gathered at the Louis Gregory Institute, and this figure reflected the steady growth of the BMG since its inception in 1987. Secondly, the brothers proudly announced a contribution of $5,968.29 to the National Bahá'í Fund. These two developments demonstrated the spiritual transformation of the participants of the BMG that was taking place. Even in the midst of the everyday social and racial burdens they faced, the brothers still showed their love for the Faith by supporting the National Bahá'í Fund.

July 30, 1995
National Spiritual Assembly of the Bahá'ís of the United States
by fax
Dearly loved friends:
    While American society crumbles on all sides, while despair and hopelessness permeates to the core of American life, the participants of the Black Men's Gathering cling to the only true salvation—namely, the Cause of Bahá'u'lláh.
    One hundred eleven black men met at the Louis G. Gregory Bahá'í Institute for a spirit-filled weekend of prayer, song, illuminating talks and consultation led by our beloved Counsellor Dr. William Roberts. We laughed, cried and shared each other's joy and pain. We expressed our love for each other in ways uncommon among Black males. Our group promised that we would take this love back to the broader society and to our Bahá'í communities.
    We humbly offer, as a token of our love and support, the sum of $5968.29 for the National Bahá'í Fund. Our prayers are with you as we enter the final months of the Three Year Plan.
    With warmest Bahá'í love,
    Black Men's Gathering—1995

Several days later, the National Spiritual Assembly of the Bahá'ís of the United States responded to the letter from the BMG and acknowledged both the participants' commitment to carrying the message of Bahá'u'lláh to their communities and their "generous contribution" to the Bahá'í Fund. The NSA also mentioned how such actions "testify to the spirit of faith that permeated the atmosphere of your Gathering." This "spirit of faith" was created through the constant prayers, songs, fellowship, and the study of the guidance, and these activities created a continuous flow of spiritual energy that created and sustained the atmosphere of the Gathering. Letters from the Bahá'í institutions provided the direction that enabled the BMG to channel that energy into service to their respective communities.

August 2, 1995
To the Participants of the Black Men's Gathering c/o Continental Counselor William Roberts
Dear Friends,

The commitment conveyed in your message and the generous contribution you made to the National Bahá'í Fund testify to the spirit of faith that permeated the atmosphere of your Gathering. We give praise for your determination to disseminate that spirit throughout each of your local communities. You have given an appropriate response to the direction given by the Universal House of Justice in its 1989 Riḍván message:

> Our primary response must be to teach—to teach ourselves and to teach others—at all levels of society, by all possible means, and without further delay. The beloved Master, in an exhortation on teaching, said it is "not until the candle is lit that it can shed the brightness of its flame; not until the light shineth forth that its brilliance can dispel the surrounding gloom." Go forth, then, and be the "lighters of the unlit candles."

We pray that your souls will continue to burn brightly to warm the hearts of all those you meet in the broader society, thereby changing their despair into the hope and joy you so assuredly embody.

With warm regards,

Robert C. Henderson

Secretary-General

National Spiritual Assembly of the Bahá'ís of the US

After receiving the letter from the National Assembly, Billy wrote to the participants of this year's Gathering. He mentioned how the annual Gatherings were similar to a pilgrimage. The Gathering also provided them with the gift of spiritual upliftment, and the brothers had a responsibility to transmit this gift to the world. Specifically, the BMG provided the brothers with a sacred space to heal their souls so that they could better heal the souls of others. As Billy wrote, this gift of healing, of love, and of devotion to the Faith had to be shared, and he reminded them of the crucial act of staying in contact with each other. He understood how easy it would be for the strong connections of love cultivated by the brothers to gradually fade in the face of the everyday, mundane activities of the world. By staying connected, the brothers could maintain the flow of spiritual energy in their everyday lives until the next BMG meeting or "pilgrimage." Billy also encouraged the brothers to remember the time and energy the Bahá'í institutions spent—in the midst of their other responsibilities—to provide guidance and encouragement to the participants of the BMG.

August 19, 1995

Participants in the Ninth Annual Black Men's Gathering

Beloved brothers,

How wonderful it was to join you in that blessed setting—the Louis G. Gregory Bahá'í Institute. Each year a sort of pilgrimage occurs where we make our way from places near and far to reconvene, to pray, to open our hearts to Bahá'u'lláh and to share and consult with one another. I feel privileged to be able to witness some of the miracles which become a reality as a result. Nothing short of the unity of souls turned to the Blessed Perfection could produce such a power, such a spirit, such a wondrously clarifying experience. This is a gift you have received and through each of you this gift must be transmitted throughout the length and breadth of this world. I call upon each of you to determine what part you will play as transmitter of this pure and golden spirit which is surely a revolutionizing element in the world. Imagine the opportunity before us!

Each of you by now has received a copy of the list of names, addresses, etc. for those who participated in the Gathering this year. Please use it wisely. Make it a point to be in touch with one another. Offer encouragement and support to each other as we encounter the inevitable challenges which mount up in this life. A simple note or telephone call brings with it a renewed joy and reflection about our shared experience. Some may have ideas to share which could enhance the teaching and consolidation work of the Faith. Let your contact be selfless and aimed solely at empowering one another in service to become better Bahá'ís.

I want to offer to you the two messages sent from the Gathering and the responses received from the Universal House of Justice and from the National Spiritual Assembly of the United States. Please note these are written with great care and sent with a potent love for each one of you. Imagine the blessings associated with prayers uttered on behalf of the Gathering and in the midst of tremendous and overwhelming responsibilities, time was arranged by the Supreme Body to pen and send a message to you.

When last I heard, over $100,000.00 (one hundred thousand dollars) was pledged for the "Silent Campaign" in support of improved facilities at the Louis Gregory Bahá'í Institute. I don't know about you, but I intend to achieve my pledge long before next July! Each time I quietly mention this little project to someone privately, they are anxious to be included as contributors. The gifts are not immense but ever so precious. In fact, it is going so well that I hope to double the amount I originally thought would be possible. Are there any among you who dares to join me? Do let me know!!

I look forward to hearing from you from time to time with news of your exciting experiences.

With warmest Bahá'í greetings / With love and affection,
Billy

1996

Since the inception of the gathering, Billy had called on the insight, support, and guidance of the institution of the Counselors. As an Auxiliary Board member in 1987, he had continually exchanged reports and sought advice from the International Teaching Center. Counselor Magdalene Carney was effusive in her enthusiasm and encouragement of the gathering, and Billy was himself appointed by the Universal House of Justice to serve as a member of the Continental Board of Counselors in the Americas in June 1988. He was the first man of African descent residing in the United States to be called to that service.

Other Counselors, while not involved in the organization and direction of the BMG, nonetheless offered a stream of encouragement for BMG activities throughout its twenty-five-year history. The following devoted souls—listed with their terms of service on the Continental Board for the Americas—included Wilma Ellis (1985–2000), Alan Smith (1985–1995), Stephen Birkland (1993–2008), Tod Ewing (1995–2000), Antonio Gabriel Marques (1998–2010), Rebequa Murphy (2000–2010), Eugene Andrews (2000–2010), and Anita Vandella Williams (2010–2015).

At the Tenth Annual BMG held at the Louis Gregory Bahá'í Institute, two former members of the Board of Counselors in the

Americas—Alan Smith from the Virgin Islands and Billy Roberts from the United States, along with a newly appointed Counselor Tod Ewing from the United States—were present. Their attendance had an impact on the assembled brothers, as this was a unique and historic moment unfolding before the eyes of the brothers not only in the context of the BMG but in their individual personal Bahá'í lives.

As a long-time participant of the gathering, Ted Jefferson recalled the poignant moment when Billy asked Tod to come to the front of the room, then also asked Alan Smith to join them. Ted felt at that moment that the spiritual impact of seeing three Black men who had been chosen to serve the Cause of Bahá'u'lláh as Continental Counselors in the same place was remarkable. He felt that these three precious souls were Bahá'u'lláh's gift to mankind. After this moving scene, Alan Smith proceeded to give the brothers a richer appreciation for the institutions of the learned,* as well as the other holy and blessed institutions of the Bahá'í Faith.

Billy then communicated to Tod that the moment had come for him to carry a mighty responsibility and that he wanted him to know that he was not alone. He told Tod that the Universal House of Justice had recognized his capacity and had called on him to serve the community in the function of Counselor. Bahá'u'lláh, Billy told Tod, would give him the strength and wisdom to serve the community well.

Billy then told Tod that he wanted to give him something that held a special spiritual significance for him. They were items that had been given to Billy and that transformed his spirit. Billy said to Tod, "I hope they will fortify you during the challenging times ahead." He

---

* The "learned" refers to the Bahá'í institutions of the Hands of the Cause, the Counselors, the Auxiliary Board members, and their assistants. (Momen, *A Basic Bahá'í Dictionary,* p. 138)

Tod Ewing at the Tenth Annual Black Men's Gathering (1996),
Louis Gregory Bahá'í Institute, Hemingway, South Carolina

then presented Tod with a small crystal box that held threads from a vacuum cleaner that was used to clean the shrine of Bahá'u'lláh, soil from the vicinity of Fort Ṭabarsí,* and chips of stone from the prison at 'Akká. Billy also presented Tod with an African walking stick that he had personally received on one of his trips to Africa. These gifts were a metaphorical passing of the baton from one brother who had served as a Counselor to another brother stepping into that mighty field of service. The gift represented a vision of the embrace of pure love between men.

The love and admiration expressed at this Gathering was heartwarming and inspirational to witness. As with any BMG,

---

* Fort Ṭabarsí was the site of a battle between the forces of the shah of Persia and the Bábís (followers of the Báb) from October of 1848 to May of 1849. (Momen, *A Basic Bahá'í Dictionary*, p. 217)

*Father and son, Nasif Habeebullah and Anthony Outler,
at the Tenth Annual Black Men's Gathering, 1996*

the presence of family members created a special opportunity for participants to develop an even stronger spiritual bond. Other participants witnessing such spiritual closeness were also enriched. With the growth and development of the Gathering, more and more families would be represented over the years, and this would result in renewed connections and relationships.

The BMG had reached a milestone—its tenth Gathering. Since the beginning of the Gathering, the brothers had grown and matured spiritually in their commitment to their Faith. They had learned to rely on the guidance during their deliberations and transmute the personal anguish and frustration so common in the daily lives of African American men into bold and enduring acts of service to their beloved Faith. They had been prepared by the careful, loving, but firm stewardship of Billy Roberts to play their unique role in the unfolding teaching plans of the Universal House of Justice. When the Universal House of Justice issued its 1996 Riḍván message to

*Black Men's Gathering, 1996, Louis Gregory Bahá'í Institute,
Hemingway, South Carolina*

the Bahá'ís of North America, it made a special appeal to African
American Bahá'ís to arise and teach their Faith in Africa, and this call
would have great influence on the future course of the BMG. The
relevant portion of that message said:

> We direct the attention of the believers of African descent,
> so beloved by the Master, to the pressing need for pioneers,
> who will contribute to the future development of the Cause in
> distant areas, including the continent of Africa for which they
> were assigned a special responsibility by the Guardian when
> the first systematic campaign was launched for its spiritual illu-
> mination. Although their contributions to all aspects of Bahá'í
> service on the home front and elsewhere will be of great value,
> they can be a unique source of encouragement and inspiration
> to their African brothers and sisters who are now poised on the
> threshold of great advances for the Faith of Bahá'u'lláh.[1]

Like their African American predecessors during the Ten Year Crusade, the brothers of the BMG arose to meet the challenge of the Four Year Plan. By the time the call of the Universal House of Justice reached the BMG participants, they had been prepared to dutifully arise and serve from their prior prayerful, reflective, and consultative annual gatherings. During these meetings, they had studied the guidance and internalized a powerful sense of their racial and spiritual identity as the "pupil of the eye."[2] As one writer described it, "these sessions [had] inspired the participants to carry the healing Message of Bahá'u'lláh to their fellow black men in American society." They were now "galvanized" by the Message, which provided them with "a sharper focus and challenging goal. The annual meetings became a means of preparing spiritually for service in Africa."[3]

Over one hundred men of African descent from throughout the United States, the Caribbean, Canada, and Africa attended this year's Gathering, which was historic for several profoundly related reasons. First, "the event aimed at deepening the participants' understanding of the history and role of the peoples of African descent. And as a result of the [G]athering, more than 45 attendees pledged to visit Africa over the following three years to share Bahá'u'lláh's message with the people there."[4] It should come as no surprise that this year's Gathering won the high praises of the Universal House of Justice for "simultaneously meeting the particular needs of a certain population while maintaining a universal spirit."[5]

Additionally, the BMG was encouraged by the International Teaching Center to bring the experience of the Gathering to the islands of the Caribbean and to Brazil. With the guidance and assistance of the Board of Counselors in the Americas, believers from these two areas attended the Black Men's Gathering in 1996 in South Carolina. One was Gabriel Marques (who would later be appointed in 1998 as a member of the Board of Counselors for the Americas) from Bahia, Brazil, and the other was Lionel Haynes from Barbados.

After their experience at the Gathering, both returned home and initiated Gatherings in their home countries.

Over the years, several contingents of brothers traveled to both these countries to support and give strength to these new Gatherings. For example, brothers from all across the Caribbean came and participated at the first Gathering held in Barbados. One of the participants in that Gathering, Arthur Powell (who would later be appointed in 2015 as a member of the Board of Counselors for the Americas), was among that group. When he returned to his home country of Jamaica, he initiated a Gathering there. The National Spiritual Assembly of Jamaica wrote a letter to this newly formed Gathering and sent copies to the BMG in the United States. That letter had an intense effect on those who participated and reinvigorated the brothers who lived on that small island nation.

1996 was a significant year for the BMG, and communications written on behalf of the Universal House of Justice to Billy, along with a letter from the Universal House of Justice to the NSA of the United States, applaud the efforts of the brothers at the Tenth Annual Black Men's Gathering.

8 August 1996

Dear Bahá'í Friend,

The Universal House of Justice has asked us to send you a copy of its message of today's date to the National Spiritual Assembly of the United States in response to the email it received from the Tenth Annual Black Men's Gathering. We are to express to you its warm remembrance of your initiation of this special event and its gratitude for the unique spirit your efforts have inspired in a succession of gatherings which focused on a particular group, to address their distinctive needs, but which also upheld the world-embracing vision of the Cause of Bahá'u'lláh. This is indeed an exemplary achievement at a time when so many other groups in the United States are gripped in the self-imposed strictures of cultural divisiveness. Would to God that the news of this accomplishment might be noised abroad as a lesson and an inspiration to others.

We are also to assure you of the ardent prayers of the House of Justice at the Holy Threshold on behalf of yourself and the members of your dearly loved family.

With loving Bahá'í greetings,

Bethany

For Department of the Secretariat

Enclosure

8 August 1996

The National Spiritual Assembly of the Bahá'ís of the United States

We were deeply impressed by the message of 28 July 1996 from the Tenth Annual Black Men's Gathering held at the Louis Gregory Bahá'í Institute. The universal spirit which it conveyed from a group of individuals who are daily pressured by the myopic cultural vision of those among whom they live and work, the certitude of the participants' commitment to the Lord of Mankind, the intensity of their desire to maintain a high standard of moral rectitude, the clarity of their under-standing of the essentials of the Four Year Plan in relation to the individual, the institutions and the community, the vibrancy of their fellowship—all evoked in us feelings of admiration and gratitude. That this exemplary gathering should have produced offers of pioneers and traveling teachers to Africa and also four pledges of deputization demonstrated the acuity of their aware-ness as to the special duties devolving upon the believers of African descent to lend needful support to the continent of their origin. It is a demonstration that must thrill the soul of our departed Guardian who dearly wished for such action to be taken increasingly by Black Americans. We warmly applaud the conduct and outcome of this gathering and assure all the dearly loved participants of our ardent supplications at the Holy Threshold that their every aspiration in service to the Cause of God may be gloriously realized through the unceasing confirmations of the Blessed Beauty.

With loving Bahá'í greetings,

The Universal House of Justice

cc: International Teaching Centre

Dr. William Roberts

By December of 1996, the time had come to begin to fulfill the pledges of the Gathering. These were the same pledges that had caused the Universal House of Justice to declare "that this exemplary gathering should have produced offers of pioneers and traveling teachers to Africa . . . demonstrated the acuity of their awareness as to the special duties . . . to lend needful support to the continent of their origin." During that summer Gathering, four brothers had pledged to travel to Africa to answer the call of the Universal House of Justice. Billy would now write to the rest of the Gathering to detail the plans of what would be a first of many trips. Those four souls who arose to travel to Africa would later be joined by five more, bringing the total to nine brothers who would ultimately make the journey.

December 2, 1996

Beloved Brothers,

I am so excited about the plans which a number of you are making in response to the call of the House of Justice to travel to Africa. It seems to me that this is a magnificent gift which has the believers in that part of the world beside themselves with joy. Each conversation I have generates more and more enthusiasm. Frankly, they can't believe that so many brothers are making plans and each area wants to have their share of the blessings of your visit.

In July, a number of you asked me to let you know when I would be travelling hoping that you could join me. Well, I have finally been able to complete those plans.

I will be visiting Southern Africa—Namibia, Botswana, and South Africa. Following two weeks there we hope to visit the Holy Land for a three-day Pilgrimage. The dates will be 10 January through 31 January 1997. If you are interested, please let me know by telephone so that I can give you the costs etc. So far Alfred Fox / Marcus Potts / Patrick Patillo / and I will be making the trip.

You should know that the friends in Southern Africa are anxious to meet as many of the brothers from the Gathering as possible. They have a wide-ranging schedule of activities planned including significant interactions in Namibia with many government officials. This will be a special bounty!

Please know you are not only welcome but encouraged to participate. The more voices who can go the stronger the spirit will be. *But please let me know quickly!*

I ask those of you who cannot participate on this journey to please offer prayers to Bahá'u'lláh for His precious blessing that we discover the bounties He has prepared for us.

With warmest love,

Your brother,

Billy

1997

In an attempt to answer the call of the Universal House of Justice, in what would be the Gathering's first of many trips to Africa, in January nine participants traveled to Southern Africa to share the message of Bahá'u'lláh with the people of that subregion. As would be the case with all subsequent travel teaching trips, the brothers who were traveling gathered for a time dedicated to spiritualization and preparation. Such sessions were sometimes held prior to leaving the United States, and sometimes they took place after the group arrived at their destination. For this trip, the session was held in Namibia. This group, which would informally be called the "Namibian Nine," included Billy, Alfred Fox, Franklin Whitson, Marcus Potts, Nasif Habeebullah, Patrick Patillo, Al Daniels, Walter Palmer, and Marvin Hughes. The brothers split into two teams. One team of traveling teachers remained in Namibia and visited Angola, while another team continued on to South Africa and Botswana.

Between January 11 and 28, the BMG travel teachers in Namibia spoke to government ministers, were interviewed on television and radio, and traveled to many areas of the country to share the message of Bahá'u'lláh. Two days after their arrival, they had an official audi-

Alfred Fox (far left) and Marvin Hughes (far right),
National Bahá'í Center of Namibia

ence (which aired on the television news broadcast) with the speaker of Namibia's legislative assembly, Dr. Mose Tjitendero. A member of the BMG delegation presented Dr. Tjitendero with a copy of the Kitáb-i-Aqdas, Bahá'u'lláh's book of laws. Dr. Tjitendero in turn gave the BMG delegation a copy of the country's constitution. In addition, one of the BMG members conducted a racial healing seminar for the Bahá'í community in Windhoek, the capital and largest city of Namibia.

Making such a trip to Namibia, with a focus on teaching and service, had an even deeper effect on the brothers of the Gathering and their relationship with one another. Patrick Patillo, one of the "Namibian Nine," first attended the BMG in 1990. Earlier that year, Patrick was introduced to Billy at a program held at the University of Michigan to commemorate the ten-year anniversary of the passing of the United States' first Black poet laureate, Robert Hayden. The program was indeed special for Patrick for multiple reasons. First, Mr. Hayden was Patrick's father-in-law. Secondly, after meeting Billy, Patrick attended the next Gathering during the coming July, as well as several travel-teaching trips over the years.

The Gathering did more than simply allow men of African descent to personally connect with one another. It created lasting and unbreakable bonds of friendship. Written just a few weeks after arriving home from their travels in Southern Africa, the following letter from Patrick Patillo to Billy Roberts illustrates such an outcome.

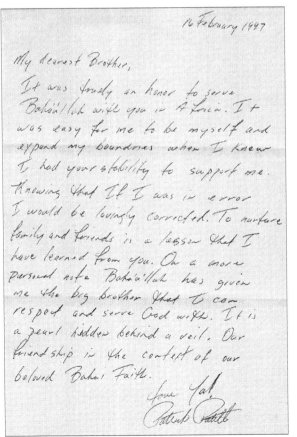

Letter from Patrick Patillo to Billy Roberts

1997 Black Men's Gathering, Louis Gregory Bahá'í Institute, Hemingway, South Carolina

As always, the National Spiritual Assembly of the Bahá'ís of the United States never wavered in its support and encouragement of the efforts of the BMG. It was this support and encouragement that guided and strengthened the BMG's efforts to serve the Faith. In turn, the BMG demonstrated their love, respect, and devotion to the National Spiritual Assembly by continuing to send it annual messages after their Gatherings. These letters between the National Spiritual Assembly and the BMG became "spiritual love letters" that warmed the hearts of all who read them.

National Spiritual Assembly of the Bahá'ís of the United States
August 9, 1997
To the Participants in the Eleventh Black Men's Gathering.
Dearly loved Friends,

Our hearts filled with gratitude as we read the July 26, 1997 message from the 11th Annual Black Men's Gathering at the Louis G. Gregory Bahá'í Institute and learned of the intensive sessions of prayer and deepening that revitalized your souls with the love of Bahá'u'lláh.

We praise the personal commitment each of you has made to develop yourself spiritually and to return to your communities resolved to "be in the forefront of the struggle for the equality of women and men." Further, we are deeply moved by your decision to establish a deputization fund in honor of dearly-loved Talia Ewing, who soaring in her divine home, most assuredly "stands ready to rush to the support of anyone" arising to further the Cause of God in Africa.

We spur you forward with the Universal House of Justice's call to "be swift in seizing your chance; be constant in your pursuits; and remain resolute in action" so that the goal to advance the process of entry by troops will soon be achieved.

As we eagerly anticipate news of your success, be assured of our prayers that His Divine Assistance is never ending.

With loving Bahá'í greetings,

Juana C. Conrad

Assistant Secretary

Initially, longtime participant in the Gathering Ted Jefferson was not interested in traveling to Africa for the teaching trips. He had an intense consultation with Billy, who reminded him that the Supreme Body—the "Source of all good [that was] freed from all error"[1]—was calling believers of African descent to fulfill a special role of teaching in Africa. Anthony Vance, a pioneer who lived in Kenya, also urged Ted to travel to Africa and encouraged him to visit Bahá'í communities in Kenya.

Having been affected by his conversations with Ray and Billy, in the summer of 1998, Ted decided to visit Kenya for several weeks as a travel teacher. Ray Collins and his wife Beverly had resided in Nairobi since 1984 as Bahá'í pioneers, and they were always happy to host visiting Bahá'ís. One day Beverly informed Ray that a man from California had come on a teaching trip to Kenya and was staying at the guest house in Nairobi. Ray asked Beverly to pick up Ted, and they offered their home to him for the remainder of his trip. Ted accepted, and thus began a lasting friendship between Ray and Ted.

Although Ray had never attended the Black Men's Gathering, it should come as no surprise that in their conversations, the topic came up. Ted explained to Ray that the Black Men's Gathering had been initiated to serve as a bulwark against the forces of racial prejudice afflicting the American nation. In time, Ray would be forever grateful to Ted for introducing him to the BMG, and he would attend the BMG for the first time in 2002.

During the rest of his trip to Kenya, Ted visited many of the friends there, including former member of the International Teaching Center Mr. Peter Vuyiya and his wife Ruth. The letter shared below, written by Mr. Vuyiya, describes some of the touching moments Ted shared while he was there.

> Peter & Ruth Vuyiya,
> Box 109,
> MoisBridge.
>
> 21st Aug. 1997.
>
> Mr. Ted Jefferson
>
> Dear Ted,
>
> We enjoyed having you with us on the farm. Your busy encounter with us and our neighbours was an indication of the success of the Bahai Black Mens Gathering in the United States. There is a lot of promise and scope for it in the teaching field of the faith in not only in Africa but for the whole black race in the entire world! We long to see more of your type.
>
> Safe journey back home.
>
> Yours lovingly
>
> PS. Your walking aid is delivered with this letter.

Letter from Peter Vuyiya to Ted Jefferson

1998

The BMG embarked on its second travel-teaching trip in January of 1998. This time, the group had grown from nine to fifteen brothers. As he prepared the men for the trip, Billy reminded them of their sacred mission in response to the call of the Universal House of Justice: "To the fifteen Men of African Descent who are responding to the call of the Universal House of Justice from the BMG, Beloved Brothers: Well, soon we will be winging our way to the continent of our origins in response to the call of the Universal House of Justice! What a joy it will be to see each one of you in the City of the Covenant—New York."[1]

The following brothers participated in this travel-teaching campaign: Jihmye Collins, Alvin Daniels, Alfred Fox, Nasif Habeebullah, Camille Herth, John Mangum, Carl Murrell, Mike O'Neal, Patrick Patillo, Richard Powell, Anthony Reid, Bruce Reynolds, William Roberts, Sam Stafford, and Larry Strickland.

This time the BMG focused on West Africa, where they split into three teaching groups that traveled to different regions. One group, comprised of Alfred Fox, Nasif Habeebullah, John Mangum, Carl Murrell, and Richard Powell visited The Gambia and rural areas in

Côte d'Ivoire, where refugees from war-torn Liberia were encamped. When the group gave talks and interacted with some of the groups of Bahá'ís and friends of the Faith, they did not have a structured approach. Invariably, a topic that continued to come up was the advancement of women. Not long before their departure, they were asked to speak at a fireside with about fifty people attending, and the advancement of women was the topic of the presentation. Also, while in The Gambia, the brothers met with the country's National Spiritual Assembly. In that conversation, the topic of the advancement of women and how it was such a cornerstone topic in many of their encounters also arose.

"Answering the Call" artwork created by and given to the fellow members of the trip by Cam Herth

After completing their trip to West Africa, the brothers made their way to Haifa, Israel for a visit to the Bahá'í World Center.

Patrick Patillo, Kiser Barnes, Cam Herth, Sam Stafford, Nasif Habeebullah, Alvin Daniels, Glenford Mitchell, Larry Strickland, John Mangum, Bruce Reynolds, Anthony Reid, Jihmye Collins, Michael O'Neal, Alfred Fox, Carl Murrell, Joan Lincoln, Billy Roberts (Photo Courtesy of Alfred Fox). Not Pictured: Richard Powell.

January 29, 1998
[Haifa, Israel]

After attending Hooper Dunbar's Thursday night study class, youth staff volunteer Stephen Vaccaro was invited by a friend of his from Senegal to come to his apartment and meet the members of the Gathering who had recently arrived from their travels to West Africa. Having researched the Black Men's Gathering and their first pioneering trip last year for a statistics report, Stephen was anxious to meet the brothers. After spending time with the group, Stephen realized how uplifted he felt to meet such devoted souls, to hear their stories, to laugh with them, and to bask in their radiant spirits. Afterward Stephen wondered to himself how many white people would ever have the opportunity to witness and be a part of the bond of these Black men. How would many of his friends of East Tennessee feel if they too encountered such love?

January 31, 1998
['Akká / Haifa, Israel]

Stephen was walking in old 'Akká with some friends when he bumped into the brothers again. He offered to show them some of the city, and he pointed out the path Bahá'u'lláh and the exiles had used to walk from the sea gate to the "Most Great Prison."* He also showed them the mosque of al-Jazzar, as well as the Turkish bath where the first pilgrim had been able to see Bahá'u'lláh. As they returned to the two vans the brothers had rented, Stephen talked with Billy Roberts about the Gathering, and he told Billy that, while writing his report, he had cried sitting in front of his computer terminal and had whispered under his breath, "I wish I were a Black man."

Billy laughed heartily. He told Stephen of how, eleven years prior, he had thought to himself, "What can I do? How can I address some of the issues facing Black men?"

Stephen was intrigued by this question. Rather than asking "why aren't they arising to serve?" or "why isn't such-and-such happening?" or "what's his / her problem?" Billy had asked himself "what can *I* do?" Now, eleven years later, Stephen thought to himself how hundreds of African American men had attended the Black Men's Gathering, had experienced transforming moments, had arisen to

---

* The prison at 'Akká. (Momen, *A Basic Bahá'í Dictionary,* p. 161)

serve the Cause with unprecedented vigor, and had responded to the call of the House of Justice to pioneer and travel-teach in "the continent of their origin"—a deed that the House of Justice wrote must "thrill the soul of our departed Guardian."[2] He also thought of how they had championed the cause of the equality of men and women and had demonstrated the power of Bahá'u'lláh's Revelation in uniting different peoples and races of the world.

This last point, the unity of the human family, touched Stephen the most. Last year, wanting to be a force for integration at his school, he had joined the Black Student Alliance. During that year, Stephen went to meetings, served on a committee, and witnessed the love, fellowship, and joy of his African American peers. No matter how hard he tried, however, he could not break through the wall of skepticism he faced from Black students in the alliance. In many ways, this experience was heartbreaking. Yet on this weekend, Stephen had been enveloped in the loving spirit of these noble men. He had become a part of this movement that was awe-inspiring to any observer or participant.

As they were all making their way back to Haifa, Stephen was hesitant to accept a ride, as he could tell the vans were more or less full. After backing away to find his own way back, he heard a number of voices saying "get in!" and "what are you talking about?" and "come on!"

Stephen stepped into one of the vans. After they arrived in Haifa, and as the brothers were hugging and saying good-bye to one another, Stephen again hesitated to join in the embracing of the others, as he did not want to feel as if he were intruding on a private moment. Billy himself approached Stephen, took him by the hand, and led him into the middle of the "pile-on." The twenty men joined in one huge embrace and recited over and over "Alláh-u-Abhá! Alláh-u-Abhá! Alláh-u-Abhá!" There were no words for moments like these, and as they drove away, Stephen's knees were weak.

That evening, Mr. Nakhjavani* gave a talk to new staff in the Seat of the House of Justice. Afterward, Stephen's friend and longtime participant of the Gathering, Andalib Khelgati, asked him to tell a few friends about his experiences with the travel teachers of the Gathering. Stephen wanted to tell them of the love, the spirit, the joy, but all he could mumble was, "I can't describe it." Then, as he tried harder, he began to cry in that crowded room. He tried to hold his emotions inside, but he could not. He exited the room and the building and walked to a quiet place adjacent to the Seat of the Universal House of Justice. There, Stephen wept and wept. The images of Billy taking his white hand and leading him into that pile-on played over and over in his mind. As he looked across the bay toward 'Akká and Bahjí, his eyes wet from tears, he felt a certain intensity and awe of the power of Bahá'u'lláh's Revelation—to bring together hearts and races, and to bring together all the peoples of the world.

Spring 1998

As the BMG increased in number, it became apparent that it would be necessary to relocate to a larger facility. Due to a variety of reasons, Green Acre Bahá'í School in Eliot, Maine, was a logical choice. This transition was not going to be easy, however. The brothers—in spite of the challenging hotel accommodations in the neighboring town of Hemingway, the long-distance drives to hotels in other areas, and the limited facilities at the LGBI—still loved the Southern Black rural culture that permeated the site and the surrounding area. The first decade of the BMG had been spent in the midst of that vibrant Black rural environment, where—probably

---

* Mr. Alí Nakhjavání was a member of the Universal House of Justice from its inception in 1963 until 2003.

for the first time in many of the brothers' lives—they had dared to bare their souls in a safe place and had felt the healing presence and love of genuine fellowship among Black men. So it was natural that some of them initially grumbled about the change in location.

As difficult as the relocation was for many of the brothers, they quickly accepted the wisdom and guidance of Billy, who they knew always had the BMG's best interests at heart. When the brothers first arrived at Green Acre, any lingering concerns soon evaporated with the realization of its obvious spiritual and physical benefits. Green Acre had more space than the LGBI, and even more significantly, 'Abdu'l-Bahá had traveled to Green Acre during His visit to the United States in 1912. The room where He stayed is located on the third floor of the Sarah Farmer Inn, and it is now used as a prayer room. What a wonderful blessing and privilege for BMG members to be able to visit this precious spiritual space any time their hearts desired. A second appeal of Green Acre was that the gravesites of Hand of the Cause of God Louis G. Gregory and his wife Louisa Gregory were located just a short walking distance away. Nothing could be more spiritually and historically significant for the BMG than to hold its annual meetings in the vicinity of the room 'Abdu'l-Bahá had occupied and the gravesite of the only African American Hand of the Cause!

Summer 1998

Particularly important in making the move to Maine successful was the love and support of the Green Acre staff and administrators. During the previous summer, to build the foundation of bringing the Gathering to Green Acre, Billy had met with Green Acre co-administrator Jim Sacco. Billy told Jim about the Gathering and its scheduling needs, and together they had worked out an agreement to begin to host the BMG this summer. Billy had explained the details and some of the logistical challenges—for example that throughout the day and evening on the first day, approximately one hundred brothers would be arriving at Green Acre Bahá'í School. Many of them had never traveled to the state of Maine, and even more of them would be visiting Green Acre for the first time. Before the brothers arrived, Billy requested that the co-administrators of the school bring the staff together to discuss what they should expect over the coming week. He was referring to the BMG participants' activities and common exuberant behavior.

July 1998
[Green Acre Bahá'í School, Eliot, Maine]

Some of the Green Acre staff members raised questions during the meeting. For a few of them, the mere nature of the Gathering, as it had been described to them, seemed foreign and at times unrelatable. Therefore, Billy took the opportunity to offer a history and to relay the vision and the purpose of the Gathering to the staff. In addition, he was able to convey to the staff the Universal House of Justice's approval of the Black Men's Gathering—in spite of its seemingly closed nature.

This session proved to be informative for the staff members, who most likely had never witnessed such a unique gathering of high-spirited men in a Bahá'í atmosphere, or anywhere else for that matter. Billy explained to the staff that men of African descent faced ongoing prejudice and racism on a daily basis in the United States. Because of this daily onslaught of racial hostility, they needed a space where they could bond with other African American men and share with each other how they dealt with the tests and difficulties of racial prejudice.

Billy also explained that the BMG offered much-needed encouragement to the men to remain active in their respective Bahá'í communities, even when they inevitably encountered challenges in their lives and in these communities. He described to the staff how men of African descent often felt isolated from each other in their Bahá'í communities and how they craved a safe place to build bonds of friendship, to support and encourage one another, and to celebrate together the spirituality and beauty of the shared aspects of their culture, backgrounds, and experiences.

This meeting with the staff and Billy was significant because the co-administrators wanted the Gathering to go smoothly. In the previous weeks and months, both co-administrators had encountered questions from the staff about the BMG's seven-day rental—which was two days longer than the usual summer programs—of the school. Jim Sacco felt an indescribable spiritual joy when he experienced the radiant love and fellowship so warmly given by the brothers.

The BMG not only had a transformative influence on Black participants but also influenced many of the Bahá'í youth who were giving a period of service to the school. Whether preparing or serving meals, or cleaning the facilities and the grounds of Green Acre, the staff could not escape the overflowing spirit of the drumming, singing, and laughter radiating from the daily BMG sessions in Unity Hall.* During meals, these youth also witnessed the unrestrained emotions among Black men as they hugged each other and occasionally broke out into spontaneous songs during meals. One young Bahá'í youth service volunteer, Autumn-Grace Dougherty, remembered how this experience touched her heart during the summer of 1998. Autumn-Grace was white and a second-generation Bahá'í—born and raised in a small town in Western North Carolina.

Autumn-Grace was a freshman at the University of North Carolina, Chapel Hill, when she decided to offer a summer of service

---

* And later in Reimer Hall.

to the Faith. She had been trained in the Core Curriculum to be a children's class teacher, and this training helped her secure a place assisting children's classes and the summer camp at Green Acre. The summer of 1998 marked her first visit to Green Acre, and she was amazed that 'Abdu'l-Bahá had visited there, that she could pray in the room where He had stayed, and that there were buildings named after Hands of the Cause.

Autumn-Grace recalled that "[the Gathering] was such a rich, spiritual experience" and that "it was very special, . . . significant . . . [and] really sacred" that she and the rest of the staff were there "to witness the Gathering." She remembered that the staff wanted to feel a part of it, and that they felt they were witnesses to those exceptional relationships. They were honored to be in the presence of the Gathering and to render any acts of service. Unlike some Bahá'ís who initially had concerns about the BMG, particularly because they thought the exclusively Black men's meeting contradicted the Bahá'í principle of racial unity, Autumn-Grace had a different experience. She felt that serving the men at the Gathering was an honor because, as she explained, "in our society there are not many kinds of . . . spiritual spaces where Black men are talking about spiritualty and supporting each other."

Echoing what some of the BMG brothers themselves discovered, Autumn-Grace noticed how you don't often see Black men being so emotional together—crying and hugging each other. But at the Gathering, it was different. In addition, she felt that as a white person, witnessing the men's emotional upliftment was very special: "It was such an environment of acceptance, [and] music was a part of it . . . like a thread that kept everybody together." She noticed how the men "would just break out into song, [and it was] very soulful." No one present at Green Acre during the BMG session could avoid being moved by the singing and drumming. Autumn-Grace described how the "music took on a significance that it doesn't take on in other [Bahá'í] gatherings." She recalled the "full participation and the booming voices in unison that created a very powerful experience."

As she observed the men between sessions as they interacted at meals and around the grounds, she witnessed what she called their "history of pain," and she "knew people were struggling." For her, witnessing "Black men caring for each other . . . was so powerful." Autumn-Grace learned more about how the BMG members cared for each other from a young African American friend who actually attended the BMG and benefited from its mentorship. She commented how she felt that the larger Bahá'í community could learn much from such an example of mentoring young Black men.

On the last evening of the BMG, the Green Acre staff was invited to the closing program. The music was so incredible that Autumn-Grace recorded it and would later play it during her time of private prayer. During the program, the BMG offered its heartfelt thanks and gratitude to the staff of Green Acre for their weeklong service to the BMG. Autumn-Grace was touched when Billy Roberts gave her and the staff a small token, a metal African pendant. She would wear it for a long time.

Autumn-Grace's experience "was so personal . . . so intense . . . it affected how deep and loving we need to be in the community . . . how supportive." As a young white woman suddenly exposed to the overwhelming spirituality of the BMG in the summer of 1998, she described her experience this way: "When you see the amount of spirituality shared in a space like that, you know what is possible for the world, and it is so transformative." She felt "so lucky to have been able to witness [the Gathering] because not everybody received that opportunity . . . It was so special." As a result of experiencing the spirituality of the BMG, she left with the feeling that "just because I'm white doesn't mean that I'm not going to feel that love and spirit. Not at all!"

1999

January 7, 1999
[Bahá'í World Center, Haifa, Israel]

To The Bahá'í World Center

Dear Friends,

Twenty African American travel teachers from the Black Men's Gathering will leave the United States on Saturday 9 January 1999 for a three-week mission to East Africa. They will all first go to Uganda for three days, then divide into three teams to cover Kenya, Tanzania, and Uganda until 26 January; after which they will visit the World Centre for a Three-Day visit.

The Universal House of Justice, in its supplementary Riḍván message to the North American believers marking the launch of the Four Year Plan in 1996, stated, "We direct the attention of the believers of African descent, so beloved by the Master, to the pressing need for pioneers, who will contribute to the further development of the Cause in distant areas, including the continent of Africa for which they were assigned a special responsibility by the Guardian when the first systematic campaign was launched for its spiritual illumination. Although their contributions to all aspects of Bahá'í service on the home front and elsewhere will be of great value, they can be a unique source of encouragement and inspiration to their African brothers and sisters who are now poised on the threshold of great advances for the Faith of Bahá'u'lláh."

Your ardent prayers for the success of their trip would be greatly appreciated.

In His Service,

Willis Burris

January 8, 1999
[Roanoke, Virginia]

Just before he was to make his way to the airport to be part of this year's Africa trip, Alfred Fox and his family had a get-together at his mother's home. His brother and sister were there, and they all enjoyed each other's company prior to Alfred's departure for several weeks out of the country. When Alfred and his mother had a quiet moment, she told him, "I have something I need to give to you."

He wondered what it could be.

She handed him her Bahá'í declaration card. Alfred welcomed the gesture, but he was also somewhat surprised. For years, his mother had been concerned about him being a Bahá'í, and she had started attending Bahá'í deepenings at his home after she came back from church on Sundays. Initially, she had been curious about what the Bahá'í Faith was and why her son had joined it. Little by little, her heart opened to the teachings of Bahá'u'lláh. Years later, Alfred's son would also declare himself to be a Bahá'í.

January 9, 1999
[Bahá'í House of Worship in Kampala, Uganda]

Twenty members of the BMG (Amir Bashir, Alvin Daniels, Leon Ferguson, Alfred Fox, Gordon Gullett, Jamey Heath, Bernard Johnson, John Mangum, Greg McAllister, Dan McCoy, Carl Murrell, Tallis Newkirk, Darryl O'Neal, Mike O'Neal, Patrick Patillo, William Porter, William Roberts, Oluyemi Thomas, William Varner, and Fred White), who would be called the "East African Regiment," began their travel-teaching trip with a visit to the Bahá'í House of Worship in Kampala, Uganda. From there they "journeyed elsewhere by foot, bus, and truck to capital cities and small villages alike, visiting the local Bahá'ís and telling others about Bahá'u'lláh."[1] While one teaching team remained in Uganda, another traveled to Ethiopia, another traveled to Kenya, and a final one traveled to Tanzania and Zanzibar.

Receipt of the BMG's contribution for the registration of the Bahá'í Faith in Zanzibar

One important component of the brothers' trip to East Africa was the journey of the team of brothers to Zanzibar, an island located east of mainland Tanzania. As far back as the 1950s, a group of Bahá'ís had lived in Tanzania. However, even though Zanzibar was a region of Tanzania, the Bahá'í Faith had not been officially recognized there because the Faith had not yet been registered with the government. When visiting, the brothers asked why the Faith had not been registered, and the Bahá'ís there explained that the National Spiritual Assembly of Tanzania did not have the funds to register the Faith. The travel teachers consulted and decided that they would assist the NSA of Tanzania by contributing the funds themselves so that the Faith could be fully recognized and would have a lasting official status in Zanzibar.

January 27, 1999
[Bahá'í World Center, Haifa, Israel]

The twenty brothers had answered the call of the Universal House of Justice for people of African descent to help "be a unique source of encouragement and inspiration to their African brothers and sisters who are now poised on the threshold of great advances for the Faith of Bahá'u'lláh."[2] Billy had now led three groups of men from the BMG to Africa for three consecutive Januarys. In addition, numerous other individuals and families had made teaching trips to Africa, and their efforts had been reinforced by still more pioneers from among participants of the BMG. Earlier this month, Billy shared with Willis Burris, a longtime participant of the Gathering who was serving at the Bahá'í World Center, the names of the twenty brothers who were then preparing to make the trip to East Africa. Willis recorded the names of the twenty brothers on a sheet of plain paper, placed it in his prayer book, and took it many times to the shrines to beseech Bahá'u'lláh's blessings on their behalf. A unique spiritual bond, beyond what was occuring at the Gathering, was certainly created between each one of these brothers and Willis. In fact, during their visit to Africa, the brothers shared an email with Willis with the caption, "Kampala will never be the same." After reading this e-mail, Willis realized that Bahá'u'lláh was working wonders through those souls and that the teaching trip in Kampala had been a success.

In anticipation of their arrival, and hoping to hear that they were now in Haifa, Willis called the brothers' hotel throughout the day. However, it wasn't until 1:45am that he got a call from Billy, who told him that everyone had arrived safely in Haifa. They all decided to meet at the Haifa pilgrim house later that morning.

At the pilgrim house, Willis and the participants of the BMG were reunited in the shadow of the sparkling beauty of the shrine of the Báb. When Willis arrived, a staff member from the pilgrim house was briefing the participants. After this presentation was concluded, Willis was able to embrace each of his brothers, some with tears in their eyes. It was the beginning of a new and different journey from any Willis had previously experienced in the company of these brothers. There was a new calm and a new confidence in his being as a result of this sweet reunion.

Standing: Alfred Fox, Gordon Gullett, Dan McCoy, Oluyemi Thomas, Michael O'Neal, Bernard Johnson, Darryl O'Neal, William Porter, Ali Nakhjavání, Carl Murrell, Leon Ferguson, Fred White, John Mangum, William Varner, Patrick Patillo, Greg McAllister, Kiser Barnes, Alvin Daniels, Dr. Firaydoun Javaheri, William Roberts, Amir Bashir, Burháni'd-Dín Afshín. Kneeling: Jamey Heath, Tallis Newkirk, Willis Burris. (Photo Courtesy of Alfred Fox.)

January 29, 1999
[Bahá'í World Center, Haifa, Israel]

Today was a bittersweet day for the brothers, as it would be the final day—at least for this trip—in Haifa. At the Haifa pilgrim house, Mr. Glenford Mitchell and Mr. 'Alí Nakhjavání, members of the Universal House of Justice, addressed the brothers. As the two men spoke, the brothers could see radiance and excitement in their faces.

Mr. Mitchell reminded the brothers of their birthright as spiritual descendants of the Dawn-breakers and of the preponderating role that the American Bahá'í community needed to continue to play in the promotion of the steadily emerging Faith of Bahá'u'lláh. He emphasized, with satisfaction, their recognition and striving for the oneness of mankind, and he reminded them of the many passages from Shoghi Effendi in which he stressed the unflinching obligations of the American Bahá'ís.

Mr. Nakhjavání, a longtime lover of the peoples of Africa, was in his element as he mingled with the brothers from the Gathering as they recounted many memory-inducing stories of their previous days. As he listened to the stories from the brothers, he even indulged the group with some of his own experiences in Africa while ultimately encouraging them to persevere in their efforts. He urged them to encourage the Bahá'í youth and also Bahá'í women to organize into groups to travel-teach in Africa.

A day so full of spiritual bounties culminated in the presentation of the BMG at the Seat of the Universal House of Justice. After the previous year's visit of the BMG to the World Center, word had certainly spread among the World Center staff of the spiritual potency of an encounter with the brothers of the Gathering.

Two members of the Universal House of Justice and five members of the International Teaching Center attended this year's devotional.

The staff also came out in large numbers to create a packed room of over two hundred fifty souls.

The program was beautiful and began with prayers and song—both of which set the stage for an evening of elation. Counselor Penny Walker welcomed and introduced Billy, who then guided the proceedings until Counselor Walker's closing comments. The audience was taken on a spiritual journey, beginning with the life of Mr. Richard Powell—an inspiring gentleman who was over seventy years old—who had gone to Africa with the group last year. With the stage of recounting their inspiring experiences thus set, and with scintillating humor and rare candor for some, the speakers shared with those in attendance a rare glimpse into that realm of unity that is generated at the Black Men's Gathering and that helps one prepare oneself to become a worthy servant of Bahá'u'lláh.

One can never hear enough of the many amazing stories of BMG members' first encounters with the Gathering. The following narrative reveals just how powerful and transformative first encounters can be even in settings outside of the regular BMG venues. In it, Frederick Landry describes his first encounter from the perspective of a young African American male who was adopted by white parents who understood the importance of connecting their son to "his roots." They were not alone in this effort. Other white Bahá'í parents, as well as interracial parents concerned with how best to connect their adopted African American or biracial sons to "their culture," often perceived the BMG as a safe space for their sons to discover their spiritual and cultural identity. Frederick's narrative helps to understand how the BMG attracted, embraced, and transformed these sons and brothers.

January 29, 1999
[Haifa, Israel]

What to think of this, my first encounter with the Black Men's Gathering . . . I've only recently arrived in the Holy Land on an eighteen-month term of service at the Bahá'í World Center. My mother had, for several years, encouraged me to attend the Gathering and had suggested that I attend with George Minter, a family friend from my hometown of Murfreesboro, TN. George, who was my mentor as a young adult, had attended several of the Gatherings in South Carolina. Unfortunately, I wasn't incredibly interested in attending. I suspect that my mother and father, both being white, and me being adopted had something to do with me dismissing the notion. I felt as if this was another attempt to connect me to my roots, and as an eighteen-year-old, I wasn't buying it.

But here I am—years later, in the multipurpose room in the Seat of the Universal House of Justice—attending a program and experiencing feelings that I have never experienced before. I'm not too sure what the Gathering is or why I decided to attend tonight, but as the spontaneous drumming and singing begins and I watch the brothers on the stage, I witness something that I had always longed to see in myself. I watch as young and old brothers alike are enamored with the spirit of the Faith. I see in those men a special power that causes me to think to myself that I want to be just like those individuals up on the stage . . .

Unlike Frederick Landry, Pierre Pickens of Detroit, Michigan had grown up around African American Bahá'í relatives and friends. Notwithstanding their somewhat different racial and cultural upbringings, both Frederick and Pierre felt the powerful spiritual influences when they participated in the Gathering. An emotional moment for Pierre occurred while he was attending the Gathering during its second year at Green Acre Bahá'í School.

July 9, 1999

Today, I experienced one of the most powerful devotional experiences of my life. It occurred at Green Acre Bahá'í School, in Bahá'í Hall. We had just finished breakfast, and before we started our devotions, I heard a few announcements informing us of requests for specific prayers. We then started prayers, and it felt like the beginning of a journey. At some point, I remember our feet tapping the wooden floor in unison as we merged into singing, "Yá Bahá'u'l-Abhá." It felt as if we were in the middle of the ocean somewhere on a slave ship with the waves rocking it back and forth, with just the sound of our voices calling on the Almighty, as that was the only thing that we had to hold on to. I could not hold my tears back, as I had never felt anything like that in my entire life. I felt unified with my ancestors, as well as with my fellow brothers, and the closeness I felt to our Creator was unparalleled.

Chibuzor Uwadione lived in Obiaruku, Nigeria and had traveled to Haifa in February, 1999 to offer a period of service. Although Chibuzor had grown up in Africa and had not endured the type of racial prejudice faced by Black males in the United States, the Gathering helped him overcome other spiritual challenges he had faced in Nigeria.

July 15, 1999

I felt that this year was sort of a spiritual rebirth in many ways for me. Earlier this year, I went on pilgrimage, and here I am attending, for the first time, the BMG. My participation at the annual Gathering of the brothers this past week was a spiritual encounter the like of which I had never experienced before. Sharing a spiritual journey with a group of brothers seeking God in prayers and in praise was incredible. Although I was visiting from the Bahá'í World Center, I found commonalities and a great deal of connection in prayers with the brothers. It was as if we all had the same problems and were all calling on God to provide us solutions to those challenges. I felt as if we were huddled in the shrine of Bahá'u'lláh and were invoking His name, and I felt as if our prayers were being answered in real time. We celebrated our humanity through prayers and music, particularly drumming, and I found inner peace and a deeper connection with my Creator.

On the last day of the 1999 Gathering, the following letter, sent by the Local Spiritual Assembly of the Bahá'ís of New York City, mentioned a notable annual effort inspired by participants of the Gathering who were members of the New York City Bahá'í community. This effort, which would become an annual occurrence, was an example of the spiritual power and creative expressions invoked by the Gathering.

July 15, 1999
Black Men's Gathering
C/o Dr. William Roberts
Dear Friends,

The Spiritual Assembly sends you its loving admiration for your spirit of consecration and your desire to serve the Faith more fully. The procession to the graves of the Hand of the Cause Louis Gregory and his wife Louisa Gregory acknowledges the important and unique contributions that these two believers made to the Cause of God. Their marriage symbolizes the striving for racial unity that continues to characterize the life of our national Bahá'í community.

Past participants in the Black Men's Gathering have returned to our community and inspired their fellow believers to reach greater heights of service. The first travel-teaching trip from New York City to The Gambia will be leaving at the time that the Gathering is taking place, and it is the Assembly's hope that this great spiritual journey to West Africa will become an annual event.

Certainly your time together will be a time to refresh your spirits, deepen your understandings of the Sacred Work, and fill your souls with courage to promote the Word of God.

With loving greetings,

The Spiritual Assembly of the Bahá'ís of the city of New York

Hillary Ioas Chapman, Secretary

On this final morning of the Gathering, the brothers, their families, and other guests (mostly from the Northeast) gathered for the last devotional at Green Acre for that year's Gathering. As the spontaneous devotions subsided, Billy invited everyone to quietly call out the names of loved ones who had passed on to the next world. Many in attendance reverently spoke the names of souls—of numerous nationalities, races, and backgrounds—who were truly loved and admired. The spirit of the moment that honored those cherished souls was tender and moving. The devotions then transitioned into a procession to the gravesite of Hand of the Cause of God Louis Gregory and his wife Louisa Gregory. After the one-mile walk, a program was held to commemorate and honor their lives.

Standing: Alfred Fox, Jamey Heath, John Mangum, Billy Roberts, Darryl O'Neal, Patrick Patillo, Harvey McMurray, Oluyemi Thomas. Kneeling: Gordon Gullett, Bernard Johnson and Fred White at the 13th Annual BMG. (Photo Courtesy of Charles Muhammad.)

Ted Jefferson and Charles Muḥammad at the 13th Annual BMG (Photo Courtesy of Charles Muhammad)

*Brothers drumming and singing at the 13ᵗʰ Annual Black Men's Gathering,
Bahá'í Hall, Green Acre Bahá'í School, 1999
(Photo Courtesy of Charles Muhammad)*

*Oluyemi Thomas, David Closson, and Ormand O'Neal on the final day of
the Gathering, Bahá'í Hall, Green Acre Bahá'í School
(Photo Courtesy of Charles Muhammad)*

Procession to the gravesites of Hand of the Cause of God Louis Gregory and his wife Louisa Gregory

2000

January 2000

The BMG traveling teachers had spent the first three years of the Four Year Plan visiting, one region at a time, countries throughout Africa. By 2000, they were set to expand their teaching activities and send travel teachers simultaneously to four regions—Southern, West, Central, and East Africa. Before the trip, all the brothers met in New York City for a couple of days of spiritual preparation. The following individuals participated in this teaching trip: James Abercrombie, Richard Abercrombie, Emanuel Ankrah, Stanton Brown, Charles Bullock, Willis Burris, Charles Carnegie, David Closson, Alvin Daniels, Dave Davidson, William Davis, Leon Ferguson, Aaron Fowlkes, Alfred Fox, Christopher Gourdine, Robert Grant, Gordon Gullett, Ronald Headlam, James Heath, Walter Heath, Camille Herth, Roger Hogan, Charles Howard, Theodore Jefferson, Bernard Johnson, Roderick Lawrence, John Mangum, Walter Mays, Charles Muḥammad, Michael O'Neal, Anthony Outler, Patrick Patillo, Pierre Pickens, Marcus Potts, Lee Ratcliff, Dwayne Rayner, Anthony Reid, Bruce Reynolds, Robert Reynolds, Todd Reynolds, William Roberts, Norris Robinson, Lloyd Seawright, Darryl Smith, Samuel Smith, Morgan Spriggs, Samuel Stafford, Bernard Streets,

Oliver Thomas, Oluyemi Thomas, Martin Varner, Michael Watt, Charles White, Phillip White, Britt Williams, Harold Williams, and James Williams.

The BMG travel-teachers formed teams and journeyed, spreading the divine fragrances, throughout the four regions. Various groups of brothers traveled to Botswana, Côte d'Ivoire, Democratic Republic of the Congo, Ethiopia, Ghana, Lesotho, Liberia, Malawi, Mozambique, Nigeria, Senegal, Swaziland, Uganda, Zambia, and Zimbabwe. The brothers had visited the Ugandan Bahá'ís the previous year, and the teaching team who journeyed there were welcomed back with sincere hospitality.

A quilt welcoming and given to the brothers when they arrived in Uganda

January 15, 2000
[Democratic Republic of the Congo]

Alfred Fox was with the team that visited the Democratic Republic of the Congo. Late during the night, when everyone else was sleeping, he was lying awake in his bed. Holding a small flashlight for some dim light, he was quietly engrossed in reading a book when Billy Roberts happened to wake up and notice him. As the hour was late, he asked Alfred what he was doing. Alfred's response was that he was practicing pronouncing words found in the holy writings because, he sincerely said, they came from Bahá'u'lláh.

Moved by this explanation, and aware that Alfred had been, in the not-too-distant past, illiterate and was still in the process of learning to read, Billy got up out of his bed, pulled up a chair, and joined Alfred in reading the text. Together they practiced pronouncing and reading the writings for some time, and Alfred frequently asked Billy, "Now what does that mean?" He was never satisfied with Billy's first answer and would often ask him for more detail. He also frequently responded to Billy's answers with, "Now I'm sure Bahá'u'lláh had more in mind than that!" Desperately hoping to return to sleep, Billy often stopped and asked him if he thought it was time for them to go to bed—to which Alfred always replied exuberantly, "Well . . . just one more line!"

Billy holding the son of pioneers Susan and Jason Sheper, Willis Burris, Alfred Fox, Christopher Gourdine, Morgan Spriggs. Limete, Democratic Republic of the Congo.

In light of the purity of his desire to know Bahá'u'lláh, and due to his humble spirit, Alfred would receive an invitation to travel to Haifa, Israel to attend the opening of the Terraces on Mount Carmel as one of the nineteen representatives of the Bahá'ís of the United States the following year.

Similar to their previous travel-teaching trips, BMG members visited, upon their return from Africa, the Bahá'í World Center, where they were able to visit the holy shrines. Some had the honor and privilege of meeting with the two living Hands of the Cause and the members of the Universal House of Justice and International Teaching Center.

Participants of the Central, Eastern, Southern and West African travel-teaching trip of 2000. Also pictured: Glenford Mitchell, Joan Lincoln, and Kiser Barnes. (Photo Courtesy of Willis Burris.)

Kiser Barnes and Billy Roberts

A testament to the Gathering's impact on the friends in Kinshasa, the capital of the Democratic Republic of the Congo, is found in Laetitia Zawadi Chigangu's letter to Billy two weeks after the brothers departed from the capital city.

February 8, 2000
[Letter from Laetitia Zawadi Chigangu to Billy Roberts]

Laetitia Zawadi Chigangu   TRANSLATION.
B.P. 181
Kinshasa I
D.R. Congo   Beloved Billy,

Allah'u 'Abha !
With a heart full of joy, I am taking advantage of Susan's trip to write a few lines to you to remind us of our time together & as a witness of our love. I am sure that you have no idea what an influence your visit to Kinshasa exercised on the Community.
All the friends are still talking about you all and every one is looking to do a teaching project in their communities. Bravo dear friends, it is due to your example and your love. Please Billy, if I wrote to Eric Dozier and Sam Sam Stafford and I asked them to get Susan's e-mail address from you, but they could also respond to the postal address above.
     Greetings to your family and to the whole Bala's family.

          Your sister in Bahá'u'lláh
               Laetitia.

Also, the National Spiritual Assembly of the Bahá'ís of Nigeria sent the following message of appreciation to the team of brothers that traveled there the previous month:

February 14, 2000
[Letter from the National Spiritual Assembly of the Bahá'ís of Nigeria to Participants of the Gathering]

We wish to express our profound appreciation and gratitude to you for the wonderful visit of our communities from January 10 to January 25, 2000. Your visit, the first of its kind, under the auspices of the call of our Supreme Body in the Message of Riḍván 153 to America for our African American brothers and sisters to visit, encourage, and inspire us to achieve the goals of the plan, left an indelible mark in the hearts and minds of many believers as well as high officials and traditional dignitaries you met during your trip . . . Significantly, your successful overcoming of the considerable hurdles involved in visiting our vast and populous country should surely dissipate the fear in many of coming here, and open the floodgate of travelling teachers and even pioneers who must need come to proclaim and teach the Faith to the largest concentration of the "pupil of the eye" on earth.

The love and joy generated by the brothers' trips was, of course, inspiring and certainly was one of the results of the Universal House of Justice's special appeal (in its 1996 Riḍván message to the Bahá'ís of North America) to African American Bahá'ís to arise and teach the Faith in Africa.

In addition to the letter from the National Spiritual Assembly of Nigeria, the following letter from the National Spiritual Assembly of Zambia to the traveling teachers to their country also conveyed heartfelt sentiments:

15 February 2000
Beloved representatives of the Black Men's Gathering,
Zambia January 2000
To our dear Brothers,

Alláh'u'Abhá and warmest greetings to you all from the Bahá'í community of Zambia.

We were so fortunate that, due to unforeseen circumstances, some of your representatives were able to spend time with us here in Zambia as part of the annual Black Men's Gathering.

Your love and joy resonated amongst us, inspired us and really touched an inner cord with the indigenous Zambian Bahá'ís. We would like to invite a representation from the Black Men's Gathering to Zambia as a part of your upcoming visits to Africa, particularly as we will be celebrating the 50th anniversary of the first Bahá'ís arriving in Zambia in 2002 and would love to share in that experience with you.

We look forward to hearing from you and meeting with you again.

Warmest love,

National Spiritual Assembly of the Bahá'ís of Zambia

cc: National Spiritual Assembly of the Bahá'ís of the USA
    International Teaching Centre

By the end of the Four Year Plan, the BMG's traveling teachers had increased from nine during the first year to fifty-three who were traveling on the fourth trip. In total, twenty-six African countries had been visited during the Plan. In a summary of the Bahá'í community's achievements during the Four Year Plan and the Twelve Month Plan, from 1996 to 2001, the BMG's traveling teaching activities were noted. Of the activities, it was said that: "The results have been uniformly successful. The host countries gained many benefits from these visits. Local believers were inspired, especially youth, and as

a consequence of this teaching, there were often many new enrol-
ments. The Americans conducted deepening programs. They met
with prominent people and garnered the interest of the media."[1]

Summer 2000

Not all the first encounters with the BMG occurred during the
annual Gatherings at the Louis Gregory Institute and the Green
Acre Bahá'í School. Some participants' first encounters occurred in
smaller local and regional BMGs throughout the years of the BMG,
as in the case of Morgan Spriggs of Aloha, Oregon:

> My experience with the Gathering began with a regional
> Gathering in the summer of 2000 in California. An intimate
> affair, that encounter awakened my soul and set the stage
> for my transformation. By the winter of 2000, I experienced
> more of the Gathering and met more magnificent Black men
> than I had ever met before in New York before our journey
> to Africa. Their spiritual energy supported me in my first trip
> abroad. I experienced the prayers of the Congolese; their praise
> of Bahá'u'lláh shimmered with bright colors propelled by the
> spiritual bliss that they were in.

After his first encounter with the regional BMG, Morgan participated in the larger annual BMG at Green Acre, and there he
experienced the full range of the spiritual and cultural power of the
Gathering.

October 14, 2000
[Louisville Bahá'í Center, Louisville, Kentucky]

Another BMG participant, Jamar Wheeler of Louisville, Kentucky,
had been an active seeker of the Bahá'í Faith since first hearing about
it in May of 2000. He had learned about the Faith from a Bahá'í

television spot from the 1-800-22-UNITE campaign. Jamar called to learn more and to express his interest in the teachings. Within a few days, he found himself reading various Bahá'í literature, seeing the name Bahá'u'lláh, and learning about His personage. Gradually, he fell in love with the Faith.

Nearly five months after first learning about the Faith, Jamar was invited to an event at the Louisville Bahá'í Center, a place he had visited many times before. This particular visit, however, was different because this evening, Jamar, at age 19, would formally declare his Faith in Bahá'u'lláh and become a Bahá'í.

After declaring as a Bahá'í, Jamar became very active in the institute process, and soon one of Jamar's Ruhi tutors told him about the Black Men's Gathering. Upon hearing about the Gathering and what it was, Jamar instantly asked if he could attend. He was told that he could participate in the Gathering by invitation only, and his understanding was that if his Bahá'í activity reached a certain level, Billy would take notice and invite him.

Of course, Jamar's perspective was not fully accurate. It was true that Billy invited participants of the Gathering to attend, but an invitation was open to men of African descent who were Bahá'ís or who at least believed in the principles of the Bahá'í teachings.

Years later, after applying for a service opportunity at the Bahá'í National Center and working in the Treasurer's Office, Jamar would be invited by Billy to join him in attending a regional Black Men's Gathering in Michigan at Louhelen Bahá'í School (which would be a special place for Jamar in his growth as a Bahá'í). In anticipation of participating in the Gathering, what struck him the most, as he watched brother after brother streaming into Louhelen, was the level of camaraderie, genuine love, and closeness that was present. These brothers had bonded through common exploits and victories claimed in the name of Bahá'u'lláh, and it became clear to Jamar that the Gathering was a sacred space imbued with the realization of and a continual striving toward Black nobility. Jamar witnessed and experienced this nobility among men who were spiritually linked to the African continent, who had endured racism, whose hearts were wedded to the Cause of Bahá'u'lláh, and who were toiling for the realization of the oneness of humanity. In addition to the regional Gathering at Louhelen, Jamar would go on to attend two of the annual Gatherings at Green Acre.

2001

In 2001, the following article appeared in *The Independent,* a newspaper in The Gambia and spoke about the need for initiating a much-needed focus on the empowerment of women in that country.

Bahá'ís Embark on Training Programme for Women
January 15, 2001
Posted to the web January 15, 2001

Banjul

The National Spiritual Assembly of the Bahá'ís of The Gambia recently embarked on a three-month training programme on the empowerment of women in the society.

The programme, sponsored by the Permanent Institute Board (PIB) of the Bahá'ís of The Gambia, is currently taking place at the Latrikunda Sabiji Bahá'í Centre, with an enrollment of forty participants.

Speaking at the opening ceremony, the head of the Local Spiritual Assembly of the Bahá'ís of Latrikunda, Mr. Abu Kargbo, said the programme is aimed at providing women with an opportunity to understand their mission, role, and responsibility as handmaidens in the family and in the community so that they will participate in community activities.

He said that once the women agree to participate in community activities, they can receive their training from other institute courses and also be part of other community activities alongside the men.

He speculated that the participation of men in the training is essential because it will enable them to understand the importance of practicing the principles of equality of men and women and the desire to practice it. He reiterated the hope that with training, the Center will support women in their efforts to develop their potential through education and training and to have access and control over their time and resources so that they can enter all fields of human endeavour and contribute meaningfully toward the advancement of the well-being of humankind.

In his closing remarks, Mr. Simon Colley, Chairman of the local Spiritual Assembly of the Bahá'ís of Lamin, pointed out that the advancement of women is what the government was talking about, which he said is in line with what the Bahá'ís are advocating. He said the training will be significant and helpful to girls and young women who have yet to marry so that they will know how to live with their husbands and also how to bring up a good family.

He concluded that the training programme is open to all Bahá'ís and non-Bahá'ís, regardless of their faith, because one of the ten fundamental principles of the Bahá'í faith is that universal education is compulsory for all.

He said that certificates will be awarded to participants at the end of their training.[1]

As mentioned previously, although one had to be invited to attend the Gathering, the invitation was basically a formality. Ultimately, Billy needed to know the spirit and intentions of the would-be participant and to confirm his age. Below is an example of many such requests for an invitation, and these requests often came from parents interested in their son attending. In this letter, Diana Malouf had written to Billy about her son Hassan and his lifelong friend. As he would do in this case and in other similar communications, Billy requested that Hassan contact him directly expressing his desire to attend.

February 12, 2001
[Email from Diana Malouf to Billy Roberts]

Alláh'u'Abhá!

I am trying to find out how to get my son, age 16, and his friend whom he taught the Faith to since the 2nd grade and is a Bahá'í, involved in the Black Men's Gathering. I realize it is by invitation, and I have spoken about it to Richard Thomas and Julius Smith, who both live in the Lansing area. Is it possible to go at their age? What is the process and when is your next gathering?

Other than that, I hope you are well and happy.

Sincerely,

Diana Malouf (Robert's sister :)

The Gathering was instrumental in that it inspired participants and gave them the courage to "own their Faith" and to share it with others. The following letter to BMG participant and New Yorker Carl Murrell exhibited the transformative power that participants of the Gathering were able to give to friends of the Faith.

April 9, 2001
[Email from Kenneth Ray to Carl Murrell]

Greetings Mr. Murrell,

My name is Kenneth Ray, and I am a new seeker. I've been under the mentorship of Mr. Lloyd Lawrence for the past several months and believe that the Báb and Bahá'u'lláh are the messengers of God for this time period. I plan to declare my faith during the twelve days of Riḍván.

Lloyd has made favorable mention to me of the upcoming Black Men's Gathering and has asked me to confer with you for an official invitation to attend. I strongly believe, as a man of African descent, that in order for Black men living in America to surmount the many obstacles that we encounter on a daily basis, we need to become stronger individuals within ourselves and our communities. This gathering provides a safe environment for us to do so and with its cathartic effects will help us to emerge as more focused and loving men, both to our communities and ourselves.

I look forward to hearing from you soon.

In the Spirit of God,

Kenneth Ray

Brooklyn, New York

Through the mentorship of Lloyd Lawrence, Kenneth Ray declared himself a Bahá'í, and he and his friend Lloyd went on the following year to initiate the devotional meeting termed *Hush Harbor* in New York.

Modeled after the annual Gathering's practice of sharing reports of their meetings with institutions of the Faith, the participants of a local Gathering in Florida wrote the following letter but first greeted and gave thanks to Billy in his role as a member of the National Spiritual Assembly of the United States. They then proceeded to give a detailed report of their activities. Such reports were essential historical documents of local BMG's activities, and they are also testimonies of ongoing spiritual transformation.

June 1–3, 2001
[Groveland, Florida]

To our beloved Brother Dr. William Roberts, member
National Spiritual Assembly of United States
Dearly Loved Brother,

We thank you for your letter of encouragement and guidance. The prayers you said for us in the room of 'Abdu'l-Bahá at Green Acre Bahá'í School were appreciated and felt by us.

Fifteen Bahá'í brothers of African descent from Florida and Georgia gathered from June 1 thru June 3, 2001 at Pine Lake Retreat in Groveland, Florida for the first Black Men's Bahá'í Gathering in the state's history. We were filled with the fire of devotion engendered by our heartfelt supplications to the Blessed Beauty.

Our spiritual journey began with the auspicious signs of a double rainbow in the eastern skies and a fiery red sunset in the west.

We received a special gift of the book *Pupil of the Eye* from Auxiliary Board members Charles Cornwell and Farah Rosenberg. The text of this book was a valuable resource to guide us in the study and reflection of the unique spiritual attributes with which we are so richly endowed, and we learned about our responsibility to manifest the full potentialities of these gifts.

During the course of the weekend, we remembered Hands of the Cause of God Enoch Olinga and Louis Gregory. We honored their memories with presentations and reflections on their lives and service. Their stories served as models and standards for us to emulate in our Bahá'í service. We also took inspiration from the life of Eduardo Durante Vieira, the first African martyr, and stories of the courage and sacrifice of the Dawn-breakers.

Now standing on the shoulders of these heroic believers, and with their memories in mind, we who have been designated as the pupil of the eye are poised to assume a leadership role in the effort to banish the injustice of racism and to "do all in [our] power to ensure that within the Bahá'í community itself the Negro and white believers understand and love each other and are truly as one soul in different bodies." We also know that we have a role in assisting our nation in addressing this issue.

During the course of our deliberations, we acknowledged that racism is a spiritual disease that has infected every aspect of American society. However, we identified strategies for dealing with racism and discrimination that are consistent with the Bahá'í teaching and our nobility as human beings.

Further, study of the January 9, 2001 letter from the Universal House of Justice has provided direction for our energies and has increased our resolve to contribute more than our share to winning the goals of the Five Year Plan.

Please remember us in your prayers as we return to our home communities to champion the Cause of Bahá'u'lláh.

With loving greetings,

The Brothers of the first Black Men's Retreat,

Groveland, Florida

There are countless stories of the paths taken by individual African American Bahá'í men on their path to participate in the BMG. In the e-mail below, Paul Baraza requested an invitation to join the BMG, which would lead him on the path to becoming a spiritually fulfilled Black man.

June 3, 2001
[Email from Paul Baraza to William Roberts]

Alláh-u-Abhá,

This year, after witnessing two historical events of the Bahá'í International Community, I feel the year wouldn't be complete without attending and being part of a Gathering that has won admiration of many who are aware of it.

I hereby request an invitation to attend the 15th Annual Bahá'í Black Men's Gathering at the Green Acre Bahá'í school in Eliot, Maine, U.S.A.

Your assistance is much appreciated.

Sincerely,

Paul Baraza

Morgan Spriggs was the only Black Bahá'í living in the Aloha, Oregon community. Although he attended his first regional BMG the previous year, Morgan was inspired to join the brothers this November on the travel-teaching trip to Liberia. The following passage conveys Morgan's experiecne at this year's annual Gathering and the impact it had on him.

July 15, 2001
[Green Acre Bahá'í School, Eliot, Maine]

This morning, I experienced my first gathering at Green Acre Bahá'í School; the percussive and melodic waves of prayer surrounded me. My brothers' chants and prayers were at times nearly too much to bear. A tremendous power enveloped my soul as one by one, people read, sang, and shouted in affirmation to the beauty of what was shared. Sitting side by side with a diversity of proud Black men, I've never been so close to people who looked like me, who wanted me to be there, and who just wanted to pray with no other issues. It took a while for me to get the courage to say a prayer, but after a time, I let go to offer my contribution.

Other African American Bahá'ís experienced their first powerful spiritual encounters at this year's Gathering as well. David L. Closson described his first experience in vivid detail, and he noted the cultural and regional backgrounds of the participants and the unique musicality of one of the participants, Oluyemi Thomas.

July 15, 2001
[Green Acre Bahá'í School, Eliot, Maine]

Arriving at this, my first Gathering, I'm thrilled to meet and know these 122 men of African descent coming from twenty-four states and the nations of Cameroon, Ghana, Jamaica, Bermuda, Canada, and Tobago. It feels like Harlem on The Piscataqua (River). In this diverse Brotherhood, there are many trained singers and professional musicians. One particular brother who stands out is Oluyemi Thomas, from Detroit. Oluyemi is always attired in West African garb, resplendent in a tall Yoruba hat; has a full beard; and wears wire-rimmed glasses. This brother is always happy, and his countenance always invites you into his presence. He's a master of the reed instruments, but his instrument of choice is the bass clarinet. I had read that this instrument is one of the hardest to master, with the embouchure being so difficult to maintain. The only time I had heard the bass clarinet played was listening to Eric Dolphy's music. At the music session preceding this after-noon's devotions, Oluyemi and a classically trained French horn player rehearsed a musical piece. The brother on the French horn was struggling to meld with Oluyemi. He stopped in frustration and said, "I can't find where this music is going." Oluyemi smiled at him and said, "You have to extrapolate the circularity of possibilities. Try the Lydian Mode." The brother looked at Oluyemi, then at me. All I could do was smile back in sympathy! When Oluyemi puts that reed into his mouth and forces air down that long, black tubular conveyance of sound, what one hears is deep prayer, a chant, an imploring to God. Oluyemi blowed and blowed, 'til he glowed and glowed.

Anisa Nizin of Ridgewood, New Jersey was volunteering at Green Acre Bahá'í School for the summertime. She and other staff volunteers experienced the Gathering as observers, but of course they interacted in various ways with the brothers throughout the week. For Anisa, there was so much inspiration, such as the beautiful devotions, the drumming, the singing, and the praying. But perhaps most influential for Anisa was the personal encouragement, love, and support she would not only witness but also experience personally. Being seventeen years old, Anisa was inspired to find her own voice while making lasting friendships with a number of brothers. Throughout the week, several of the participants encouraged Anisa to hone her passion for writing. At the time, she was on track to embark on a different major when she enrolled in college. However, her experience with the Gathering helped her feel more confident and decide that what she really wanted was to write poetry, so she ended up studying creative writing in poetry when she was in college. Anisa can remember at that Gathering, Anis Mojgani taking her aside, encouraging her, and sharing his poems with her. For her, these moments were precious.

On one of the last days of the Gathering, Nasif Habeebullah—"Uncle Nasif"—pulled Anisa aside and said to her in that matter-of-fact / loving style he was known for: "Come on. I want to take you for a walk." Anisa agreed, and on that walk, Nasif urged her to follow her spiritual path. He said that he wanted her "to just pray up," to do the best in her life, and to value herself.

Anisa reflected on Nasif's words and said to herself, "Yeah, I need to do that—I do need to value myself!" She loved his counsel.

The warmth and encouragement that she received at the Gathering did not come only from Nasif. "Uncle Bruce" Reynolds—longtime participant of the Gathering—also pulled Anisa aside to say how happy he was that she was there and that he was proud of her. He told Anisa how he was sure that her father—Joel Nizin, who was known to many brothers and who was a supporter of the BMG—was proud of her as well.

Being in an atmosphere of genuine love proved to be invaluable for Anisa during such an impressionable time in her life. She felt protected and supported, and she would carry those feelings with her for years to come.

Green Acre Bahá'í School youth volunteers: Anisa Nizin and Toni Robison—
May, 2001 (Photo Courtesy of Kelly Yazdani)

Joel Nizin, Anisa's father, was a Bahá'í of Jewish descent who had married an African American Bahá'í. He had such positive sentiments toward the Gathering that he was truly disappointed that he would never be able to attend as a participant because he himself was not Black. Still, he understood that the Gathering was an incredible experience for those who were able to participate and that it provided a support network for Black Bahá'í men.

Being married to someone of another race and having a multiracial home provided Joel with valuable insights to appreciate the need for the BMG. His longtime friendship with Billy and his interactions with African Americans who attended the BMG—including his daughter Anisa's experience—allowed him to gain a unique insight into the transformative power of the Gathering. In addition, his friendship with a devoted youth participant of the BMG, Trevor Nightingale, who lived with the Nizin family for some time, no doubt increased his connection to the Gathering.

Perhaps one of Joel's most significant impressions of the BMG was how it inspired participants to become more involved in the larger Bahá'í community. As an example, a dear African American friend of Joel's had always stood on the sidelines of Bahá'í community life, while his wife had always been more involved in Bahá'í activities. Joel saw firsthand how his friend, after participating in the Gathering, came out of his shell and became more active in his local Bahá'í community. It was a revelation for Joel to observe the differences between interacting with African American brothers on the sidelines and then watching as they became more engaged in community life after attending the BMG.

The BMG expanded and enriched the diversity of Bahá'í devotional styles. For example, Joel had attended, over the years, many Bahá'í devotionals whose style was very polite and reserved. He experienced just the opposite in BMG-inspired devotionals often held in local Bahá'í communities. He lovingly described these prayer sessions as boisterous, with brothers stomping up and down and singing in loud voices.

Joel had had a taste of this unreserved spiritual fervor before. As a medical student at Howard University in Washington, D.C.

in the 1970s, he had experienced a similar spirit when some of his African American friends invited him to an African Methodist Episcopal church. He enjoyed attending the church immensely, and he was particularly struck by the freedom of expression, which he also observed and connected with in the BMG. For Joel, the true testimony of the spiritual influence of the BMG was not only the effect it had on the brothers who attended but also how it affected the devotional style of the larger Bahá'í community.

Joel's admiration and appreciation of the BMG increased during some precious moments when some of the brothers would come through the New York / New Jersey area on their way back from pilgrimage after travel teaching in Africa. On one occasion, Michael O'Neal of Savannah, Georgia and his son, Darryl O'Neal, who was fresh from pilgrimage, stayed with the Nizin family and gave a fireside while at their home.

Joel was also able to attend the last day of the Gathering and to thereby fulfill, in a small way, his desire to be part of the BMG. Since he lived in New Jersey, Joel was planning to spend the night at a local hotel that Friday evening and drive to Green Acre the next morning for the devotional that was open to the community. Billy heard of this and instead invited Joel to room with him. That evening, Joel was able to engage with the brothers and join them in prayer and devotions. He and Billy stayed up late into the night engaging in deep conversation. The next day, Joel took part in the morning devotions and also in the procession to the gravesite of Hand of the Cause Louis Gregory and Mrs. Louisa Gregory. The invitation from Billy and his time there was such a sweet occasion for Joel—an experience that he would never forget. Of all his wonderful Bahá'í experiences, Joel ranked his time and experiences with the Gathering very high on the list.

Eugen Yazdani from Tucson, Arizona was another staff volunteer who was serving at Green Acre Bahá'í School during the BMG at

Green Acre in 2001. Eugen had originally been introduced to the BMG from his cousin several years prior. Eugen's cousin had done a period of service in the late 1990s at the Louis Gregory Bahá'í Institute and had brought back with her an audiocassette of the Gathering's music. Throughout his adolescent years, Eugen and his family would go on teaching and family trips and would play this music. He and his family would connect over the music, and many years later, Eugen would find himself teaching his own children those same songs.

Having grown up in the country of Chad, Eugen always wanted to do his year of service in Africa. However, obstacles seemed to always get in the way of that plan. So in October of 2000, Eugen began his ten-month period of service at Green Acre. After he arrived, Eugen was told by other long-term staff members that if there was one thing that would surely be a highlight event of one's period of service, it would be the week of the Black Men's Gathering. This opinion would certainly be one that Eugen would agree with when his final week of service coincided with the Gathering.

During his time at Green Acre, Eugen and other staff volunteers stayed in the basement of Green Acre's "Fellowship House." This building also happened to be where the Gathering was held that year due to campus construction and ultimately the demolishing of "Bahá'í Hall," which had been the home of the BMG since it moved to Green Acre in 1998. During the week of the Gathering, any time Eugen was in his room during his off-hours from serving, he could hear the music, the singing, and the prayers of the Gathering upstairs. Even though he was not a part of the BMG, Eugen felt the spirit of the devotions whenever he was sitting in his room. Of course, he was also able to engage with the participants of the Gathering in other settings during the week.

On the last full day of the Gathering, similar to other years, the brothers celebrated their experience throughout the week with the

Green Acre staff. Following prayers, the members of the Gathering offered a performance where the staff were greeted, thanked, given gifts, and invited to participate with their own reflections. This tradition was a way to give to those staff, who had selflessly served the BMG all week, an expression of gratitude and to demonstrate the brothers' loving appreciation. Among others, Eugen stood up and spoke from his heart. He talked about his observations during that week and was moved to tears by the environment of love and appreciation surrounding him. He felt that he was now spiritually galvanized and prepared to move on to his next path of service—which would take place in the next several weeks—to go travel teaching to Cameroon. Eugen expressed how blessed and fortunate he felt to have witnessed the spirit of the Gathering and to be able to take part in it. He was ready to take that spirit to Cameroon on his next path of service.

"Pile On" during the program with the Green Acre staff, 2001
(Photo Courtesy of Kelly Yazdani)

This was the fourth annual BMG held at Green Acre Bahá'í School. An impressive number of 104 participants attended from various parts of North America as well as from the Bahá'í World

Center. The BMG was blessed with the presence of two Counselors—Counselor Eugene Andrews, who was one of the original twelve who attended the Greensboro meeting in 1987, and first-time visitor Counselor Firaydoun Javaheri. The integration of youth was one of the bright spots of this annual BMG.

July 20, 2001
The National Spiritual Assembly of the Bahá'ís of the United States
Dearly Beloved Apostles in the Cause of the Blessed Beauty,

It is with great humility and honor that we, the participants of the 15th Annual Bahá'í Black Men's Gathering, received your heartfelt letter of July 19. We were moved to tears by your conveyance of love, inspiration, and encouragement.

As we are humbled by your perception of us being "signs that the meek have inherited the earth" and "symbols of universal salvation" we pray to and rely upon Bahá'u'lláh to assist us in being worthy of so lofty a station amidst all mankind. Through our arising to serve Him we are assured of Divine assistance. Your offering of the sweet savory words of 'Abdu'l-Bahá was most comforting to us and will be used as a source of guidance in all of our endeavors.

This year's gathering was the fourth at Green Acre Bahá'í School. It was attended by 104 brothers from the United States, Canada, the Virgin Islands, Bermuda, and Haifa. We were blessed by the presence of Counselor Eugene Andrews and also, for the first time, a member of the International Teaching Center, Counselor Firaydoun Javaheri. Throughout the week, the gathering was filled with soul-stirring spiritual enrichment. Intense prayer and song permeated our hearts and souls as we supplicated to Bahá'u'lláh and the Concourse on High. A special healing prayer was offered on behalf of our beloved brother Jack McCants and beloved sister Patricia Locke.

We applaud the efforts of the Green Acre staff whose dedication greatly contributed to the success of the gathering. Their level of service was worthy of 'Abdu'l-Bahá's vision of these sacred grounds.

With a sense of urgency, we deepened and consulted on the January 9 letter and 2001 Riḍván message from the Universal House of Justice and the Five Year Plan of the National Spiritual Assembly. Assured of the assistance of Bahá'u'lláh, we embrace the Plan with confidence and resolve. The clarity and conciseness of this Plan ushering in the Fifth Epoch allows us to better focus our energies on training institutes, devotional meetings, and children's classes. Other areas of consultation included the Kingdom Project and the National Fund. In a spirit of sacrifice and love, pledges and contributions were made to both funds.

In accordance with the Five Year Plan, the youth were an integral part of the gathering. They demonstrated exceptional maturity, wisdom, and commitment to the Plan and will play an active role in fostering a culture of Bahá'í life upon returning to their communities. Many discussions were facilitated by youth, along with presentations of community projects, music, and poetry.

We were very excited to learn of the upcoming travel-teaching opportunities in Liberia and Brazil in response to requests from the World Center.

The gathering will culminate with the traditional processional by friends from the northeast region to the gravesites of Hand of the Cause Louis Gregory and wife Louisa. A special tribute has been planned for this occasion.

We are eternally grateful for your support and guidance as we aspire to assist in building the Kingdom of God on earth.

With a heightened sense of love and reverence for the National Spiritual Assembly, you are in our hearts and prayers. We love you, we love you, we love you.

In loving Bahá'í service,
15th Annual Bahá'í Black Men's Gathering

Since 1996, the Brazilian Bahá'í community had held a conference called the "Bahá'í Encounter for Afro Descendants" that had the goal of increasing the self-esteem of the participants, as well as to encourage the deepening of local community members' spiritual understanding, and supporting them in their personal transformation. The conference also focused on promoting, within the community, the principle of the oneness of humanity. As the Bahá'í Encounter for Afro Descendants initiative grew and evolved, along with affirmations from the Universal House of Justice, the Gathering's goal of travel teaching to Brazil was cemented; and it was a natural fit for a BMG trip to coincide with the conference, which Gabriel Marques had initiated himself with the consultative assistance of Billy Roberts.

August 7, 2001
[Email from Gabriel Marques to the Black Men's Gathering, Attn: Billy Roberts]

Salvador, Bahia,
04 August, 2001
Dear Billy Roberts,

I have the joy to inform you of the date of the 6th Bahá'í Encounter for Afro Descendants to take place in Salvador, Bahia from January 25, 26 and 27, 2002.

I would like to suggest that a group of the friends from the United States might stay a few days after the event so that we may carry out some activities with the Black Movement in

Brazil with whom we have had a good deal of interaction, thus strengthening our ties. If these friends can arrive in Brazil 4 or 5 days before the event, this time can be used to visit some of the small Bahá'í communities outside the city of Salvador, [and] they would participate in the Encounter at the Regional Bahá'í Center in Salvador, and then the friends from the U.S. would participate in the activities with other institutions here in Salvador and / or in other cities of Brazil.

Considering that Salvador, Bahia is one of the most visited cities in Brazil, especially in the summertime (January–February), I recommend that flight reservations be made as much ahead of time as possible.

Depending on the interests of the friends, one option to consider is to purchase a Varig AirPass in the United States, which allows you to visit three or four different cities in Brazil at a very reasonable price.

One of the characteristics of the Encounters that we have realized in Brazil is the participation of both men and women, [and the Encounter is] open also to people who are close to the Faith. (In general, we have around 80 to 100 people.) I would appreciate it if you could share the last few programs of the Black Men's Gathering so we can study how to prepare a good program.

I look forward to hearing your thoughts on these ideas soon.
Gabriel

Plans were then made for a trip to Brazil, and they were also then made for another trip to the continent of Africa. At the previous year's Gathering, the group had decided to send traveling teachers to Liberia. The brothers made this decision based on the reports of the men who had gone travel teaching to Africa in January, 2000, and from the consultation two of those travel teachers had with the National Spiritual Assembly of Liberia. Thus, the BMG decided to create a sustained effort to support the Liberian NSA's teaching and consolidation efforts. In their annual message to the Universal House of Justice, the brothers shared this decision, as well as other highlights from their annual meeting at Green Acre. In response, the Supreme Body wrote, "We joyfully applaud the goal of your Gathering to assist the Liberian Bahá'í community under the guidance and direction of its National Spiritual Assembly, a community that is still recovering from the pangs of a debilitating civil war."[2]

On November 6, 2001, ten BMG members embarked on their important travel-teaching journey to Liberia—the African country settled by former slave ancestors in the early 1830s and where the first African American Bahá'ís pioneered during the Ten Year Crusade (1950–53). In undertaking this trip, the brothers were following in the sacred footsteps of these precious souls. The ten brothers who made this trip included Stanton H. Brown, Jolyon M. Clark, Jr., Aaron Fowlkes, Gordon Gullett, John McDay, Ormand O'Neal, Lee Ratcliff, Billy Roberts, Morgan Spriggs, and James Williams.

In a report to the Universal House of Justice following the trip, Billy wrote, "I am happy to report that ten brothers from the BMG have completed a travel-teaching trip to Liberia in response to the commitment made during the Gathering this past July 2001. The visit was simultaneously very challenging and extremely rewarding." He continued, "Unexpected opportunities to demonstrate patience, detachment, perseverance, and selflessness were abundant, beginning with an announcement upon takeoff from the United States that the airline we were traveling on, Sabena, was as of that flight to be out of business when we landed."[3] As Billy would later report, the rewards of the visit began as soon as they arrived, when they

Morgan Spriggs, Ormand O'Neal, Jolyon M. Clark, and two Liberian friends

were met by their Liberian Bahá'í brothers and sisters: "The believers in the Liberian community were outstanding in the midst of persistent difficulties and few resources in the country. The greeting of members of the National Spiritual Assembly from the moment we stepped into the country, and the continuing presence of one or more of them throughout the entire time—even up to the farewell at the airport—was remarkable. We were and are so grateful."[4]

The BMG travel teachers visited schools and governmental officials, including the Speaker of the Parliament; the Minister of Foreign Affairs; the Minister of Gender Development; the Minister of Health; the Minister of Education; the Minister of Internal Affairs; the Minister of Information; the National Press Union; the Inter-Faith Council; KISS FM National Radio; and the National Television InterFaith Program. They also visited rural Bahá'í communities, where they witnessed vivid expressions of African Bahá'í life. In one

James Peabody (member of the Liberian NSA), Mr. Appleton (member of the Liberian NSA), Aaron Fowlkes, Lee Ratcliff, (unidentified Deputy Minister of Education of Liberia), James Williams, (unidentified member of the Liberian Department of Education), Stan Brown, Mr. Moses Garza (member of the Liberian NSA), Georgia Caine (director of the Liberian NSA's External Affairs Committee)

village, a celebration was in progress for the Birth of Bahá'u'lláh. It was a beautiful program filled with prayers and readings, speeches about the birth of the Founder of our Faith, dancing, songs aplenty, and a banquet table of delicious food for all to share.[5]

The BMG team took particular notice of the Bahá'í children, who were present and participated in every way. Their songs and recitations of passages from the sacred text—in both English and in their tribal language *Krahn*—deeply moved the brothers. The team also took note of the influence of the Faith on women and gender relations in the community, and they observed that Liberian Bahá'í women were prominent in leadership roles and that their participation represented a strong foundation of community life.[6]

Billy Roberts with children in a remote village outside of Monrovia, Liberia
(Photo courtesy of Ormand O'Neal)

The brothers were astounded by the Liberian Bahá'ís' detailed understanding and practical application of the House of Justice's January 9, 2001 message to the Counselors. Clearly, these wonderful, spiritually mature souls had captured the spirit of the House's guidance, and they had obviously thought through the concepts of the guidance and had applied them on every front. Everywhere the team of brothers went, they witnessed and participated in village-wide core activities, such as devotionals, study circles, and children's classes. The children attending these classes were the same ones who earlier had been quoting passages from the sacred writings.[7]

The brothers brought with them an electrical generator for the Liberian Bahá'í Center, materials to set up two lending libraries of Bahá'í sacred texts, and funds for fifteen bicycles to be utilized for teaching trips in these rural areas.[8]

One might wonder what the effects were of the BMG's trips to Africa. Of course, it is impossible to fully comprehend the total effect and influences that the brothers had on the individuals and communities with whom they came in contact; however, the following story highlights one outcome.

Years later, when Billy and his daughter were in Accra, Ghana visiting the friends, they were invited to a meeting of coordinators of the junior youth spiritual empowerment program in West Africa to learn about their experiences in the junior youth program. Those participating traveled to the meeting from all over West Africa. When Billy and his daughter entered the room, they noticed a visible stirring among some of those present.

When Billy asked what was going on, the moderator of the program said that some of the young Liberian people were saying that they knew Billy.

Billy replied, "How can this be?"

Two of the young men then stood and greeted Billy. They said they had met him in their village, along with other men from the United States ten years prior. They said that when they met these Black men, they had been very young—only nine or ten years old—but that meeting them had been the first time they had heard about the Bahá'í Faith. The youth recalled that the reason they had gone to see them was because these Black men were distributing hard candies, and the youth had wanted a share. With a smile, they said that they had remained after the candy had been finished because they had been hoping that the men would give out more. The children had then listened to the discussion between the brothers, the Liberian children, and the Liberian adults. They began to understand that the Bahá'í Faith was for everybody. In addition, these Liberian children said to themselves that if these men had traveled so far from their home to tell the Liberian people about their faith, then they would look into it. They began participating in children's classes, then junior youth groups, and now—ten years later—they were not only junior youth animators but were also coordinators of the junior youth spiritual empowerment programs in their country.

After hearing the youths' story, Billy recalled the words of a recent message from the Universal House of Justice: "But what gratifies us beyond this is the certain knowledge that victories will be won in the next five years by youth and adults, men and women, who may at present be wholly unaware of Bahá'u'lláh's coming, much less acquainted with the "society-building power" of His Faith."[9]

To Billy, these precious young men were incredible examples of this truth. Their growth and transformation elicited feelings of amazement and humility from everyone at the meeting.

When the brothers returned from their trip to Liberia, the opportunity for them to fulfill the BMG's commitment to travel teach to Brazil was on the horizon.

December 14, 2001
[Email from Billy Roberts to the Members of the Black Men's Gathering]

Members of the Black Men's Gathering

Dearest Brothers:

At last, I have secured information regarding our upcoming visit to Bahia, Brazil as promised in our July communication to the Universal House of Justice from the Gathering this past summer.

We will depart from Chicago on or about 19 January and return on or about 2 February 2002. Our entire time will be spent with the believers in the Bahia area. During three of these days we will participate in the Gathering for Brazilian Bahá'ís of African descent in the region, which was established about four years ago after experience was gained from the Black Men's Gathering by members of the Brazilian Community.

Now we have the opportunity to further assist our fellow believers through this special visit.

Cost for the journey will be US $2500 for each person, which includes airfare, ground transportation, and meals. (Meals purchased individually must be covered by each person.)

I would like to hear from you by Thursday, 20 December 2001. Please send a bank check or money order with the amount ($2500) along with your valid passport and two passport photos to me at the address above.

Please note that the airfare costs for this trip may increase if we are unable to secure at least 20 people to travel, thereby allowing us to access group airfare rates.

I send this letter to you with excitement and enthusiasm. The believers in Brazil have expressed amazement that we would think them important enough to visit at this historic moment. What an opportunity to bring joy to their hearts and simultaneously fulfill our promise to the Supreme Body.

Please let me hear from you soon.

With loving greetings,

Your brother,

Billy

Reggie Newkirk, a long-time participant of the Gathering who lived in Saskatchewan, Canada, demonstrated the love and sacrifice and commitment that was commonplace among the Gathering. Although unable to attend the trip to Brazil, Reggie selflessly wanted to support someone else's participation.

December 16, 2001
[Email from Reggie Newkirk to Billy Roberts]

Hi Billy,

Your comments and perspectives are most appreciated. I am wondering if there is a youth who could use a few dollars. I have a little that I could contribute to assist one of the younger brothers—if you think it will be helpful. Tallis and I both are planning to attend the [Gathering]!

Love and best wishes,

Reggie

2002

Before embarking on any travel teaching trips, the BMG requested prayers from the Bahá'í World Center for protection and success for their efforts to serve the Faith.

11 January 2002
The Universal House of Justice
PO Box 155
Haifa, 31 001 Israel
Beloved Friends:

The group of 19 men listed below will depart for a travel teaching visit to Salvador, Bahia, Brazil beginning 19 January through 2 February 2002 in fulfillment of the commitment made by the Black Men's Gathering to you this past July.

We humbly request your prayers on our behalf that the Ancient Beauty may protect and even multiply our meager efforts in service to the Cause.

With loving Bahá'í greetings,
Billy Roberts

Dr. William Roberts—South Hadley, Massachusetts
Marcus Potts—Salem, Virginia

Alfred Fox—Roanoke, Virginia

Ted Jefferson—Santa Cruz, California

Oliver Thomas—Detroit, Michigan

Oluyemi Thomas—Oakland, California

Robert Grant—New York City, New York

Aaron Fowlkes—Framingham, Massachusetts

Richard Bruce—Shrewsbury, Massachusetts

Monroe McCarrell—Chicago, Illinois

Richard Posey—Chicago, Illinois

Patrick Patillo—Ann Arbor, Michigan

Dr. Richard Beane—Chapel Hill, North Carolina

James Heath—Los Angeles, California

Lee Ratcliff—Oakland, California

Gordon Gullett—Oakland, California

William Varner—Atlanta, Georgia

Jihmye Collins—San Diego, California

Dr. Harvey McMurray—Durham, North Carolina

The travel-teaching journey to Salvador, Brazil represented a major milestone in the BMG's service to the Bahá'í Cause. Brazil's large population of people of African descent made it a logical choice for a BMG travel-teaching team. This trip continued the BMG's earlier travel-teaching efforts to Africa to establish friendships between Bahá'ís of African descent throughout the African diaspora. As always, the BMG sought and received the guidance and blessings of the Universal House of Justice. Additionally, individual members of different institutions encouraged the participants of the Gathering and offered their personal wishes. The following two letters are from Dr. Peter Khan, who was a member of the Universal House of Justice from 1987 to 2010, and one written on behalf of the Universal House of Justice, respectively.

January 13, 2002
[Email from Peter Khan to Billy Roberts]

Dear Billy,

What a wonderful action you and your brethren are contemplating! Your message brought joy to my heart and lifted my spirits for the entire day. My only regret is that I am unable to join with you and go through the wonderful and inspiring experiences which await the group in Salvador Bahia.

I see this action as one further step in the fulfilment of the spiritual destiny of the American nation, and of the peoples of that continent.

I will await eagerly news of the accomplishments of the group.

Kindly convey to them my great love and good wishes as they embark on this most important mission. I will be thinking of them during the entire period they are away, and will be remembering them in my prayers.

With Bahá'í love,

Peter

January 15, 2002
[Email from Department of the Secretariat to Billy Roberts]

Dear Bahá'í Friend,

Your message of 13 January 2002 has been received at the Bahá'í World Centre, and you may be assured of the prayers of the Universal House of Justice, as requested.

With loving Bahá'í greetings,

Department of the Secretariat

January 28, 2002
[Fazenda Coutos, Bahia, Brazil]

Fazenda Coutos was a relatively poor community with small, closely situated homes and a population of approximately 42,000 residents. Most appeared to be under the age of thirty. Few people drove cars along the narrow streets, which were often filled with children and young people walking or playing. Men often sat at small, makeshift tables playing dominoes at all times of day, and young girls were often caring for small babies of their own. Yet, a real sense of community permeated Fazenda Coutos. People knew their neighbors in a way that is uncommon in most communities in the U.S.

After the brothers arrived in Brazil, one of their hosts, Liese Florez, and Billy drove the Fazenda Coutos teaching team to their housing assignments. The group was to stay at the site of a Bahá'í-inspired Social and Economic Development project—a three-story building that served as an educational center for local children and youth. The project was initially financed mostly by Bahá'í funds, but because of the recognized impact that the project had on the community, it was now being supported primarily by local government funding. It should be no surprise that there were good relationships between the government and the educational center, where staff members were comprised of Bahá'ís and friends of the Faith. Although the building had initially served as a day care center, it soon grew in scope and was now home to a vibrant literacy program, and a community soccer team. Later, a radio station was introduced!

The brothers split into four teams, some with the task of visiting homes and inviting residents to a public meeting to be held a few days from then. One of the teams, which included Billy, met with youth who were studying radio and receiving job training. Some were Bahá'ís and some non-Bahá'ís, but in total, there were about thirty young people. Billy talked about goal setting, motivation, and determination. The most important part of this encounter occurred during the responses to the question Billy posed: "What does this course mean to you?" There were some who said the course changed their lives—it either caused them to alter their lifestyle, or it gave meaning to their lives. The recognition by these young men of the transforming power of the training was, of course, very touching to everyone present.

Another group visited both non-Bahá'ís and Bahá'ís and invited them to the planned meetings over the next two days. Another group—which comprised Aneri Santiago (an Auxiliary Board member who resided in the Fazenda Coutos community), Jamie Abercrombie, and Aaron Yates—had a very special experience. This team had gone to visit Bahá'í homes. In one of the homes they visited, they met the sister of a Bahá'í who had previously shown no particular interest in the Bahá'í Faith. However, after discussing the Faith and, especially, after reading a prayer for steadfastness, the sister began sobbing and declared that she wanted to be a Bahá'í. She said that, even before the brothers had said a word, something about this encounter had moved her. Her heart was obviously already prepared for the moment.

On Monday night, a devotional was held outside on the roof of the home of a Bahá'í who served as the cook for the education center. The brothers brought chairs up to the roof and placed them in a circle. About forty people assembled in this rather small space, and the number only grew as the night progressed. Although there were many in attendance, the evening was humble and intimate with the only light coming from a single bulb on the roof and a nearby streetlight. A large group of children and youth were present, with the younger children seated on the floor in the center of the circle. The brothers offered many prayers and led the Gathering with many songs. At the conclusion of a very wonderful meeting, the residents commented on the significance of the brothers coming to Bahia. Some felt that this was an experience that would permanently change their community for the better. Billy told the children and youth that the brothers' coming should teach them that everyone can make a difference in their Bahá'í and local community and that *their* actions could make a difference to others.

January 30, 2002
[Fazenda Coutos, Bahia, Brazil]

Two days later, the brothers devoted their day to inviting local Black men to a meeting at the education center that evening. During the afternoon, the brothers used two teams to go out and extend invitations to the local men in the streets and in their homes. They soon discovered that the language barrier made communication difficult unless someone in each group was able to speak good Portuguese. The brothers then decided to merge their two teams, and they continued to visit with many of the local men in their homes. They played games with them in the streets, and simply developed relationships and engaged in conversation with them. Many nodded in assent to the question, "Will you come?" Despite receiving positive responses to their invitation, the brothers had no way of knowing how many would actually show up.

The brothers had invited people to come at 8:00pm, and a few of the young men they had invited began to arrive, on time, which was a bit of a surprise in itself. The plan also included holding a separate meeting with women, led by Aneri, while the brothers met upstairs with the men. Slowly but surely, the reception room began to fill up with people as small groups of men drifted into the building. Unfortunately, there was a class being held in the upstairs classroom where the meeting was to take place, so things would not able to begin until 8:30. The brothers realized that more people than they anticipated had responded to their invitation, but they feared that if the meeting did not get started soon, their audience would drift away. After engaging those present in conversation, the brothers realized that the men were there with sincere interest and that the scheduling challenge was a nonissue.

Finally, around the half-hour mark, they were able to get everyone upstairs and start the meeting with introductions of the brothers from the Gathering. Then each person in the audience gave their name and the community where they resided. The brothers then described the BMG and why it existed. Then they gave an introduction to the Bahá'í Faith and established a connection with Bahia and its importance to the Bahá'í Faith in Latin America and to the world. The brothers discussed the nobility and unique gifts of Black people and explored the issues of the lack of self-esteem that arises out of racism, poverty, and lack of opportunity. There were several excellent questions and offerings from the men in attendance, which included a lengthy statement from a young Catholic priest who had decided to come after the brothers met him on the street earlier in the day. His comments were positive and complimentary of their efforts. By all accounts, the local men felt that in Brazil, skin color was not as much of a handicap as lacking an education and lacking financial resources. The men acknowledged, however, that darker-skinned Brazilians were, on the whole, more at a disadvantage in the job market and in other areas. Aside from the six members of the Gathering, fifty men, fifteen boys, and twenty-seven women attended the evening meetings. The women gathered in the downstairs meeting but joined the brothers upstairs at the end of the program. After the prayers, songs, and overall presentation, which was very well received by the audience, a beautiful moment occurred at the conclusion of the meeting, when one of the young men from the community declared as a Bahá'í.

February 1, 2002
[Bahia, Brazil]

On their final day in Bahia, the brothers gathered with the Regional Council and other members of the Brazilian Bahá'í community who had made the trip possible. The brothers presented gifts to the Council and the others who gathered. The Regional Council, in turn, gave each of the brothers a small painting representative of Bahia. The Bahia friends thanked the brothers profusely in an emotional and moving scene.

Billy then asked members of each team to stand and express their thoughts and to relate some of the significant stories from the areas where each team had been assigned. Some of the brothers related stories of teaching successes, while others told of the wonderful prayers and songs that had touched hearts in the area. Counselor Gabriel Marques expressed his appreciation to the BMG and suggested that, instead of the Brazilian Bahá'ís making individual comments, they should line up, walk by each of the brothers and look into their eyes without speaking or touching. As the brothers looked into the faces of their new friends whom they had come to know and love in such

Alfred Fox and Ted Jefferson in Bahia, Brazil, 2002
(Photo Courtesy of Alfred Fox)

a short time and then began to contemplate the fact that they would very soon be parting, they became emotional. There were tears in the eyes of some, and others offered a light touch of a hand as they passed. Everyone was silent, and the moment was quite special for all.

The following letter stands as a powerful example of the impact that the brothers would often have on those that they would meet in their travels. Maria de Fátima was a Bahá'í who opened up her apartment to house two of the brothers on the Brazil trip.

April 11, 2002
[E-mail from Maria de Fátima to Richard Posey and Robert Grant (as members of the Brazil Travel Teaching Trip)]

Salvador, March 15, 2002

Dearly loved friends in Bahá'u'lláh: Richard Posey and Robert Grant,

I hope you've had a happy trip going back and arrived well at your hometowns.

With the selfless help of Shanta, our Bahá'í friend, I'd like to write you, in English, about what my heart is feeling, while I think of the heavenly experience that I and the community of Salvador enjoyed, during those days of January 2002.

The gift Bahá'u'lláh gave me, having you with me at the apartment, cannot be described, for there are no words that can describe it adequately. I was not totally aware of the beauty of the two jewels that were there, of the immensity of the shine and the beauty that irradiated throughout the entire environment, until our friend Edvaldo could transmit to me a few glimpses of that enchantment.

You and the other African Americans led us to paradise here on earth, you made us live what we did not know deeply, spirit and love bonded together. You were 19 angels in our midst, and you left us all spiritually inebriated. How I reflected upon the generosity I found in each one of you! How I learned from what I saw and perceived in you! Salvador is no longer the same, since you came, and it laments, as we do, the feeling left by your [absence]. An experience like that is unique and represents a true bounty from God. The friends here knew how to take advantage of it and drink from the fountain, to the last moment.

In Aracaju, the town where my family lives (do you remember?), where I went, taking you in my heart, I went through victories and crisis. My grandson was born beautiful and healthy, and brought us joy. Eight days later, suddenly, my son's father, my ex-husband, died, leaving our hearts full of pain. . . . [H]e was very dear to all the members of my family, and to very many friends. His heart was enlarged, and he was known for the greatness of his heart. He was . . . the father of three daughters, and the two families shared their suffering together, united. It was very beautiful! Bahá'u'lláh gave [me] the comfort of being near my son, on vacation, to comfort him, and cheer him spiritually.

I am very happy, for I now feel my mother and all my family are much more open to the Bahá'í Faith, and to knowing Bahá'u'lláh. I believe that the meeting that night at my apartment, your direct teaching to my mother and aunt, the prayers, your luminous presence and loving kindness helped make this happen. Thank you very much for the unremovable mark you have left in my life! May Bahá'u'lláh bless you always!

Know that you always have a home in Brazil,

Love,

Maria de Fátima

The following letter was written by Heather Marques, an American believer, member of the National Spiritual Assembly, and the American Consul in Brazil. She was married to Counselor Gabriel Marques, and her letter to Billy is noteworthy on many levels. The BMG gave an expensive set of drums to the friends in Brazil. By donating these instruments to the Afro-Brazilian youth, the BMG was affirming an African-diaspora cultural connection and the emerging role of the youth in Bahá'í devotions. Music has always connected people of African descent throughout the world and played a vital role in their religious life.

April 11, 2002
[Email from Heather Marques to Billy Roberts]

Dear Brother Billy!

I want to share some good news with you regarding the percussion instruments the brothers donated to our region. A percussion band has been founded in Areia Branca (the community where Cosme lives, where Harvey [McMurray] stayed) and the youth there are really responding. From the start, it was clear that the instruments were to be used to bring out the Sacred. At Naw-Rúz, the band played for the community of Lauro de Freitas, and they were a big hit! The friends from Lauro de Freitas who are carrying out the activities in Areia Branca decided that in order to be in the percussion band, you had to be in a study circle! The interesting thing is that although the band is a BIG Hit, there are youth who are more interested in the teachings from the study circle than in the band! It is quite a learning experience for all involved. We had a weekend seminar on socio-economic projects, and it came out that the friends from Lauro de Freitas are not quite sure if the percussion band is part of a socioeconomic project or if is a tool for teaching the Faith. I'm sure that will all become clearer in the future. For right now, it is a stimulus for a young vibrant community to grow together.

Much love to you and to the brothers!

Your sister,

Heather

Oliver Thomas and Ted Jefferson at the 16th Annual Black Men's Gathering (2002)

Participating in the BMG inspired a wide range of creative artistic expressions in music, poetry, drumming, singing, and painting, among others. With the growing number of musicians that were becoming involved in the Gathering, another music CD was produced with a selection of music created and inspired by the Gathering. Tributes, poetry, and traditional songs were also featured on the produced CD.

One of the selections from the 2002 CD was Anis Mojgani's poem "I Hear the Drums Drumming." Anis, who would go on to be recognized as Oregon's tenth poet laureate, spoke of cultural and racial identity and personal growth in a dynamic and soul-stirring way. Not all the selections featured on the Gathering's CDs were from the participants themselves. Below is one example of how the BMG inspired Anisa Nizin, the Green Acre staff volunteer who was also a young poet. The poem she referenced was included as part of the CD for this year's Gathering.

16th Annual BMG CD cover art

Ronald O'Neal, Ormand O'Neal, Michael O'Neal, Billy Roberts, Louis O'Neal, Darry O'Neal and Ray Rudolph at the Green Acre / BMG Saturday Picnic

July 11, 2002
[Email from Anisa Nizin to Billy Roberts and the Members of the Black Men's Gathering]

Dear Uncle Billy,

Throughout the year a number of men from the Black Men's Gathering have asked me for a copy of the poem I wrote last year; however, due to the large number of activities I was involved in, I did not really get a chance to send it. So, here is a copy of the poem. . . . I hope all is well with you and that the Gathering goes well, and if it is even a fraction of what I caught a glimpse of last year, it will be fabulous. I am about to undertake a period of service, probably returning the beginning of next summer from Guyana, Trinidad, and Jamaica. Prayers would be greatly appreciated, and please send my love to all of the men attending. It was such an indescribable experience that I still think about all the time. I was just one of the touched souls who experienced a part of it, and I am so grateful for that. Here is the poem, take care and I hope to see you sometime soon after my travels so I can tell you stories. Bahá'í love.

~Anisa Nizin

Beaming light in their eyes
Aching creases in their ever-present smiles
Open arms ready for hugs
Embraces from their brothers
Embraces to their uncles
Embraces with their fathers
All united for a short span of time
But building love and bonds that last
Forever and a dime
This gathering of men
This gathering of the finest deep gems
Of black men
The black men's gathering
Where there is no oppression caused suffering
No hate or disunity
Only coming together and discovering
What wonder lies in each and every one in
This divine meeting
The beating of their hearts
The beating of the drums
The singing of their songs
The laughing from their souls
All come together in perfect harmony
If only one of these black men was me
Then I could experience this
Phenomenal occurrence that
Leaves the public in awe from amazement
And the participants enraptured from their evolvement
But I must cry from afar
And realize that I can still
Breathe in the essence that
Wafts in every direction

Spreading to the touched and untouched hearts
Who can't help but be inspired
Just by catching a glimpse of
The splendor of these black gems
These black men
These glorious individuals
At their gathering
The black men's gathering

16th Annual Black Men's Gathering
Green Acre Bahá'í School
Eliot, Maine
July 19, 2002
Universal House of Justice
Bahá'í World Center
P.O. Box 31 001
Haifa, Israel
Beloved Supreme Body,

The palpable spirit that underscored this year's 16th Annual Black Men's Gathering was rendered by ninety-nine black men, twenty-four of whom were young adults intoning prayers and chants that soared to the angle of ascent.

Arriving at Green Acre, the Gathering was embraced by the loving green expanse upon which the Master walked, and the almost completed new classroom facility, a testament to a partial fulfillment of the Kingdom Project. The Gathering was opened with fervent prayers, songs to lift the spirits, and drums praising and petitioning the ancestors for strength and guidance. Each morning passages were read from *Call to Remembrance* to keep us ever mindful of the supreme sacrifices of the Blessed Beauty.

16th Annual Black Men's Gathering, Green Acre Bahá'í School, Eliot, Maine

In the first consultation of the Gathering, we vowed to fulfill the charges of the "Annual Message of the National Spiritual Assembly of the Bahá'ís of the United States Riḍván 2002," especially the study circles which "are growing quickly and show great potential to stimulate spiritual vitality, community development, and teaching."

We vow to inculcate your letter of 26 April 2002 to the National Spiritual Assembly of the Bahá'ís of the United States, in part, to ". . . be doubly mobilized to counter the march of forces of darkness that are wreaking fear and confusion in the hearts of people everywhere."

We vow, in accordance to your Riḍván Message 2002, to devote our energies to "devotional meetings, children's classes, and youth programs within the framework of clusters."

From the April 26 Message, under the skillful leadership of Dr. Roberts, we extracted lights of guidance that compelled us to explore the vastness of the institution of the Funds, International, Continental, National and Local, deriving a new understanding of how we can be better contributors and inspire others to do the same.

In our determination to facilitate involvement of younger brothers in all our activities, two did a brilliant job of facilitating a lively discussion on authenticity: others have been asked to take on other duties, and they were more than willing to accept.

Many were highly receptive to the invitation to travel teach in Bahia, Brazil.

Three international pioneers from Kenya, The Gambia, and Surinam stimulated the Gathering with excitement and anticipation as they shared with the brothers the challenges and rewards of pioneering.

For two nights in the moon-struck darkness, we entered the depths of a replicated Síyáh-Chál,* brilliantly designed by artist Lloyd Lawrence, and emerged in a heightened and reflective mood.

Counselor Eugene Andrews, whose presence further charged the Gathering, joined us on Thursday evening and shared with us narratives of his recent trip to the Cape Verde Islands, a familial sojourn and a journey of the soul. He weaved a spellbinding discourse on the progress of the soul in our contingent world of travail.

Our weeklong Gathering ended with a procession and memorial program presented brilliantly by a contingent of young men from our midst at the graveside of Hand of the Cause of God Louis Gregory and his wife Louisa Gregory. All present, including many believers and their guests from across the Northeast Region, were moved and awestruck by the power and reverence displayed on this occasion.

The overflowing expressions of love from you, the Supreme Body of our Faith, will lead us to new levels of commitment, service, and obedience. We are abundantly grateful.

The Men of the 16th Annual Black Men's Gathering
July 2002

As the Gathering's letter to the Universal House of Justice mentioned, the devotions of the BMG included a solemn and reverent atmosphere in the replicated atmosphere of the Síyáh-Chál, and the programs to honor Hand of the Cause of God Louis Gregory

---

* The Black Pit. The subterranean dungeon in Ṭihrán where Bahá'u'lláh was imprisoned with many other Bábís in the summer of 1852. (Momen, *A Basic Bahá'í Dictionary*, p. 211)

Program at the gravesite of Hand of the Cause of God Louis Gregory and his wife Louisa Gregory

Billy Roberts laying flowers petals on the graves of Hand of the Cause of God Louis Gregory and his wife Louisa Gregory

and his wife Louisa Gregory were moving as well. Each year, Lloyd Lawrence and a team of brothers would plan and carry out penetrating and powerful memorial programs.

Some of the greatest gifts to the BMG were the responses received from the Universal House of Justice to letters sent from the Gathering. These letters from the Supreme Institution affirmed that the BMG was aligning their efforts with the current Plans and that the Universal House of Justice was pleased with them. The following is the response to this year's letter to the Universal House of Justice.

To: Participants in the 16th Annual Black Men's Gathering
c/o Dr. Billy Roberts
U.S.A.
Date: 25 July 2002
Our hearts were uplifted by the message from your recent gathering at Green Acre which so eloquently conveyed the deeply felt expressions of your sentiments of faith and devotion, your aspirations in response to the call of the Five Year Plan, and your eagerness to assist with the teaching work in other lands, including Brazil. Rest assured of our loving appreciation of your principled strivings. Our heartfelt prayer at the Holy Threshold on behalf of each and all of you is that the Blessed Beauty may ever reward your unrelenting efforts with His divine confirmations.
The Universal House of Justice

Like many other African American Bahá'í men drawn to the BMG by the need for Black male spiritual bonding, Ray Collins wrote a letter to Billy in which he expressed his appreciation for the contributions Billy made to the African American Bahá'í community. Notwithstanding his pioneering experience in Africa, Ray credited the BMG for providing him with an unprecedented experience of Black male bonding.

August 2002
[Email from Ray Collins to Billy Roberts]

Dear Billy,

I wanted to send you a note some days ago but my spirit was so invigorated by the BMG that I could not form the words (I still can't). Nonetheless, I wish to attempt to express my deep appreciation for the contribution you have made to the African American Bahá'í community through your leadership of the BMG. I thank God that I have lived long enough to experience the deep spiritual bonds that I now have with my fellow Black male believers. This is something I have longed for and dreamed about. Even my pioneering in Africa, while wonderful, did not produce the same spiritual elation that I gained from participating in the BMG for the past two years. I know that a mere "thank you" is insufficient but I am sure that in [the] future more eloquent scribes than I will find suitable words to describe your accomplishment. May God's blessings be upon you and yours.

Warmest Bahá'í love,

Ray

On Sunday, September 29th, many participants of the BMG living in New York and New Jersey held a devotional that was open to both Bahá'ís and non-Bahá'ís. The devotional was held at the historic Evergreen Cabin* in the community of Teaneck, New

---

* In 1912, 'Abdu'l-Bahá visited Teaneck (West Englewood) at the Bahá'í property where Evergreen Cabin is located. Evergreen Cabin is commonly known as the Cabin in Teaneck. (https://www.wilhelmproperties.org/-property-history.html)

Jersey, and it was hoped that it would be the beginning in a series of upcoming devotionals intended to imbue the communities in the New York / New Jersey metropolitan area with the spirit and energy of the Gathering. The community was further encouraged that the devotional was initiated and was wholeheartedly supported by the spirit and foresight of Auxiliary Board member for Propagation Karida Griffith and the Auxiliary Board member for Protection Hooshmand Sheshberandaran.

The following is an emailed report of the devotional sent by assistants to the Auxiliary Board.

October 1, 2002
[Email from Lloyd Lawrence, Ormand O'Neal, and Dwayne Rayner to participants of the devotional gathering in Teaneck, NJ]

Alláh-u-Abhá friends,

Sunday, September 29th, 2002:

What an afternoon at the Cabin in Teaneck! Did we invoke the Concourse on High? Were we in the presence of the Spirit of 'Abdu'l-Bahá? While we tried to take one step, did God take two? And for those who attended, were they happy, overjoyed, their hearts uplifted?

Whatever the case may be, this "Gathering" was one of the most joyous events that we have ever been involved [in]! And [it was] definitely a step toward the building of our community life, a central aim of the Five Year Plan.

We thank Bahá'u'lláh for giving us His Faith to share with the world! Thank you to our beloved Auxiliary Board members, Karida Griffith (Propagation) & Hooshmand Sheshberanda-ran (Protection), for their audacious wisdom and encouragement to initiate such a loving event, which was graced by the presence of our endeared member of the Board of Continental Counselors, Rebecca Murphy.

The "Gathering" was attended by approximately seventy-five people, of which no less than fourteen were there to inquire about the Faith. It began with the beating of the drums (Ishmael, you're beautiful!). Next, Artemus Stover gave a brief introduction on the nature of the devotional. Then we started singing "Oh Lord my God!" We then prayed. And sang. And prayed and sang!

The prayers were powerful, the singing inspiring! So many beautiful voices were in harmony (Clive Herrings' voice, a treasure!). By the way, the women "carried" us in the singing as each participant was given a beautiful song book prepared by brothers Kenneth Ray and Lloyd Lawrence. At one point during the devotional, the singing led to more drumming, which led to dancing (and yes Talibah got happy!).

We ended the devotional portion by singing and marching to the song "Done Made My Vow to the Lord!" in which there was 100% participation! It was exciting to see everyone having such a wonderful time!

The brothers then set up and served dinner that included rice, beans, baked and curried chicken, collard greens (Will's grandma's style!), salad, cornbread, hamburgers & franks, and for dessert, (Stormin Ormin's) homemade carrot cake! So we ate! And ate, fellowshipped, and ate some more, until folks were fully satisfied. The devotional began around 2:00 pm and ended around 6:30 pm (4½ hours!!) This is definitely the first but not the last of such a wonderful community building event.

Thanks goes to all the brothers who assisted in planning this wonderful gathering; we worked together and really made it happen.

Lastly, much love and thanks to Dr. William (Billy) Roberts for his guidance not only as founder of the BMG, but as a brother, father, and friend to so many of us! "ET CU SHEY!!!!!!" (JOB WELL DONE!!!!!)

Your brothers,

Ormand, Lloyd, and Dwayne

After receiving the report of the devotional, Auxiliary Board member Karida Griffith's response letter of appreciation revealed the powerful spiritual impact that BMG-style devotionals were having on Bahá'í community building throughout the country. She was so moved by the gathering that she planned to share it with the Counselor and the International Teaching Center.

October 1, 2002
[Email from Karida Griffith to Participants of the Teaneck, NJ Devotional Gathering]

Dear All,

I can't get over how amazing the devotional gathering was! It was one of the greatest events I've ever attended as a Bahá'í. Really. It is so fulfilling to see the vision of the House of Justice at work in our community.

Hooshmand and I cannot say enough about your amazing service. And we're hearing the buzz from all of you that this is only the beginning . . .

FYI, we are asking the assistants (Ormand, Dwayne & Lloyd) to put together a brief report of the event, so that we can give it to Counselor Murphy, and subsequently the International Teaching Center. The ITC will definitely want to hear about this incredible contribution to the achievement of the Five Year Plan goals.

Thanks to all of you who worked to put it all together.

With great love & appreciation,

Karida

Auxiliary Board member for Protection Hooshmand Sheshberandaran repeated the admiration for and appreciation of the
BMG devotional mentioned above by Karida. He added how the
BMG contributed to key aspects of community building: opening
new chapters in the community, in the region, and empowering
the African American voice in "taking its rightful place and shaping the Bahá'í communities in this region." His e-mail was a truly
remarkable statement of the BMG's influence on the larger Bahá'í
community.

October 1, 2002
[Email from Hooshmand Sheshberandaran to Participants of the Teaneck, NJ Devotional Gathering]

My dear and esteemed Brothers,

I can only echo Karida's sentiments.

Together you have taken a historic step.

You have opened a new chapter in this region.

It is the opening of a new chapter for the community in
what it experienced, opening of a new chapter in the field of
service by you, and opening of a new chapter in the African
American voice taking its rightful place and shaping the Bahá'í
communities in this region.

Yá Bahá'u'l-Abhá.

With deeply thankful and loving greetings,

your brother,

Hooshmand

Counselor Rebecca Murphy, who was herself in attendance at
the devotional gathering, was also so moved that she wrote to the
National Spiritual Assembly and included the account from the
organizers of the occasion held just a few days prior.

October 2, 2002
[E-mail from Rebecca Murphy to the National Spiritual Assembly of the Bahá'ís of the United States]

Dear Friends,

This weekend I attended a devotional gathering at the Cabin in Teaneck. It was a wonderful, vibrant event. It was initiated by three assistants to the ABM who had attended the Black Men's Gathering. I send it to you just so you get the flavor of some of the activities. I have encouraged the ABMs to do more of these devotional gatherings throughout the region.

Your sister,

Becky

2003

A month after the 15th Annual Black Men's Gathering in July 2001, the Universal House of Justice sent a message to the brothers in which it praised the decision of the BMG to provide opportunities of service for youth: "That you will, among other activities, be sending traveling teachers to Liberia and Brazil shows how far-reaching is your devotion to the work of the cause. The great promise of your ultimate success lies, we feel certain, in your decision to include youth in your activities so that they can transmit to the future the enduring benefits of your exemplary initiative."[1]

In January, 2003, the BMG made good on its decision when it dispatched fourteen youth traveling teachers on their own teaching trip. After arriving in Chicago for their spiritual preparation and visit to the Bahá'í House of Worship, the youth assumed that Billy Roberts would be joining them on their journey to Brazil. After arriving at the airport, they learned that this would not be the case. In fact, Billy had previously decided to not accompany the youth because he wanted to empower them by giving them responsibility. He wanted them to know that he and the brothers saw them as men who could be trusted.

The costs of the trip had been "covered by a combination of deputation from the BMG itself and from the International Teach-

Standing: Brian Williams, Anis Mojgani, Teddy Lawrence, Anthony Outler, Dwayne Rayner, Andre Ballew, Haydar Barnes, Teo Henry, Artemis Stover. Seated/Kneeling: Harish Anderson, Darryl O'Neal, Derik Smith.

ing Center (ITC)." After the trip, the BMG reimbursed all the funds so that the International Teaching Center would be "able to assist others in their desire to be of service." Expressing the gratitude of the BMG for the ITC's support of the youth travel-teachers, Billy wrote, "the opportunity to serve the cause in this way had an extraordinary impact on the region they visited, especially the youth of Bahia, and as important a wondrous effect on each one of the traveling brothers from the gathering." In addition, he continued, "the power of your commitment and confidence in the gathering and these individuals in particular added to their determination to become outstanding servants in the field. We humbly thank you for this." The youth who went on this trip were Harish Anderson, Andre Ballew, Kiser Haydar Barnes, Miles Henderson, Teo Henry, Teddy Lawrence, Anis Mojgani, Darrell O'Neal, Louis O'Neal, Anthony Outler, Dwayne Rayner, Derik Smith, Artemus Stover and Brian Williams.[2]

As mentioned previously, in 1996, Gabriel Marques of Bahia, Brazil first attended the Gathering in South Carolina and returned home to initiate a Gathering in his home country. By 2003, the Gathering in Brazil, named the "Encounter of African Descendants," was in its seventh year of deepening its participants' spiritual understanding and paving the way for personal transformation. In January, Billy wrote the following inspirational e-mail to their Gathering:

January 29, 2003
[Email from Billy Roberts for the Encounter of African Descendants 7th Annual Meeting]

To The Seventh Encounter of Bahá'í African Descendants ~ Salvador, Bahia

Dearly loved Coworkers:

It is with great joy that I greet you and remember with a throbbing heart the time we enjoyed together a year ago. How our hearts were bonded together is an expression of our common Faith and love for Bahá'u'lláh and the realization of the mission to change the world which has been placed before each of us. I will forever cherish that spiritual union we experienced together.

As you gather together, please know that the Black Men's Gathering celebrates your achievements and sends you our admiration and praise. The recent visit of fourteen younger brothers from the BMG last month reinforces the joy we already feel as we witness your growth there in Bahia.

The prophecies of the Master about Bahia are becoming a reality day by day through the raising up of strong believers who are pillars of the Cause of God in that region. His spirit must be rejoicing to see the youth taking hold of the reins of the Cause and taking it to new heights only they can visualize. The Youth of Bahia are our champions, and we long to see each of you growing in capacity and strength. The study circles, devotional meetings, and children's classes you are attending are central to the progress you are enjoying, so please don't stop. Keep on and on and on!

Please be assured prayers for your every success will be said in the Mother Temple of the West here in Wilmette.

With a loving heart and huge embrace,

Your brother,

Dr. Billy Roberts

Highlighting this years' Afro-Descendants Gathering, the Bahá'í World News Service published the following story:

In Brazil, African descendants plan for better society
February 2, 2003

Drumming and dance were features at the Afro-Descendants Gathering in Brazil.

SALVADOR, Brazil — More than 170 men, women and children attended a conference of people of African descent in Brazil to gain a deeper understanding of their heritage and to plan to construct a better society.

The "Afro-Descendants Gathering" was held in the Regional Bahá'í Center in Salvador, Bahia, from January 31 to February 2, 2003. It was sponsored by the Regional Bahá'í Council for the States of Alagoas, Bahia and Sergipe.

The seventh such gathering in Brazil since 1996, the conference had the aims of increasing the self-esteem of the participants, deepening their spiritual understanding, assisting them in their personal transformation, and promoting the principle of the oneness of humanity.

"The aim was to gain a deeper perception and appreciation of African cultural heritage that had an enormous influence on Brazilian culture during the centuries of slavery," said Mr. Gabriel Marques, a member of the Continental Board of Counsellors, a senior advisory body that forms part of the Bahá'í administration.

"Brazil was the last country in the world that abolished the institution of slavery—in 1888," Mr. Marques said. "The wound is still too fresh, and the Brazilian population is just beginning to overcome this problem."

In order to better understand racial prejudice and how it operates in today's society, the participants spoke in a session of their personal experiences of day-to-day discrimination.

Then they examined the contributions made by "Afro descendants" to technological and scientific development in both ancient and modern times.

Participants also studied selected Bahá'í principles such as the oneness of the human family and the need for "unity in diversity."

Children mixed with youth and adults at the Afro-Descendants Gathering held in Salvador, Brazil.

In one session, they studied the text where Bahá'u'lláh compared "the colored people to the black pupil of the eye."* Two ophthalmologists then explained the vital function of the pupil to the eye, comparing it to the contributions people of color make to humanity.

Participants also discussed how they could build a better society. They concluded they should make greater efforts to promote the moral education of children, study the Bahá'í sacred writings regularly, and seek to spiritualize themselves,

---

* 'Abdul-Bahá said that his father, Bahá'u'lláh, had made the comparison between Black people and the pupil of the eye, and 'Abdul-Bahá himself said, in a letter to the first African American Bahá'í, Robert Turner: "Thou art like unto the pupil of the eye which is dark in color, yet it is the fount of light and the revealer of the contingent world." Mr. Turner visited 'Abdul-Bahá in the Holy Land in 1898. He was the butler of Mrs. Phoebe Hearst, an early American Bahá'í.

their families, and their communities through participation in devotional meetings and study circles, which involve learning about their own spiritual nature, and acquiring the skills and motivation to take effective action.

The gathering was permeated with music and dance. Istvan Dely, a Hungarian musician who resides in Colombia, was a featured guest. An accomplished drummer and percussionist, he spoke of the spirituality of the African heritage.

"Not having any books, (Africans) used the power of music and dancing as a channel to express their veneration of the spiritual world," said Mr. Dely, who has been closely involved in the revival and integration of the arts and African percussion in Bahá'í study circles in Africa and the Caribbean.

Two special events preceded the gathering. The first was a visit to the region by fourteen young American men who had participated in the Black Men's Gathering, a Bahá'í event held in the United States aimed at rejuvenating the souls of the participants and enkindling in them a spirit of Bahá'í service to humanity. They dedicated two weeks to the promotion of community life activities in the area.

The other event was an African mask workshop involving twenty-four youth from the region. The idea behind it was to develop the individual artistic abilities of the youth and also to learn how to incorporate the arts into study circles.

The masks decorated the venue of the gathering, and the young people who made them explained the feelings or specific virtues they sought to express in their masks.

March 2003
[Saskatchewan, Canada]

Concern and apprehension seized Reggie Newkirk as the dates of the Seventeenth Annual Gathering drew near. His heart pounded with anxiety as he considered not attending this year because it seemed too expensive. Then, he disappointedly wondered how he could think this way when he knew how beneficial the five previous gatherings had been for him. Reggie consulted with his family about his concern. Tallis (Reggie's son), who was part of this consultation, was the person who had persuaded Reggie to attend his first Gathering. When Reggie shared his doubts about whether he should attend, Tallis felt it was unthinkable that his father would consider not going this year. For Reggie, it all boiled down to this question: given the tremendous benefit he derived from previous Gatherings, could he afford *not* to attend this year's session? In addition to answering this, Reggie's wife made it known that his attendance at the gathering was not negotiable. She felt he should go, and that was that!

The impact that the Gathering had on participants was well-known to many who had never even attended the BMG themselves. Frequently, like the following example, a family member, friend, or a member of a Bahá'í institution would reach out to Billy to request that a certain person be invited to attend the BMG.

April 16, 2003
[Email from Kambiz Rafraf (member of the LSA of Dallas, Texas) to Billy Roberts]

. . . On another note, there is an African American man in our community, who declared over two years ago. His name is Tommy Taylor. Is it possible for you to invite him to the Black Men's Gathering this year? It would be very meaningful and inspiring for Tommy and the Dallas Bahá'í community if he is able to attend. I am not sure if he is able to attend, but I thought I would mention it to you.

With love,

Kambiz

Sometimes it took several attempts to invite brothers to the BMG. Some longtime Bahá'ís needed to be convinced that the BMG was supported by the Bahá'í institutions and not at odds with the Bahá'í principle of racial unity. Interestingly enough, two brothers, Burton and Julius Smith, were second-generation African American Bahá'ís and had never experienced anything like the BMG growing up in a Bahá'í community. But it would take more than a first or second invitation for Burton to find himself at the Gathering, as demonstrated in the account below.

May 17, 2003
[Bahá'í House of Worship, Wilmette, Illinois]

Burton Smith of Lansing, Michigan had recently been approached by his eldest brother Julius to go to the fiftieth anniversary of the dedication of the Bahá'í House of Worship in Wilmette, Illinois. Initially, Burton had declined the invitation from his brother, but later Burton called Julius and explained that he had had a change of heart. They then left shortly for the Bahá'í House of Worship. When they arrived, they were fortunate to be able to take their photo on the steps of the House of Worship. Interestingly, their parents had taken a very similar photo fifty years before at the House of Worship's first dedication ceremony.

After the program, they both ran in to Billy Roberts, who put his hands on Burton's shoulders and lovingly asked him why he had never before attended the Gathering. Burton remembered that years before, Patrick Patillo—a fellow friend—had asked him the same question when they were at Louhelen Bahá'í School.

Burton's response was that he had not been invited—to which Billy replied, "Well, consider coming."

Burton filed the information away and spent the rest of the evening with his brother.

June 30, 2003

Regional Bahá'í Council of the Northeastern States
June 2003
To the Friends in the Northeastern Region
Dear Bahá'í Friends,

Saturday morning, July 19, 2003, will be a wonderful occasion for our Northeastern community. The Bahá'í Black Men's Gathering, which will be meeting at Green Acre Bahá'í School for the sixth time, has invited the friends in the Northeast to the closing day's activities and a joyous celebration.

The friends may start arriving at 8:00 AM at Reimer Hall on the main Green Acre campus. Prayers begin at 9:00 AM, after which begins the procession to the graves of Louis and Louisa Gregory. In the words of one participant it is a "process of transformation, a preparation, a being made fit to serve His Cause."

Following the memorial meeting and procession you are invited to return to the Green Acre campus where a barbeque lunch will be served for a nominal fee (approximately $10) and we will be treated to fellowship, music and jubilant tributes. (If you intend to stay for lunch, please advise and register in advance with the Green Acre Bahá'í School by calling [the office].)

This day will be a special and spiritually significant time when the men of "The Gathering" embrace their fellow believers and join forces praying for the release of spiritual energy from the Concourse on High to be directed at the achievement of victory in this Region. During the Four Year Plan, the Twelve Month Plan and the Five Year Plan, members of the Gathering have systematically visited the African and South American continents providing service, forming lasting friendships and teaching the Cause of God. The Regional Bahá'í Council of the Northeastern States invites your participation in this precious experience. It is a unique opportunity to unite with men of African descent from all over the world to bring power to our community. It would be wonderful to see all of the diversity of our community participate in this event: Persian, European, Hispanic, Asian, African American, American Indian, young, old, women, men, children, junior youth, and youth.

In the words of the Supreme Body regarding the Black Men's Gathering:

"The universal spirit conveyed from a group of individuals who are daily pressured by the myopic cultural vision of those among whom they live and work, the certitude of the participants' commitment to the Lord of Mankind, the clarity of their understanding of the essentials of the Four Year Plan in relation to the individual, the institutions and the community, the vibrancy of their fellowship—all evoke in us feelings of admiration and gratitude."

"This is indeed an exemplary achievement at a time when so many other groups in the United States are gripped in the self-imposed strictures of cultural divisiveness. Would to God that the news of this accomplishment be noised abroad as a lesson and an inspiration to others." —The Universal House of Justice, 8 August 1996

Please inform each member of your community of this Saturday morning gathering, July 19, at Green Acre. The barbeque begins around noon and the celebration lasts the whole day. If you intend to stay for lunch, please advise and register in advance with the Green Acre Bahá'í School by calling [phone number], or send an email to [email address].

With loving Bahá'í greetings,

Regional Bahá'í Council of the Northeastern States

July 12, 2003

As Reggie Newkirk made his last leg of the journey to Green Acre, he wondered if anyone at the Gathering would remember him. Would he be quizzed for having missed the last three years? Would there be an entire new group of men attending whom he did not know? Would he end up being alone among the men? His answer would soon be apparent to him. Within a short period of time, after the start of the Gathering, Reggie had connected with old and new brothers, all of whom welcomed him as if they were longtime friends.

This year, one of the defining elements of the Gathering was the focus on the training institute and how important it was in the framework for action. In its Riḍván message of 1996, the Universal House of Justice had called for the establishment of institutes worldwide, in order to provide systematic training in the fundamental verities of the Faith and to develop capacities to build communities animated by the vision of Bahá'u'lláh. All around the world, training institutes were experimenting with different curriculum. In the United States, there existed two such curricula—those developed under the Ruhi Institute and those of the Core Curriculum.

After reading the Riḍván message delivered to the Bahá'ís of the world in 2003, Billy decided to respond to the call of the Universal House of Justice and set up an accelerated training during the Gathering for brothers who were interested in becoming tutors. He decided to reach out to the Magdalene Carney Training Institute and Louhelen Bahá'í School to get a list of those members of the Gathering who had experience in facilitating these types of courses. One of the individuals identified was Pierre Pickens.

There were countless special moments during the BMG that revealed the genuine love shared among the brothers within the Gathering. One element, which often was overlooked or which was mistakenly omitted from descriptions of the Gathering, was laughter. Laughter became part and parcel of the weeklong camaraderie, and it was also present in the Core Curriculum training that was led by Pierre. As he was going through the materials, different brothers would comment, praise, or share particular thoughts.

What stood out amusingly, however, was one particular brother who was very animated and who would ask questions or interject his point—no matter how strange it sounded or how it made him look—with a determination to grab everyone's attention. It made for a very comedic atmosphere. Near the end of the training session, the participants were asked to go around the room and share what stood out for them regarding the material studied on the four prerequisites of spiritual education (knowledge, wisdom, spiritual perception, and eloquent speech) and how it would apply to their efforts going forward.

When it was this particular brother's turn to share, he stood up and proceeded to walk around the room and direct everyone to close their eyes.

As every other participant closed his eyes, this gentleman proceeded slowly to vocalize, one at a time, each prerequisite. Walking slowly and taking about thirty-second pauses, he started with "knowledge." Then, continuing to walk around and pausing every half minute, he began singing, "wisdom." He repeated the same pattern for "spiritual perception," and when he was ready to say the last prerequisite, an extended period of silence fell over the room.

Out of respect for the brother's dramatization, most participants kept their eyes closed until finally, some realized that the dramatic effect of the final pause was simply because the brother had forgotten the fourth prerequisite. "What was the last one?" the brother asked. He had to ask this question numerous times to let people understand that he really couldn't recall the last prerequisite. In the end, everyone erupted into laughter and in unison stated, "Eloquent speech!"

In addition to the accelerated training in the institute process, this year's Gathering was blessed with the presence of Counselor Gene Andrews and Dr. Robert Henderson, Secretary of the National Spiritual Assembly of the Bahá'ís of the United States. Although only able to spend a day at the Gathering, both of these admired men spoke to the Gathering, and they were able to inspire each brother in attendance with uplifting stories from their experiences across the country and the world. Their words encouraged the Gathering and inspired all the brothers to work toward the goals of the current Five Year Plan.

17th Annual Black Men's Gathering, Green Acre, Eliot, Maine, 2003

On each of the Gathering's travel teaching trips, Billy always brought back gifts for the brothers in attendance at the following BMG. With last year's trip to Bahia, Brazil, Billy had purchased bracelets, which he gave to the brothers. The gift would be a continual reminder of their Brazilian brothers and sisters as well as the spiritual connections formed.

A gift to the BMG participants from the 2002 travel-teaching trip to Bahia, Brazil

In the following letter to the Universal House of Justice, the BMG expressed excitement to be meeting in the newly completed Harriet and Curtis Kelsey Center. With an impressive number of 108 participants attending, one of the understandable highlights of this year's Gathering was the eighty brothers who received intensive tutorial training in the Fundamental Verities and the Ruhi Institute courses.

July 19, 2003
Dearly loved servants of the King of Glory,
    We greet you in the name of God the Most High!
    Once again we have convened the Black Men's Gathering, however, this time we meet in the newly completed Kelsey

Center at Green Acre Bahá'í School. It is a very beautiful center and our meeting is truly a spiritual conference of joy and upliftment, with an underlying pledge to transformation, so vitally necessary for the successful achievement of the remaining goals of the Five Year Plan. Led by Dr. William Roberts, one hundred eight black men, so poignantly aware of the plight of their brothers and sisters in the cities of America, registered their personal commitment to any and all marching orders we will henceforth receive from our beloved Universal House of Justice.

From the opening session, the atmosphere was charged with a strong dedication on the part of the brothers to acquire those skills that will be necessary for the successful functioning in the institute process. Toward this end, more than eighty brothers, over a two-day period, received intensive tutorial training in the two curricular sequences: Fundamental Verities, and Ruhi. The brothers vow to continue this training in their respective communities so that they can become competent facilitators in service to their Assemblies and the waiting souls in their clusters.

In order to understand the "perplexities" of the times, we took to heart your recommendation to study the letters of Shoghi Effendi mentioned in your Riḍván 2003 letter. We established three workshops that elucidated our understanding of the present hour and the need to prioritize our efforts to only those activities that will achieve the goals of the Cause. Additionally, we gained further knowledge through seminars on the law of Ḥuqúqu'lláh, deepened on your January 17th, 2003 letter, and explored the communiqué from our beloved National Spiritual Assembly titled; "Blazoning The Name of Bahá'u'lláh."

Our hearts were further motivated and challenged by Counselor Eugene Andrews and Dr. Robert Henderson who both arranged to spend a day with us. They encouraged the brothers to look at ourselves anew. Dr. Andrews encouraged us to continue in building momentum and to assume greater responsibility for advancing the Cause in our communities, while Dr. Henderson fired our appreciation about the relationship between the brothers, and Bahá'u'lláh.

The report of the successful trip by the younger brothers to Bahia, Brazil earlier this year emboldened us to the realization that with your supplications to the Blessed Beauty on our behalf, we can move those mountains that have encrusted and immobilized our hearts and minds.

We would like to take this opportunity to express our sincere appreciation for the continued support of the Black Men's Gathering and your encouragement to actualize those spiritual potentials of the heart that we are just now dimly perceiving through the pupil of our eyes.

We love you from the bottom of our hearts.

Sincerely,

The Men of the 17th Black Men's Gathering

c/o William Roberts

As customary, the BMG sent its letters/reports to various Bahá'ís institutions. This one shared the activities of the Seventeenth Annual BMG with the Continental Board of Counselors:

July 19, 2003
[E-mail from the Black Men's Gathering to the Continental Board of Counselors]

Dearly beloved Counselors,

We, the participants of the Seventeenth Annual Bahá'í Black Men's Gathering, bring you our heartfelt greetings from the newly erected Harriet and Curtis Kelsey Center at the Green

Acre Bahá'í School in Eliot, Maine, the spot signally blessed by the footsteps of our Beloved Master. We would now like to share with you highlights of the week's events.

The 108 participants of the Gathering immersed themselves in an atmosphere of unconditional love, transported themselves to the realms of the spirit through the purity of fervent prayer and song, and became melded into a single soul through radiant fellowship. We began each day's devotions with the ancient vibrations of African drums and percussion instruments. These warriors of Bahá'u'lláh reconsecrated their souls to the mission of the Five Year Plan and to blazoning the name of Bahá'u'lláh.

Launching the events of the Gathering, a most significant gift was offered to the brothers in the form of an intensive facilitator / tutor training in Ruhi Book 1 and the Fundamental Verities sequence of courses, immediately bringing over eighty men of African [descent] into the fold of tutors / facilitators, a sorely needed fuel for the development of the training institute process, the "engine" of the Five Year Plan. We are grateful to The National Teacher Training Center at the Louhelen Bahá'í School and the Magdalene Carney Regional Training Institute for their tireless efforts in preparing the materials needed and also for training six of our participants to facilitate these courses. The brothers were exhilarated with enthusiasm and joy for being offered these bounties!

The following evening, Dr. Roberts, our leader, acknowledged the commitment and efforts of the brothers in the area of promoting and stimulating devotional activity throughout the United States. Particularly noteworthy were the efforts of the brothers in Florida, New York, New Jersey and Illinois as they traveled in and also outside their regions to hold devotionals at a variety of venues, ranging from Cluster Reflection Meetings to the Annual Conference of the Association for Bahá'í Studies in Toronto, Canada.

On the fourth day of the Gathering, we consulted on the great challenge of raising children and youth by connecting their hearts to Bahá'u'lláh. We concluded that this can be best accomplished through community support, garnered from universal love, where every child is seen as our own and every adult as a sister, brother, aunt, uncle, or grandparent.

Six dynamic workshops were conducted allowing for engaging discussions and deepening on Blazoning the Name of Bahá'u'lláh, the Law of Ḥuqúqu'lláh, the January 17th, 2003 letter from the Universal House of Justice to the Bahá'ís of the World, and the three letters mentioned by the Supreme Body in its Riḍván 2003 message from the World Order of Bahá'u'lláh. Due emphasis was placed on the recent messages from the World Center.

The Gathering was energized with the presence of Counselor Eugene Andrews and Dr. Robert C. Henderson, Secretary-General of our National Spiritual Assembly for a day. Counselor Andrews emphasized the need for us to claim our communities spiritually, while Dr. Henderson gave an awe-inspiring conveyance of Bahá'u'lláh's suffering and His mission to redeem humanity from its present condition. We also had the participation of three Auxiliary Board members and two members of Regional Bahá'í Councils throughout the week.

Our closing celebration, open to everyone from across the northeast, was enchanting! The entire assemblage of friends formed a one-mile procession to the gravesites of Hand of the Cause of God Louis G. Gregory and his wife Louisa for a sacred devotional remembrance.

We thank you for your wisdom, encouragement and bound-
less love and hold you in our thoughts and prayers.

With Warm Bahá'í Greetings,

The Participants of the Seventeenth Annual Bahá'í Black
Men's Gathering

C/o William Roberts

The participants, numbering 108 strong, came from as far north
as Canada and of course from the northeastern, southern, midwest-
ern, and western United States. Some traveled from other countries.
They came by plane, car, and bus. They carried with them the best
of provisions—hearts throbbing with the love of God, prayer books,
and favorite sacred writings—for their sojourn at Green Acre. Some
participants brought with them djembes, cow bells, tambourines,
guitars, congas, and portable keyboards. Many of them sported
dashikis and other attire representative of their African heritage.

As mentioned previously, this year's Gathering featured a different yet important agenda—a training in the Ruhi and Core Curriculum Fundamental Verities courses. In total, forty-two men took the
accelerated tutor training in Ruhi Book 1, and thirty-six took the
Fundamental Verities training. Both courses were covered in fifteen
hours over both days.

This year, the Gathering spent one morning studying and consulting on the Riḍván 2003 message. Each of the brothers had to make a
choice of attending two of six workshops. The workshops that were
offered were "The Goal of a New World Order," "America and the
Most Great Peace," "The Unfoldment of World Civilization," "The
Right of God," "Building Momentum," and "Blazoning the Name
of Bahá'u'lláh" (a program of the NSA of the United States).

Another highlight at the Gathering was hearing from the fourteen young men, from age 18 to 28, who had volunteered to travel
to Brazil. The youth gave a presentation on their experiences and

reported how they had worked hand in hand with local Bahá'í youth to teach children's classes, host devotional meetings, and tutor study circles. Those at the Gathering heard many touching (and funny) stories of the youths' time on the trip while also hearing about the lessons they learned. All the youth agreed that they had not anticipated the degree to which young Brazilian Bahá'ís were in the forefront of the teaching and consolidation activities, as well as the institute process.

At the central BMG and local Gatherings, different brothers often brought with them new forms of art and ways to celebrate devotionals. This year's Gathering brought new songs to the ears of Reggie Newkirk. This year, he learned quite a few new songs that were sung at the annual Gathering. One of the songs that touched him very deeply had these lyrics: "Done made my vow to the Lord. / And I never will turn back. / Oh, I will go. I shall go / To see what the end will be."

As this song was being sung, one of the elders stood up and started to move around the room in a dignified step movement. Soon he was joined by the rest of the Gathering as the brothers moved—first, in single file and then in multiple lines (because of space limitations)—taking steps in unison, singing in harmony, and affirming the vow that each one, in his own mind and heart, had made to his Lord. Ultimately, they moved in serried lines, as if they were receiving their marching instructions from 'Abdu'l-Bahá Himself.

July 28, 2003
[Email from the Universal House of Justice to the Black Men's Gathering]

Your message from the most recent Black Men's Gathering reflected the quickening spirit we have come to expect from the integrity of your efforts to achieve increasing measures of spiritual transformation in your individual lives and higher levels of service to the Cause of Bahá'u'lláh. We are greatly pleased that you are succeeding in your endeavour to attune your actions to the vital purpose of the Five Year Plan. You may rest assured that you are remembered in our ardent supplications at the Sacred Threshold.

The Universal House of Justice

cc: National Assembly of the United States

Many BMG participants kept a journal to record their personal reflections, feelings, and experiences at the Gathering. These brothers felt obligated to write down such important and transformative experiences so that they could share them with others. Although his actual journal is not reproduced here, the following communications from Reggie Newkirk (who had not participated regularly in the Gathering) to Deborah Kirton, who was serving at the Bahá'í World Center, illustrates the transformative value of the BMG.

July 28, 2003
[Email from the Reggie Newkirk to Deborah Kirton]

Hi Deborah,

FYI, attended the Seventeenth Annual Bahá'í Black Men's Gathering. It was a grand event. I started writing notes to myself following the sessions of the gathering in order to be able to share with you something of the feeling and spirit of that event. Nothing I can write would convey to anyone all that happen[ed] or that was. As inadequate as these personal reflections are—"here they be for ya." The spirit of Maya Angelou's comment was most definitely evident during the gathering:

"Everything in the universe has rhythm. Everything dances."

Truly this was a healing event for me.

Reggie

July 28, 2003
[Email from the Deborah Kirton to Reggie Newkirk] *

Dearest Reggie,

Firstly, thank you so very much for sharing w/me your personal recollections of the BMG; rest assured that what you shared went from your fingers and heart to my eyes and spirit only, and shall go no further!

When, several years ago, the BMG first came to the Bahá'í World Centre en route to their return to the US, I was blessed to attend the session which was held in the flat of a couple who was then serving here—he was from Nigeria and she was from Australia. I so vividly remember the experience that should I close my eyes now, I can see the moonlit radiance of the men's faces, hear the resounding bass texture of their voices raised in glorification of their Lord, feel the trembling of their awe and submission to a Power Whose might and forgiveness had given them a new beginning and identity, and I can touch the force of their spiritual magnetism. These men were spiritual warriors and servants of Bahá'u'lláh and, Reggie, I don't think in my entire life I have ever seen a collection of such beauty in one place!!!

I recall sitting in that couple's flat which was designed to accommodate a family of three, at most, but which was filled from nook to cranny w/about 60–70 people strong, and thinking in my mind, "so this is the true reason why we are hated and feared as a people." That reality hit me like a ton of bricks when I looked into the eyes and faces of these beautifully imperfect but spiritually exceptional specimens who represented the core essence of black masculinity, b/c at that moment, I finally

---

* Shared with permission.

understood why there was racism and hate prejudice—it was
b/c those who control and maintain the status quo are seized
w/an obsessive compulsive fear of the unique spiritual power
and humility to be found w/in the children of "the pupil of the
eye." You mentioned in your reflections that the only thing to
fear is fear itself—Lord is this ever true! When the children
of the pupil of the eye clear away the material / mental agita-
tions and dirt from their vision and completely understand,
embrace, and fulfill to the maximum capacity what each and
every one of them has been endowed w/by the Creator, then
their spiritual beauty and energy become like loadstones which,
through the inherent power of the Word of Bahá'u'lláh, will
attract the hearts of men. When you humble yourself before
Bahá'u'lláh, He will lift you up toward the heavens, and this
scares the be-Jesus (not to be disrespectful) out of those whose
misguided beliefs force them to see us as theirs to exploit and
oppress.

What you scarred, broken, flawed and amazingly beautiful, glorious, kind-hearted, affectionate, and mighty Black
sons of Bahá'u'lláh provide to each other and obtain from the
One Source during these annual "pauses" which occur at the
BBMG is what I wish for every Black man on this planet. You
seek from God first and submerge yourselves in the healing
balm of His Revelation and you experience, maybe, I would
imagine for the first time for many of the men, the inner
beauty and reflection of Bahá'u'lláh residing tall and strong w/
in yourselves and those of your other brother-friends.

I am so very happy for you that w/the love and support of
your wife and family you were able to attend this year's gathering; I placed the names of your entire family on the prayer list
of the Universal House of Justice and, inshallah, maybe next

year you may be granted your heart's desire, in that you will be able to attend the BBMG w/both sons.

God bless you Reggie.

With warmest Bahá'í greetings,

Dk

Here is another example of the wonderful confirmations the BMG received from the International Teaching Center. The bringing of joy was indeed mutual.

July 31, 2003
[Email from Gene Andrews to the Black Men's Gathering]

Dear Friends,

I am pleased to report to you that the International Teaching Center received with warm appreciation the message of July 24, 2003 from the participants at the Seventeenth Annual Bahá'í Black Men's Gathering at Green Acre Bahá'í School in Eliot, Maine. The news that 108 friends immersed themselves in prayer and song and at the same time participated in intensive institute courses brought them great joy.

The Teaching Center wants you to know that they will offer heartfelt prayers in the Holy Shrines that from this recent conference a great impetus will be given to the growth of the Faith in every area where the dear believers reside.

With loving Bahá'í greetings,

Gene Andrews

Member, Continental Board of Counselors for the Americas

Cc: International Teaching Center

Counsellors Birkland, Huerta, and Murphy

National Spiritual Assembly of the Bahá'ís of the United States

The following two letters are from two young African American Bahá'í men to Billy Roberts. Both letters demonstrate the respect these young Bahá'í men had for Billy as the organizer and an elder of the Gathering. Many brothers considered Billy a guide, a spiritual "uncle," and a surrogate "father," and they often sought his advice and encouragement as they explored their paths in life. All this was made possible by their involvement in the nurturing fellowship of the BMG.

July 31, 2003
[Email from Sultan Stover to Billy Roberts]

Hey Dr. Roberts,

Well it's been about two weeks since the gathering, and remember when you asked me what I wanted to do and I said "go pioneering"? Well, I just got a job at the School of the Nations in Brasilia, Brazil. I will be teaching visual arts and drama. Things are moving really fast; I am waiting for my visa, and I leave on the 6th of August and possibly sooner! I will be there on a two-year contract (hopefully more).

Once I get there and get settled, I will email you again to let you know that everything worked out.

Well! I will see you next year at the gathering and let you know how it is going!

Is there anything I have to do as far as administrative Bahá'í stuff to be counted as a pioneer?

Your Brother,

Sultan

August 1, 2003
[Email from Frederick Landry to Billy Roberts]

Alláh'u'abhá Dr. Roberts,

Thank you so much for your call this evening! It was wonderful speaking to you tonight. As I said, I'm doing well and am still very much in thought and reflection about my week at the Gathering :). I am in a constant plight to bring the latent spirit (that I know is in me) to reality, and to be a more loving, more spiritual, and more sensitive soul. I am ever-so grateful that I now have a friend, a brother, an uncle, and a father who is such an example for me! I thank you so much Dr. Roberts for your love, your sensitivity, and your straightforwardness. I have attached the promised picture :).* The hard copy is soon to follow.

Much Love,

Frederick

It was always wonderful for the Gathering to hear of stories that either commented on or conveyed the deep and powerful effects of the Gathering. Kambiz Rafraf, who encouraged Billy to invite the then-new Bahá'í Tommy Taylor to the BMG, wrote the following e-mail shortly after the 2003 BMG held at Green Acre.

August 1, 2003
[Email from Kambiz Rafraf to Billy Roberts]

Dearest Brother Billy,

I just wanted to share with you that Tommy Taylor shared with me and also shared at the Feast that the Black Men's Gathering was the best trip and experience of his life. He said that the most memorable moment at the gathering was when a special speaker recounted Bahá'u'lláh's hardships in the Síyáh-Chál prison and the unbearable conditions there. Tommy remembered the emotional faces and tears from the memorable story. Another special moment Tommy remembered was the visit to the Louis Gregory gravesite. He recounted the many prayers that were said there and the sprinkling of the rose petals

---

* This photo is featured on the final page of the book.

on the grave and the distinct African drums playing in the background. "God is sufficient unto me," "Make me a hollow reed," And "Is there any remover of difficulties" [continued to] ring in the ear as Tommy and J.P. returned home.

Thank you on behalf of all of us for such a great gift and experience for our dear brothers, Tommy and J.P.

Loving greetings,

Kambiz

The San Diego brothers made their mark last year with their first local Gathering. In fact, this had actually been the first local Gathering held in the United States, as the BMG before then had been held in a centralized format. As a small token of remembrance, an inspired piece of artwork in the form of a button was created and given to each brother in attendance.

Artistic creation by Jihmye Collins commemorating
First Annual San Diego BMG

This year, a second local BMG would be held in San Diego, and Jihmye Collins would fulfill the pledge he had made to the centralized Gathering at Green Acre that summer to continue the important work of holding a local Gathering for brothers in and around San Diego.

August 4, 2003
[Email from Jihmye Collins to BMG Participants in Southern California]

Alláh-u-Abhá!

Dear brothers, greetings!

As we who attended the Seventeenth Annual Bahá'í Black Men's Gathering (BMG) at Green Acre are finally coming back down to earth, part of my service commitment to the local area is to coordinate the Second Annual BMG in San Diego.

Although there has been no specific date set, it is likely that it will be held in November again. I will await further word from Dr. Billy Roberts before determining which three-day weekend and [get] the information to you in a timely way.

As the Bahá'í world has gone past the halfway mark of the Five Year Plan, there is much work to be done towards its fulfillment, and we brothers have great roles to play in our service to the Blessed Beauty. Fellowship and a course of study, along the lines of the regular BMG, will be important components in preparing each of us for this service, while giving a taste of what was a most joyful time had by all at Green Acre while being in a "learning mode."

I anxiously anticipate getting back in touch with each of you with dates, so that you can get on the bus "making your vow to the Lord."

Sincerely, your brother,

Jihmye

This year, the Gathering consulted on holding a travel-teaching trip to Trinidad and Tobago, and they decided that they would contact the National Spiritual Assembly about the possibility of such a trip. In addition, many of the brothers' wives expressed an interest in being part of one of the Gatherings' travel-teaching trips! As such, Billy's communication to the NSA included the request that the brothers' wives accompany them on the trip.

August 7, 2003
[Email from Billy Roberts to the National Spiritual Assembly of the Bahá'ís of Trinidad and Tobago]

National Spiritual Assembly of the Bahá'ís of Trinidad and Tobago

Mrs. Shahnaz Jamalabadi, Secretary

Beloved Friends:

The 17th Annual Black Men's Gathering concluded its proceedings this year with an overwhelming expression of determination to exert in ever more diligent terms resources to advance the process of entry by troops as outlined in the Five Year Plan. In response to a message sent by the brothers of the Gathering, The Universal House of Justice stated in part: "Your message from the most recent Black Men's Gathering reflected the quickening spirit we have come to expect from the integrity of your efforts to achieve increasing measures of spiritual transformation in your individual lives and higher levels of service to the Cause of Bahá'u'lláh."

The Black Men's Gathering has for many years undertaken among other things traveling teaching initiatives to countries throughout the world to assist the believers in those regions with their efforts to promote the Cause of God and their local community development process. Our approach is to engage with the believers as an assistance to them, to encourage them in their work, and to participate in their community activities. We would like to include your country as our destination this year.

Our hope is that we could plan a visit during or near the end of December during the time when many people have the Christian holidays off from work. Our idea is also to invite the wives of our members to accompany us on this journey if they are able.

Please let me know if this is a possibility. I would appreciate hearing from you quickly since much has to be planned in a short amount of time. The brothers are extremely excited by this possibility and await your response.

We know that your richly blessed community has already achieved many victories and we pray to be able to enhance and support you in the realization of many more.

I can be reached in these ways at the Bahá'í National Center in the United States.

Please accept special greetings and know you are in our thoughts and prayers.

With deepest appreciation,

Your brother,

Dr. William Roberts

for the Black Men's Gathering

cc Universal House of Justice

Counselor Rebequa Murphy

The NSA of the Bahá'ís of Trinidad and Tobago responded favorably to the Gathering's interest in a travel teaching opportunity in their country.

August 19, 2003
[Email from the National Spiritual Assembly of the Bahá'ís of Trinidad and Tobago to Billy Roberts]

Dear Dr. William Roberts,

The National Spiritual Assembly sends you its warmest greetings.

We warmly extend invitation to the Black Men's Gathering, including the wives of your members, to visit our country.

Please let us know what kind of activities you would like to do during your visit in Trinidad and Tobago.

Beside the activities you intend to do, there are possibilities of organizing activities in the University Media and External Affairs by the Bahá'í Institutions.

We appreciate receiving the intended date of the Black Men's Gathering visit to our Country (arrival and departure date), and also how many are coming and what kind of accommodation would the "Gathering" expect.

We are looking forward to seeing you all.

With loving Bahá'í greetings,

The National Spiritual Assembly of

the Bahá'ís of Trinidad and Tobago

Shahnaz Jamalabadi, Secretary

During this year's Gathering held at Green Acre, in addition to writing to the World Center, the Gathering also wrote to the Regional Bahá'í Councils. The following letter from the Regional Bahá'í Council of the Southern States is an example of the impact that BMG letters, reports, and participants' testimonies were having on Bahá'í institutions and community life. Here the Council makes reference to the brothers who "serve as spiritual instruments of the Cause of God" through the United States and Canada.

August 29, 2003
[Email from the Regional Bahá'í Council of the Southern States to the Black Men's Gathering]

Participants of the Seventeenth Annual Bahá'í Black Men's Gathering

Dearly loved friends serving the glorious Cause of God,

The Regional Bahá'í Council of the Southern States rejoices with you and is deeply touched at reading your inspiring and powerful letter reporting on the spirit and events of this year's Bahá'í Black Men's Gathering. Your letter was reinforced by the moving testimonials from one of our members who attended the gathering and returned with clearly visible joy and sense of fulfillment from the richly endowed experience.

We have visions of the soul of our beloved Hand of the Cause of God Mr. Louis G. Gregory rejoicing at the spirit and devotion of your meeting and your journey to the place of burial for him and his blessed wife, Louisa. Our hearts too were warmed in hearing the recount of the special devotional service at the gravesite.

We are confident that through this spiritually uplifting experience you are energized to play a more expanded, enriching, and sacred role in the advancement of the Five Year Plan as well as the continual enrichment of your souls and the spiritual conquest of the planet.

The Council knows we are blessed to have in the Southern States, the other Regions and Canada such empowered workers who serve as spiritual instruments of the Cause of God. We praise your efforts and hope the labors you exert will generate into extraordinary victories in the Five Year Plan.

Our prayers and love are with each and every one of you as together we press on to serve our Lord.

With deepest love and admiration,
Regional Bahá'í Council of the Southern States
Mahyar Mofidi
Secretary

After the intensive trainings had concluded at this year's Gathering, the names and contact information of those trained in each curriculum were sent to each Regional Council in the United States. Below is the communication to the Regional Bahá'í Council of the Western States. Nine brothers in this region had undergone training to facilitate the Fundamental Verities Curriculum and Book 1 in the Ruhi curriculum.

September 24, 2003
[Email from Billy Roberts to the Regional Bahá'í Council of the Western States]

Regional Bahá'í Council of the Western States
Charleen Maghzi, Secretary
Dearest Friends:

I am happy to share with you the names of those participants of the Black Men's Gathering who were trained to be tutors of Book 1 in the Ruhi Curriculum and as facilitators of the Fundamental Verities Curriculum at our July session.

Our commitment to energetically support the work of the Five Year Plan through Devotional Meetings and now through Study Circles adds to the much-needed resources required for advancing the process of entry by troops.

Please forgive me for the delay in sending these added resources for the Institute Process to you, but the demands here at the Bahá'í National Center have only now eased a bit.

I ask that you forward them to the appropriate coordinator of the Regional Training Institute Board so that these souls may be pressed into service as soon as possible.

With loving appreciation for your many efforts in His service,
Your brother,
Billy Roberts

Fundamental Verities Facilitators: Owen Creightney, Leon Ferguson, Teo Henry, Ted Jefferson, Teddy Lawrence,

Michael Mathenge, Lee Ratcliff, Ronaldo Raeheim, Morgan Spriggs
Ruhi Facilitators: Stan Brown, Gordon Gullett, Jamey Heath, Walter Heath, Charles White

November 28, 2003
[Blazoning the Name of Bahá'u'lláh Conference, Nashville, Tennessee]

Burton Smith was again invited—this time by Bruce Reynolds—to attend the BMG next year. Bruce was as direct as Billy had been earlier that year, and he said to Burton, "Why haven't you been to the Gathering?"

At that point, there was nothing else for Burton to say, and he decided to see what this Gathering was all about. He contacted Billy later that Thanksgiving weekend and promised that he would be at the next Gathering.

Billy's response was somewhat jovial but loving: "I have a way of making people keep their promises!"

As promised, Burton and his brother Julius would attend the next year's Gathering. The Gathering would be exceptionally memorable for Burton, as it would be the first of only two Gatherings he would be able to attend with his brother. Julius had been diagnosed with stage 4 cancer, and Burton would of course hold on to and treasure the time they spent together at the BMG.

December 11, 2003
[Email from Joe Dolphin to Billy Roberts]

Dear Dr. Roberts,

I write to inquire about the possibility of attending the Black Men's Gathering in Green Acre next year. I am a Bahá'í of African descent living in Barbados. I am currently going through the Ruhi process and I also serve on the National Spiritual Assembly. I recently spoke to Lionel Haynes and based on his suggestion as well as that of Dorothy Whyte, I would appreciate the opportunity to participate in the Gathering in 2004.

Thank you,

Joe Dolphin

Between December 25 and January 3 of 2004, the BMG embarked on the travel-teaching trip to the twin islands of the Republic of Trinidad and Tobago. Ten of the brothers participated and were accompanied by their wives. The names of the brothers who traveled individually and the names of the brothers who traveled together with their wives are listed here: Richard E. Bruce, Beverly and Willis Burris, Jihmye and Susan Collins, Philippe Copeland, Al and Gwen Daniels, Alfred Fox III, Nelson and Jean Freeman, John W. Mangum Jr., Ervin and Merrie Milton, Mike and Ruth Paiya, Marcus and Judy Potts, Matthew Potts, Lee Ratcliff and Monica Al-Bajari, Billy Roberts, Sam Stafford, Dawn and Oliver Thomas and Charles and Velura White.

In a report of the trip to the Universal House of Justice, the BMG wrote, "The special privilege we enjoyed of visiting the homes of the believers, praying fervently with them, eating with them, chatting and just supporting each other in warm Bahá'í fellowship, may have been the most significant part of our sojourn." They also reported that they "participated in significant media interviews on televisions, radios and various newspapers." They were "hosted at two welcome receptions, one in Trinidad, hosted by the National Spiritual Assembly of the Bahá'ís of Trinidad and Tobago and the community, and the other in Tobago by the Local Spiritual Assembly of St. Andrews." And as a crucial part of their teaching efforts, they "sent representatives to pay courtesy calls on the president of the Republic, the Honorable Dr. Maxwell Richards and the Chief Secretary of the Tobago House of Assembly, Mr. Orville London."[3]

Marcus Potts, Judy Potts, Sam Stafford, Hamid Farabi, His Excellency George Maxwell Richards, Billy Roberts, Velura White and Charles White (Photo Courtesy of Marcus Potts)

2004

In 2004, Counselor Stephen Birkland wrote to BMG participants, praising their service, and highlighting in particular the inclusion of institute courses in the recent BMG program. He also acknowledged the efforts of the BMG in developing and introducing devotional sessions to areas where the brothers lived.

31 January 2004
To the Participants in the 17th Annual Bahá'í Black Men's Gathering
Dearest Friends,

Your letter of 25 July 2003 briefly describing the activities of your most recent gathering which included a review of some of your associated activities around North America was received with much joy. I apologize for not responding on behalf of the Counsellors until now. While I haven't written sooner please know that you are often in my prayers and thoughts.

Your efforts to prepare yourselves for higher and higher levels of service along with your actual services during this past year were part of the consultation of the Continental Board of Counsellors this week as we met in plenary in Sao Paulo, Brazil.

Your example of including institute courses as a part of your program last summer was noted and we prayed that most of you have continued to progress through the entire sequence of courses, one of the two essential movements of the 5 Year Plan.

Also noted was the example of devotional sessions you have developed and introduced to more and more clusters where your participants reside. (I have shared my personal experience with many of my colleagues of presenting at the Association for Bahá'í Studies conference last summer just following one of these sessions and how the spirit of the conference was affected by this wonderful group of Black Men.) This service of developing and refining devotional sessions in the clusters, one of the three core activities of the Plan, reflects your deep understanding and "consciousness of the spiritual dimension of human existence," as the Universal House of Justice has written.

The Counsellors regularly pray for all of your efforts within the framework of the 5 Year Plan, during the time you are together and while you are serving in the field, both in your own clusters and internationally.

Thank you for every little thing you do in the path of the Blessed Beauty.

With loving gratitude,

Stephen Birkland, Member

Continental Board of Counsellors in the Americas

The following letter to Billy Roberts is also a precious reminder of how the BMG encouraged and inspired brothers to get involved in the institute process. One can feel his devotion and love for the Ruhi courses as he shares his and other friends' experiences. The story of the youth raising funds for the Faith is priceless, as is his reflections during his obligatory prayer about his son, Jamal.

May 7, 2004
[Email from Bill Wilson to Billy Roberts]

I just wanted to write and say hi.

I wanted to tell you that I've got only 1 more book to go in the Ruhi sequence before I'm finished with this part of the sequence. I've yet to complete Book 4, although I'm in a study circle that [is] close to completing it. The Assembly just recently completed Book 3, and as part of the practice, actually taught a children's class at [our weekly Bahá'í "school."

It was a sight to see. Old folks [were] singing songs, coloring, and memorizing the Writings of our Beloved. We had 8 members take the course together and all 8 taught [at the children's class]. The Assembly is beginning Book 4 in a couple [of] weeks. Since Book 5 is not part of the sequence in these parts yet, we'll get to Books 6 and 7 by the fall. At any rate, if you're planning on holding study circles during the BMG, I'd be happy to tutor any of the books.

I'm sure you've heard about this from Alloysia or some other avenue, but a couple of youth in Clifton Springs wanted to do something to help the National Spiritual Assembly. They asked a nearby Assembly to host a potluck dinner where the friends would pay for the foods and all money collected would be sent to the national fund. The text of the e-mail sent to the friends is below. The results from the event were impressive—$5,319.00. I've included the email to the friends about the success.

Finally, I was saying my obligatory prayers one morning, not too long ago and had a rather profound experience relating to the BMG. Actually, I may have been reacting to the beauty of the idea. At any rate, I saw Jamal, my son, attending [a] junior session of the BMG, facilitated by older members, who had also brought their sons to the event. The novelty of this was that the kids were not teens, but pre-youth. What came to me was generations following generations in this beautiful cycle. I don't know whether you've any plans for this kind of event in the future, but I thought I'd pass it along.

Be assured of my prayers for your success and happiness in this world and the next.

Your little brother,

Bill Wilson

This year would be Neysan Sturdivant's first significant experience with the Gathering. He had heard of it many years before but had diligently avoided attending. Nevertheless, over the years before he first participated, he began to have a feeling that maybe he should check it out. Due to several factors, however, he was not able to attend. Additionally, for a variety of reasons, he was very apprehensive about participating. When he was finally able to attend the Gathering, Neysan had a spiritual awakening, similar to the experience he had had in 1995 when he traveled to Israel on his year of service. He wrote the following passage describing his first experience at the BMG.

July 10, 2004
[Green Acre Bahá'í School, Eliot, Maine]

I think a big push for me to come to the Gathering was that my son was on the way, and I felt that I needed to do some things before he was born. It was also special to be here with my dad. I looked around, and there were a couple of other father-son attendees. We walked up to Sarah Farmer Inn, and my dad knew folks and I didn't, but everyone was greeting me as if we did know each other. More and more people were greeting me as me, and not as my father's son. I felt welcomed and accepted without people knowing me—I felt warm. I was like a kid who had his warm, cozy blanket. The air around the gathering comforted me, and I could tell that I was free to be myself without having to worry about whether I was going to offend someone or anything like that—I could just be me. And then we had prayers for nearly three hours. It took me three or four days to get a prayer in. I could tell that part of the gathering meant being able to simply socialize with others and talk. I was having wonderful conversations and developing friendships—ones that I knew were going to help me strengthen my marriage and family life through hearing others, their input, and their history and advice. I could easily say that I knew this experience would be invaluable to me.

Like Neysan, Hassan Malouf of East Lansing, Michigan attended his first gathering in 2004. As you will recall, Hassan's mother had contacted Billy in 2001 with the hope that her son would attend the BMG, and Billy had let her know that Hassan would need to call him.

Ultimately, Hassan would contact Billy. Hassan had experienced somewhat of a tumultuous childhood, particularly because of his experiences at school. There, he was constantly seen as and labeled as the "bad kid." In the summer before his sophomore year of high school, he found himself beginning a process of investigating spiritual truth, turning more toward God, and rejecting many social relationships—especially those in high school—that he had established over the years. For more than a year, Hassan spent much of his time in silence and reflection. Sometimes he was able to count the words he had spoken during the course of a single day on one hand.

He longed for deep bonds of friendship, but he found himself only becoming more and more isolated in an attempt to ward off many of the toxic relationships and influences that had been part of his life. At the same time, he was spending much more time in prayer and meditation, which marked a new and dramatic shift for him.

Still, this period of solitude was a blessing for him. In the midst of this personal transformation, he was introduced to the institute process and began taking Ruhi Book 1. The study circle allowed Hassan to be among people whom he felt were sincere, and because he felt accepted, he was able to open up his heart to a degree. When he contacted Billy about attending the 2004 BMG, Hassan had already been praying that the BMG would provide him with the opportunity to truly heal from the painful experiences he had endured throughout his life.

July 12, 2004
[Green Acre Bahá'í School, Eliot, Maine]

When Hassan arrived at Green Acre, he fervently prayed for his emotional healing. Before his introduction to the Gathering, he was, of course, moved by the brothers sharing their experiences, and he also forged genuine spiritual bonds with many of the participants. He had rarely experienced such feelings during the past several years. As he considered his personal introduction and what he would say, he found himself begging Bahá'u'lláh to please let him just be completely truthful. Even at this early stage in the week, the hardened shell around his heart was already breaking away, and the intensity of the brothers' prayers was melting away his aloofness. In fact, when he stepped through the doors of the prayer room and heard the drums, the phrase "Ancient of Days,"* for some reason, was powerfully in the forefront of his mind.

---

* Refers to Bahá'u'lláh.

When it came time for Hassan to stand up and introduce himself to the group, he did not expect for the spiritual effect to be so powerful as to take a firm grip of him and render him unable to speak. As he was struggling to say a word, a familiar voice—Burton Smith's—offered Hassan a quiet, gentle prompt: "Tell them about your mom and dad."

Hassan tried to follow the advice he had heard, but a rush of emotion again rendered him unable to finish his thoughts. He was overwhelmed with pain and joy, but he tried to collect his thoughts, and through his tears, he was able to share that his parents had visited Green Acre together before he was born. Then, somehow, he was able to share the deepest secret in his heart—that he just wanted to be able to show love.

Putting these feelings into words was hard, but once he had spoken, he felt as if the shell around his heart had finally loosened and fallen away completely. This was a major moment of healing in Hassan's life, and he felt that by the grace of God, through the Gathering, much of the healing for which he had been searching had been granted.

Sundiata Spencer was also attending the Gathering for the first time in 2004. Although he was a declared Bahá'í, Sundiata admittedly did not fully believe in God when he was invited to go to the Black Men's Gathering.

In the two years leading up to his eighteenth birthday, Sundiata had helped the Habeebullah family in Decatur, Georgia with their junior youth group, which was known as the "Umojah Souljahs." The Habeebullahs' son Raphael had introduced Sundiata to the Faith. While finishing up their junior youth group one Friday night at the Bahá'í Unity Center in Decatur, Georgia, Nasif Habeebullah revealed to Sundiata, as gently as he could, that Sundiata would not be able to go to the BMG because he was not a Bahá'í. Nasif's understanding that one had to be a Bahá'í was not accurate, but because he wanted so badly to go, Sundiata declared as a Bahá'í with words but not true feelings.

Sundiata then traveled to the Gathering and was awestruck by the spiritual intensity of the prayers. One morning, during devotions, he felt as if he were being lifted up to the top of a mountain, from which he was able to look down at his life—a life that seemed simple and distant. All his worries seemed petty. He felt the soft yet sharp authority of God that demanded trust. Here, at his first Gathering, Sundiata was learning and experiencing what it meant to believe in God, and he also found that his decision to become a Bahá'í was being confirmed.

However, he was discovering that trusting people was, for him, far more difficult than trusting God. Often at the Gathering, an older brother, after offering some advice on life or giving him a long embrace, would say, "I'm proud of you" or "I love you." Sundiata always took these gestures as something to be casually said but not to be felt deeply or taken seriously. Years later, however, after his heart had opened even more fully, he would shower the same love and encouragement on others. As it would turn out, a small group of young men who had been in his junior youth group would attend the BMG as well. Over the years, watching these young men participate in the Gathering, Sundiata's heart would swell with pride at seeing how these young brothers had grown and matured spiritually. Sundiata would continue to participate in the Gathering for many years and went on to pioneer to China and also to Uganda.

July 17–18, 2004
[En route from Eliot, Maine to East Lansing, Michigan]

Dale Mitchell had driven his son Brandan and Hassan Malouf to the Gathering a week ago. During their drive from Michigan to Maine, Hassan mentioned that he had not been in touch with his father in many years due to his father being incarcerated. Their conversation uncovered many wounds that Hassan resisted discussing during the drive east.

Green Acre co-administrator Jim Sacco, staff, and youth volunteers

Now that he had opened his heart at the Gathering, Hassan found himself yearning to reconnect with his father, and he prayed on several occasions that God would enable both of them to reestablish their relationship. He had only been three years old when he had last spoken to his father, and now, he was not even sure how to go about finding him. He knew only that his father was incarcerated somewhere in New York. After talking with Dale, Hassan was ready to find his father. Hassan contacted his mother as they were driving home from the Gathering, and after a while, she was able to determine his father's whereabouts. Although it was out of their way, Dale adjusted their destination to upstate New York, where the federal prison that held Hassan's father was located.

After driving the rest of the day and part of the next, they arrived at the prison. Soon after going through the processing room, Hassan waited at a table until his father came out. Within a few minutes, the two of them were at last able to reconnect with each other. Hassan was able to share his involvement in the Bahá'í Faith with his dad, and his father told him about many family members whom Hassan had never met. Although reuniting with his father was one of the most challenging things Hassan had ever done, he was nonetheless glad that he had reached out to him. At the same time, Hassan realized that life in prison was taking a toll on his father and that he might not be around for much longer.

2005

In the following letter, Billy provided an update to Gene Andrews on, among other things, the state of the BMG related to the challenges of growth.

March 29, 2005
[Letter from Billy Roberts to Counselor
Eugene Andrews]

Dear Gene,

Thanks for the wonderful letter and the news of the exciting activities in Broward County over the weekend. I am hoping that Lauderhill will provide valuable experience for the country about reaching into communities that are in need without treating people in a paternalistic way. It looks like this is being achieved magnificently and is thrilling to watch from a distance.

I know the brothers will want to hear a lot about this at the Gathering. Hopefully Dwayne Rayner will be there to share his experience along with you.

Gene, Bruce Reynolds called to tell me that he already has a hundred brothers registered for the Gathering this year and I have not sent out an announcement yet. This brings us to moving to a new level in its development, and I'd like to share some ideas I have seeking your input.

This year has seen a larger number of "mini-BMGs" around the country, in New York City, South Carolina, Chicago, Kansas City, Florida, northern California, San Diego, Los Angeles, Detroit, Atlanta, Boston, North Carolina, Washington DC, southern Virginia, New Jersey, and Rochester, NY. Other efforts, smaller in scale, are taking place and growing in size. You are aware of the emphasis on the two essential movements and the commitments made last year to reach out to invite non-Bahá'ís to participate. We have witnessed striking evidence of receptivity and responsiveness beyond anyone's expectations.

A growing body of devotional meetings done in the spirit and style of the BMG are presenting themselves everywhere you look. The music and drumming so common at the BMG is now accepted in many places as a part of the devotional experience, not only among believers of African descent but far beyond. In greater Chicago, for example, we have a devotional (BMG style) twice a month, with one held at the Temple and the other held at the Chicago Center. There is also a group of people—Bahá'ís and non-Bahá'ís—who grew out of this experience and who now drum together weekly. They are men and women—Black and white and Latino—and they are focused on spiritual expressions stemming from their appreciation of the power in the revelation of Bahá'u'lláh. Just amazing!

I am now thinking that it will be difficult to continue beyond this year with only the one national / international BMG experience we have at Green Acre. The space is limited, making participation for all those who wish to participate impossible, and the model limits the number who can effectively be heard as well. Processing a group of more than a hundred is a major task that becomes more difficult each year. My thinking has led me to developing the "mini-BMGs" in a more deliberate way and to reserve the Maine Gathering for those who will lead the mini-BMGs. These will likely be "elders of the Gathering" who are all ages and others who are demonstrating leadership in their areas. Young men, regardless of their current involvement, would also be invited to this experience at the same time, providing a platform for their development. I am reminded of a message from the House of Justice a couple of years ago urging consideration of this for the future.

Well, dear brother, sorry to ask for yet another request, but I hope you will share some thoughts with me about this, as I will need to formulate a plan and share it with others soon.

Please give Nancy my love and know that I keep you both close to my heart.

With much love,

Billy

Over the next few years, the decentralization that Billy described would occur, thereby placing a strategic focus on addressing the needs of the men of the Gathering.

At the heart of the Black Men's Gathering was the hope and desire that those who were participants in the Gathering would experience personal transformation (and also be responsible for effecting such a transformation in others). The following letter from a Local Spiritual Assembly represents the type of transformation and contributions to one's community for which the Gathering was commonly known.

May 26, 2005
[Letter from the Spiritual Assembly of the Bahá'ís of San Diego to the Black Men's Gathering]

Dear Dr. Roberts and Men of the Gathering,

We greet you at this time of great anticipation of the good fortunes of our shared Faith, imbued with a sense of urgency in furthering the goals of the Five Year Plan, during these last precious months.

Mr. Jihmye Collins, one of your staunchest supporters and steadfast attendees, has served the San Diego community for twenty years as a Local Spiritual Assembly member. At the Annual Election this past Riḍván, the community allowed him the opportunity to pursue other avenues of spiritual service other than serving as an Assembly member. The new Assembly has already given responsibilities to him that were heretofore unasked.

The Assembly would like to mention a few of the qualities that have made Jihmye's service so unique and memorable. Throughout his length of service we could always count on him to provide frank and loving comments during consultation; be among the first to arise to carry out all decisions of the institution; provide opportunities for what we lovingly call "tension relief" during intense meetings; exhort the friends to arise to higher and higher levels of service; and to find every occasion to blazon the Name of Bahá'u'lláh in his work and in his extensive social interactions. The individual members of the Assembly have already missed his presence at our meetings, bringing illumination to issues that sometimes were cloudy and operating as the "pupil of the eye."

We send this message to you because we have recognized that the Black Men's Gathering has done much to enhance his innate qualities of loyalty, steadfastness, devotion and purity of heart, manifesting them into deeper understandings of his important role in Bahá'u'lláh's Cause and spurring him on to actively involve himself in the core activities of the Five Year Plan. We wish to thank you for establishing and maintaining this important vehicle for empowerment, support and education for the many Black men who journey to Green Acre each July.

We stand ready to assist you in any manner which may be needed, and wish to assure you that the Regional BMG, if again determined to be held in San Diego, will continue to receive the Assembly's complete support.

Warmest Bahá'í love,

The Spiritual Assembly of the Bahá'ís of San Diego

In addition to the qualities the Spiritual Assembly mentioned here, one important contribution that Jihmye Collins made to the Gathering was his use of the arts. Each year, as part of his service to the BMG, Jihmye, a lifelong poet and painter, created a piece of artwork with a particular theme and gave it to the Gathering. The following paintings by Jihmye are a selection of his gifts to the participants of the annual BMG.

From its very beginning, the Gathering provided a welcoming and nurturing environment for artists. Drummers, singers, musicians, poets, rappers, and painters were all able to blossom and share their artistry with the other brothers. Billy ensured that all artists were made to feel welcome, and one did not have to be a professional artist to express himself in the Gathering. Everyone was encouraged to raise his voice or share his talent with the other brothers.

The BMG's emphasis on the arts and artists reflected the guidance of the Universal House of Justice:

BMG artwork creations by Jihmye Collins for the annual BMGs—from top clockwise—1997, 1998, 1999, 2002, 2003, 2004. Center: 2005.

Van Gilmer

Participating in devotions, Alfred Fox drums, and Hassan Malouf plays the Native American flute.

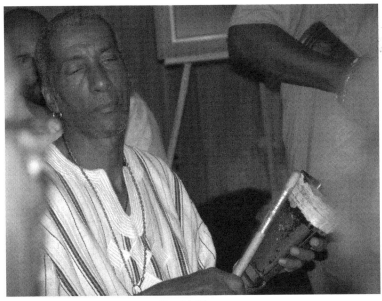

David Closson

*Nasan Fitz-Henley and Aaron Yates rapping the song "B.A.H.A.I.,"
July 16, 2005*

In all their efforts to achieve the aim of the Four Year Plan, the friends are also asked to give greater attention to the use of the arts, not only for proclamation but also for the work in expansion and consolidation. The graphic and performing arts and literature have played and can play a major role in extending the influence of the Cause . . . Shoghi Effendi held high hopes for the arts as a means for attracting attention to the Teachings . . . "The day will come when the Cause will spread like wildfire when its teaching will be presented on the stage

232

or in art and literature as a whole. Art can better awaken such noble sentiments than cold rationalizing, especially among the masses of the people."[1]

The BMG artists constantly awakened "such noble sentiment" among participants, especially when they first encountered the powerful display of artistic wonder during the sessions. During the 2005 Annual BMG, first-time participant Melbourne Mapp described how the arts impacted his transformation:

July 10, 2005
[Green Acre Bahá'í School]

My first and most memorable and transformative experience occurred on the first day of the Gathering in Maine in 2005. Shortly after leaving the dining hall and moving towards the first session . . . it was the sounds of the drums . . . first off in the distance . . . then as I reached the hall the drumming was clear, succinct, and live. The drumming, rhythms and music just took a hold of me. Down to my very essence, I felt the spirit of the Ancestors . . . spinning round in joyous embrace of the proceedings . . . here was a sea of brothers of many hues and shapes and sizes . . . and the expression of joy . . . emanated from their being. The room was pulsating with the spirits of those present and those who have transitioned on . . . and they were beaming with gladness.

Every year there were several participants who attended the Gathering for the first time. One of those individuals in 2005 was PJ Andrews. His father Kevin (who was the brother of Counselor and the 1987 Greensboro meeting attendee Gene Andrews) had been coming to the Gathering since the South Carolina days. Billy, who was close to the family, decided to invite PJ to come to the Gathering by suggesting it would be a special opportunity to do something meaningful with his father.

PJ recalled that he came to the Gathering with an incredible amount of emotional baggage. He had no strong sense of purpose or commitment to anything in his life, and he was looking for an escape from reality rather than a way to address his own struggles. PJ had connected sporadically, at best, with God throughout his youth, and he was apprehensive during his journey to the Gathering. Nevertheless, from the moment he arrived and was met and embraced by a group of his father's friends, he knew the Gathering held a certain spiritual power, though at the time, he was not fully conscious of its source.

July 14, 2005
[Green Acre Bahá'í School]

From time to time during the week, Billy checked in with PJ to see how he was doing. At one point, PJ sent him a hastily written note that read, "I have a few questions," to which Billy responded quickly and to PJ's satisfaction.

The next day Billy sat down across from him during lunch. He looked at PJ with a knowing and probing smile on his face and said, "So it seems like you're having a good time here."

PJ smiled back and said, "Yeah, I guess I am."

Billy responded with the same smile and said, "And?"

Still smiling, PJ told him to find his dad. At this point, Billy and PJ both knew that PJ was ready to declare his faith in Bahá'u'lláh. After PJ's father arrived, the three of them left the dining room and went into the Sarah Farmer room. They all cried, shared prayers, and PJ signed his declaration card. That evening, during a group consultation session in the Manny Reimer Hall, Billy called PJ up in front of the 120 or so men assembled at the Gathering and told them that PJ had an announcement.

PJ stepped forward and expressed to everyone that during the introductions, when he had told everyone that he was a Bahá'í, he had not told the whole truth, as he had not yet declared his faith. Then he announced that he had just done so. The room opened up with cheers and applause, and everyone cheered PJ's father and called him up to join PJ in the middle of the room. Together, they were surrounded by concentric circles of the group seated all around them, and they were weeping as they embraced each other. Billy asked PJ to share a prayer. Nervously, PJ quickly chose the first prayer in the first section of the prayer book someone had given to him. As he began to recite the prayer, each word pulled tears out of him, but they were tears of gratitude. It was clear that he was grateful—beyond his own ability to put his emotions into words—to God and to Bahá'u'lláh for having enabled him to recognize and love Them. When he read the line, ". . . Whose presence is my dearest wish and highest aspiration . . ." PJ fell to his knees.[2] His father lifted him back up to finish reading the prayer. As he rose to his feet, PJ felt the presence of God and the love and support of the 120 men sharing that moment with him. Van Gilmer stood up and began to sing with such fervor that PJ's tears flowed even more heavily. Everyone joined him in singing a prayer put to music by Van Gilmer, "What tongue can voice my thanks to Thee?" Van then walked toward PJ and embraced him. Soon after, PJ made his way back to his seat. Although he was not able to see clearly through his tears. He sat down next to friends, all of whom were crying with him.

The participants of the 19th Annual Black Men's Gathering reached out to the National Spiritual Assembly of Australia to share the purposes and activities of the BMG in the United States, and they gave a detailed report of the most recent Gathering. They suggested that the Australian Bahá'í community might be interested in the BMG style of devotions and mentioned that a member of the Gathering was currently pioneering there. Later in the year, the first ever Black Men's Gathering would be held in Melbourne, Australia.

July 16, 2005
[Email from the Black Men's Gathering to the National Spiritual Assembly of the Bahá'ís of Australia]

The National Spiritual Assembly of the Bahá'ís of Australia
Dearly loved Friends,

The participants of the 19th Annual Black Men's Gathering send you its warm and humble greetings from the Green Acre Bahá'í School in Eliot, Maine, United States!

For the past two decades, Bahá'í men of African descent have gathered in a spirit of unconditional love and fellowship, embracing and sharing experiences with others whom Bahá'u'lláh likened to "the pupil of the eye." These men gather in an atmosphere of safety and brotherhood, expressed by so many participants to be unlike any other atmosphere on the globe, where they experience a unique opportunity to know and love God while also learning how to know and love themselves. This year, the gathering is pleased to announce that over 120 black Bahá'í men are in attendance from all over the United States as well as various parts of the globe. We write to you with particular delight and enthusiasm, as one of the gathering's participants, Frederick Landry, has recently pioneered to Australia and presently lives in Melbourne, Victoria.

The gathering, founded and facilitated by a member of the National Spiritual Assembly of the Bahá'ís of the United States, William Roberts, provides daily experiences that are always special and unique. The mornings at the gathering include traditional African drumming followed by an hour or two of powerful prayers and song. We continue the day's events by reading and consulting on a particular message or letter from the Bahá'í World Center. Each day also includes the sharing of learnings and successes of the past year, as well as the development of strategic and systematic plans for the year to come.

Each year the gathering reads and consults on the Riḍván Message and discusses its implications for the Bahá'ís of the world and in particular for the members of the Black Men's Gathering. The members of the gathering are committed to continuing to advance the Cause through the directives of the Supreme Body in the final months of the Five Year Plan by continuing to conduct children's classes, plan devotional gatherings and facilitate study circles. What may be of particular interest to the Bahá'ís of Australia is the style of devotionals that have developed at the annual and local gatherings and devotionals all over the United States. In these, a particular spirit continues to be captured where African drumming, prayers and songs are offered in a unique format where those present are encouraged to participate, as they feel moved. We are confident that you will be pleased to welcome such devotionals in the spirit and style of the Black Men's Gathering and have asked that our brother Frederick bring this with him upon his return to Australia.

At this year's gathering, we were fortunate to be visited by a member of the Continental Board of Counsellors for the Americas. Counsellor Eugene Andrews addressed the gathering urging the brothers to continue to focus our energies on the three core activities as well as ensuring that we are focusing on our community of interest thus leading to an increase in human resources and ultimately more souls being attracted to the Faith. We pledge to do this and are empowered by his words describing the spirit and fruits of this gathering of black men by declaring, "This is the make a difference Gathering."

We ask for your prayers as the participants leave here and return to their homes all over the world to put into practice our individual commitments and assure you of our prayers for your service and the entire Australian Bahá'í community.

With loving Bahá'í greetings,

Participants of the 19th Annual Black Men's Gathering

19th Annual Bahá'í Black Men's Gathering

Green Acre Bahá'í School

Eliot, Maine

United States of America

A similar message was sent to the National Spiritual Assembly of the Bahá'ís of France where Pierre Johnson was living.

16 July 2005

National Spiritual Assembly of the Bahá'ís of France

Dearly loved Friends in the Cause of Bahá'u'lláh,

It is with radiant hearts that we, the 123 men of the 19th Annual Bahá'í Black Men's Gathering, joyously send you our heartfelt greetings from the sacred grounds, blessed by the footsteps of the Beloved Master, of the Green Acre Bahá'í School.

We are pleased to report that William Pierre Johnson, from the greater Paris Bahá'í Community (Nanterre), was a participant in attendance this year along with men from Honduras, Canada, Barbados, Australia, Bermuda, and the Virgin Islands as well as those from across the United States.

Girded by the encouragement of the Universal House of Justice and in firm dedication to the goals outlined in The Five Year Plan, the men of the Gathering have directed their focus to spreading the healing Message of Bahá'u'lláh among those individuals who are members of traditionally and/or racially marginalized communities in their respective countries. This goal will be realized chiefly through the systematic approach to growth provided by the Universal House of Justice. The core activities; raising the number of trained Ruhí Study Circle tutors and completion of the full sequence of the Ruhí courses; the carrying of the BMG-style devotional gatherings to individual local communities; and active facilitation of children's classes are the mode of operation.

We were blessed with the attendance of Dr. Eugene Andrews, a member of the Continental Board of Counsellors. His intense focus on the Five Year Plan and its final year's requirements greatly assisted us in our understanding, planning and commitment.

Our weeklong Gathering was again expertly guided and facilitated by Dr. William Roberts, Treasurer for the National Spiritual Assembly of the Bahá'ís of the United States who has organized and has led this effort for nearly twenty years.

It is our sincere hope that the spirit of our Gathering will soar over France and be felt by your beloved Spiritual Assembly and all of the believers whom you serve. Our love and our prayers are with you.

With Loving Bahá'í greetings,
The Participants of the 19th Annual Black Men's Gathering

The following is yet another example of how the BMG influenced Black Bahá'í men throughout the diaspora. In this letter to Billy, Oswald Hinds from Bermuda shares his appreciation for an "experience of unique proportions."

July 28, 2005
[Email from Ozzie Hinds to Billy Roberts]

Greetings Billy,

I wish to express my gratitude for being part of the BMG this year. Without a doubt it was, for me an experience of unique proportions. The outpouring of love and fellowship and the intensity of prayers were on a level I've never experienced before . . . Thanks so much for sharing and advising me like a real brother. Thank you.

I've spoken to CJ (Derick) and he is doing much better and is very keen on getting ahead with a BMG here in Bermuda. A number of the other friends are keen also. We will keep you abreast on this.

Billy on the final day at Green Acre, I am sorry I missed you as you wanted me to bring some items for the friends. I was all over the place looking for you until I was told you had just left. I'm sorry.

We will be having a gathering shortly of all the Bahá'í men during which Derick and I will talk a bit about the BMG. We would dearly wish to have copies of the letters from the UHJ sanctioning these gatherings to share with the friends. We do believe it can convey a lot and assist in gaining support for our BMG.

Again many thanks and I look forward to hearing from you, Ozzie.

The following is a response to an earlier idea for a pre-teen or teen BMG that Bill Wilson shared with Billy. Billy supported the idea and suggested that it needed further consideration. This idea was the fruit of years of BMG reflection and service in local Bahá'í communities.

July 29, 2005
[Email from Billy Roberts to Bill Wilson]

Dear Bill,

I am resending this note to you because it seems that you expressed an idea that may be nurtured in at least one local BMG. The idea for pre-teen or teen BMGs is a great idea that needs consideration.

Perhaps you might like to develop the idea and share it with others.

Hope you are well, and I look forward to hearing from you about this year's Gathering and how Omo experienced it.

Much love to you,

Billy

July 29, 2005
[Email from Bill Wilson to Billy Roberts]

Billy,

I'm considering it; and I'm going to develop a BMG-like program for pre-teens and teens. They are a very vulnerable group; those that survive often lose something precious in the process. I'll consult with Lori about starting a group in our home soon. We need to focus on the three core activities in our neighborhood; but I think there is a need to specialize these activities for pre-teens and teens.

Bowale should be the Elder, not me. He is really eager to serve this Cause. He is contacting lots of folks, men and women, about the upcoming BMG; soliciting support, contacting brothers, etc. I think we're going to pull off a very successful local BMG.

As for his enjoyment of the BMG at Green Acre, he was quite taken away with it. He was transformed by his pilgrimage, and the BMG advanced that transformation. He was given new insights about the 5-year plan and his role in that process. I know he wants to continue the Ruhi sequence until he becomes a tutor. We also talked about his conversations with some of the brothers. He enjoys talking far more than I ever will, but he's a willing partner in that process.

For me, the Gathering was a time of rejuvenation. Being able to pray at the grave of Hand of the Cause Louis Gregory is a Paradise of delight. This year, each morning, from Sunday to the following Saturday, I walked to his grave and said 3 Tablets of Aḥmad, the Fire Tablet, the prayer for the Northeastern States, the marriage prayer beginning, "Glorified art thou," the prayer for the Hands of the Cause, "Light and glory . . .", the Healing Prayer and various other invocations. It was a glorious way to begin a wonderful day. I'd almost always see one or two of the brothers, Dennis or Derrick, running or walking to the grave and I always beat Lloyd and Ken; who'd only walk. They would come each morning as I was just finishing my prayers. I spent time in 'Abdu'l-Bahá's room in Sarah Farmer Inn. It is sooooo peaceful there; I quickly become full when I pray in that exalted Spot.

The memory of the Gathering plays softly in my mind and heart as I go through my days; every moment was precious and they are wrapped in a golden haze of love. It was wonderful beyond words. The strength I derived from the Gathering made it possible, by the way, to bring a level of spirit to the Wednesday devotionals that was absent before. A number of people have told me how very, very special that evening was I wrote about recently. All from the BMG . . .

Love,
Bill

During Hassan Malouf's visit with his father last summer, (the first in over fifteen years), his father shared with him the addresses of relatives with whom he could visit. Although he was appreciative of his father's willingness to connect him with his extended family, at the time Hassan was not ready to reach out to these family members.

July 29, 2005
[Email from Hassan Malouf to those present at the 2005 Black Men's Gathering]

Alláh'u'Abhá all my loved family,

I wanted to let you know that last year after the BMG, I met my dad for the first time since I was about three years old. Perhaps even a little younger. He said, "This is the beginning of a new chapter." The truth of what he said became even more true last night. Last year, after the 2004 gathering, he gave me the address of my grandmother. For the whole year, I did nothing with this address. Then after this year's 2005 gathering, I wrote my grandmother a letter and sent her a picture to let her know that I loved her and the rest of the family and to tell her how I was doing. This was the first time in my life I had contacted her. Last night I got a phone call on behalf of my grandmother from my Aunt Denise. She left a message saying they're happy to hear from me and that they send their love. I called them back and spoke with my grandma, an aunt, an uncle, and a couple of cousins.

I've now connected with my father's side, the side that is of African descent. My new aunt told me that prior to receiving the letter to my grandma, they had had no idea where I was or how I had been doing for the past twenty years. The night before the letter arrived, they were speaking of me at the dinner table and wondering what I looked like and what was going on in my life. The next day, the letter from me came in the mail with my picture in it.

Now they want me to visit this summer. I don't know if I can. I want to, and perhaps I could even bring an uncle to Hush Harbour* . . . who knows, but, at the Gathering I asked

---

* Hush Harbor is a BMG-style devotional gathering in New York City.

God, if it is His will, to connect me with and bring the Faith to this side of my family. And I wondered if maybe last year was the first step in that direction. Only time will tell, but I admit I think that is what's happening. After my long message, I ask for prayers for God's message to successfully reach them and for those who are ready to get involved in the core activities of the plan and perhaps to attend the BMG of New York and of Jersey. I thank everyone for being my family that I love.

Your fam,

Hassan Malouf

P.S. A lot of them—actually, it seems most of them—live either somewhere in the state of New York, in New York City, in Jersey, or in the East Coast area.

August 1, 2005
[Email from Billy Roberts to Hassan Malouf]

Dearest Hassan,

Special and loving greetings to you. I am very proud of you and admire your courage to take this step. Your ability to utilize the support that you received from the Gathering this year and last is a testament to the power of the experience and a demonstration of our Faith in action. I am sure that the Blessed Beauty and members of the Concourse on High heard your prayers and assisted by paving the way to prepare the hearts for your willing actions. Be comforted that this will happen again as you plan to meet them face-to-face for the first time.

You must know and remember that all the brothers of the Gathering are with you and especially our dear Ted who is looking over your shoulder from the next world. Please don't forget to ask him for his help. Trust me, he is especially capable and experienced with these kinds of challenges.

I will pray for your success in the Temple here in Wilmette and am ever available to support you through yet another maze of your family history and am sure that you will find your way through with a bright and beautiful rainbow at its conclusion.

With much love and a huge Uncle "Billy-embrace,"

Billy

Seeing the personal transformation of Hassan is inspiring, and it is no exaggeration that the spiritual influences from the BMG had a significant role to play. Hassan was fortunate enough to reconnect with his father, and it also led to a spiritually powerful and meaningful reestablishment of the relationship with his parents in ways that would be too long of a story to write here. The time Hassan spent with his father in this world would be brief, as his father would pass away the following year. After completing his studies at Michigan State University, Hassan would go on to dedicate virtually all of his adult life to pioneering and serving indigenous communities in South Carolina, the U.S. Virgin Islands, and the countries of Dominica and Guyana.

Throughout its history, the BMG has been under the guidance and blessing of the Universal House of Justice. And the Gathering has always tried to be worthy of its trust by aligning its activities to the current teaching plans. In the following letter, the Universal House of Justice applauded the BMG for their "disciplined focus" in adhering to the current plan. They encouraged the BMG by stating that they "warmly embrace" the BMG's "express intention to keep within the terms of the Five Year Plans in relation to the core activities and the institute process . . ." This, in turn, would increase the contributions of African American Bahá'ís to the evolution of clusters throughout the country.

August 3, 2005
[Email from the Universal House of Justice to participants in the 19th Annual Black Men's Gathering]

Participants in the 19th Black Men's Gathering

c/o Dr. William Roberts U.S.A.

Dear Bahá'í Friends,

The consistency with which your activities have adhered to the requirements of any current Teaching Plan is the point that struck home as we read the message from your 19th annual gathering. You are to be wholeheartedly applauded, for this disciplined focus will ensure an ever-greater success as you embark on a decentralized effort aimed at extending the experience and learning that have distinguished your endeavors for well-nigh two decades. We warmly embrace your express intention to keep within the terms of the Five Year Plan in relation to the core activities and the institute process—an intention signaling as it is more intensively acted upon the welcome prospect of an increase in the continual contributions of African Americans to the evolution of clusters throughout your country. Our ardent prayer on behalf of you all is that this eager expectation may be fulfilled through the unceasing confirmations of the Blessed Beauty.

With loving Bahá'í greetings,

The Universal House of Justice

cc: National Assembly of the United States

At the summer's Gathering, the brothers wrote to Counselor Gene Andrews outlining their decision to increase an outward-looking orientation by decentralizing the annual BMG. He responded, commenting that he was pleased to hear about the brothers' commitment to the Five Year Plan, which served the African

American community by promoting children classes and devotional meetings. These activities, in turn, had the potential to bring more African Americans into the Faith.

August 7, 2005
[Email from Gene Andrews to participants in the 19th Annual Black Men's Gathering]

Dearly loved Brothers,

I was so pleased to receive your July 16, 2005 letter outlining your plan to undertake a more outward orientation through the decentralization of the annual Black Men's Gathering and your commitment to the core activities of the Five Year Plan.

Your decision to decentralize is a timely step that will serve you well during the next Five Year Plan.

Your future service to the African American Bahá'í community and the American Bahá'í community in general is indeed very promising. Initiating children's classes in African American neighborhoods, hosting devotional meetings, and tutoring study circles will no doubt bring an ever-increasing number of Brothers and Sisters to the Cause.

In my brief time with you at Green Acre I was so encouraged by the exciting stories of successful initiatives in Atlanta, "the new" New York, Detroit, and others. This is clearly a new day for the BMG and I look forward to hearing the exciting success stories and learning that will take place in the coming year.

Remember . . . JUST DO IT!

With loving Bahá'í greetings and admiration,

Gene Andrews

A Bahá'í brother from Barbados shared another touching testimony of the spiritual and emotional transformation he experienced at the BMG. Each testimony is confirmation of how the BMG experience opened the heart and removed the armor of Bahá'í men of African descent.

August 11, 2005
[Email from the Lionel Haynes to Billy Roberts]

Dear Brother Billy,

I am most grateful that you, the brothers in the USA, allowed me to join you this watershed year! I am way too impetuous for my age and would have been crushed had I not attended this year!!! I thank you and Bruce for your extraordinary patience, even longsuffering!

In 1997 I was ambushed by the spirit of the Gathering, not knowing then what transpired at these gatherings. This year I was a "veteran," so I knew what to expect in terms of impact of feelings. Wrong!!! A hundred years of poker faces and masks and armor and flippancy in emotional situations don't dissipate in one fell swoop so I weep silently, head in hands and heart in anguished release. And it was the young men's introduction that did me in.

This cutting you planted in 1987 is now fruiting, and it is not difficult to see the efficacy of these fruits on the Bahá'í community and beyond. I think it is wonderful that we have the capacity to transplant a branch of this tree anywhere we please with the knowledge that the fruit will be the same. The leaves, blossoms, fragrance and even sweetness of the fruit may vary according to the richness of the soil and the skill of the husbandman, but the fruit of service will ever be that.

I felt that this gathering was a defining moment in the history of the Faith in the Americas. Reference to it as our Badasht may be ill-conceived and inappropriate, but that is how I feel about this year's gathering. We are armed with the tools to sculpt a model of a Bahá'í community this world needs desperately. The major ingredients are love, patience, and unconditional acceptance—attributes I have seen at work constantly in the conduct of the gathering. Mind you, I have seen the cracks appear under stress, but I have also seen the quick repair work woven with the cement of humor and good judgement . . .

The Pupil of the eye of humanity has something to show the world. We have a spirituality forged by long suffering expressed in our devotions, which are diverse and deeply felt in their regional fragrance. It is a spirituality rooted in its love for Bahá'u'lláh and transposed on all His creatures. It is a spirituality that says, through its interactions to even the weakest of us, "I love you brother." It is a spirituality that manifests itself in harmless banter and good-humored dissing, as well as in serving each other, accommodating each other, and preferring each other to ourselves. This tree is a true Bahá'í community, the model we are looking for, and we the birds who have nested in its branches know only too well the difference!

Adding to this, BMG men are actively involved as tutors and facilitators; as the near-extinct male children's class teachers; as home visitors nurturing spiritually the aged and the shut-in; as hosts of uplifting devotions; as peacemakers and bridges of unity in our communities, with the love of God extended to all in our wide embrace; as encouragers and enablers in a world thriving on criticism and cynicism; as sensitive Black men speaking the language of the heart and ministering to the spiritually needy.

I have work to do here in Barbados. But I also have made a commitment to sell this idea of Black men growing, serving, and transforming our community and our world. I am looking forward to us getting participants from across the Caribbean to Tobago in November for our planting of this cutting from the BMG tree!

I know you are a busy bee with no time to read these long e-mails. I ramble no more.

Regards to the family. Mine is well, each loved one.

A Billy-embrace back at you,

Much love and gratitude

Lionel

The BMG-style devotional (known as Hush Harbor) in New York City was becoming a dynamic and integral part of the spiritual offerings of NYC. This devotional—and others like it—demonstrated to the larger society the transformative and community building power of the BMG. The following email exchanges and also the published article from the Bahá'í World News Service portrays this remarkable initiative.

October 5, 2005
[Email from Carl Murrell to Billy Roberts]

Hi Billy,

Your note reminded me . . . the BMG devotional in NYC is absolutely out-of-control (in a good way). It has totally outgrown the space that it is in. Last month I came late, and other late-comers were standing on the sidewalk peeking in. Lloyd & Ken are exploring other venues in which to hold it. People from all over the place attend, not just NYC, and I dare say that it is the one place Bahá'ís feel no anxiety bringing guests and spouses who are not Bahá'í.

Finally, I'll share an anecdote told to me by Clyde Herring. There is a Bahá'í woman in her community whose husband is not particularly religious. In consultation, they decided that they would like their two sons to participate regularly in some spiritual activity and settled on the monthly BMG devotional in NYC. After a few months of the boys' attendance in the devotionals, the father was approached by a colleague, who invited him and his sons to attend a professional football game with him as his guests. The father politely turned him down. One of his sons, who I can only imagine was stunned at his father's response, asked if he had understood correctly that his dad had just turned down free tickets to a professional football game. His father responded that it was BMG Sunday and that that took priority.

God is Most Glorious!

CM

October 5, 2005
[Email from Billy Roberts to the BMG Participants]

Dear Brothers,

Here is yet another example of the incredible import of your activities. Perhaps the New York brothers will now consider having two or more sessions—like they do at mega churches— thereby allowing more participation. I know help is needed so let's all pray they develop strong backs in the meantime.

With much love and admiration for the trail blazers in the City of the Covenant,

And for each one of you as well,

Billy

Devotional meeting pulses with energy
November 28, 2005

NEW YORK, United States—The sounds of African drums and soaring voices burst out over a normally quiet lower Manhattan Street lined with antique dealers and four-story apartment buildings.

It was a recent Sunday morning, and the pulsating energy was coming from the New York Bahá'í Center where a drum circle was being led by African American men, with people from a variety of ethnic backgrounds joining in.

Drummers send out energy and inspiration during a Hush Harbor devotional meeting at the New York Bahá'í Center. (Photo by Mike Relph)

The gathering was a striking example of a new and growing feature of Bahá'í community life: community devotional meetings designed to engage the world at large through uplifting and inspirational prayers, music, readings, and more.

In this case, the monthly event also offers a striking antidote to the sometimes subtle, sometimes overt sense of racial segregation that still pervades American society.

Called the "Hush Harbor Devotional," the gathering takes its name from meetings held by slaves who hung wet fabric on tree branches to stop their voices carrying while they were praying and planning escapes.

"The whole idea is to extend that idea of a safe place, not just for Black folks but for everyone that comes to the devotional," said Lloyd Lawrence, one of the organizers.

"I think we free people up from their own cultural limitations," Mr. Lawrence said.

William Roberts, a keen observer of the progress of the devotional, said many newcomers are surprised that they feel so comfortable in an environment that is led by African American men.

"In the larger society, people are made to fear Black men," said Dr. Roberts, who himself is African American and serves as a member of the National Spiritual Assembly of the Bahá'ís of the United States.

Dr. Roberts said that at the Hush Harbor Devotional gathering people are helped to feel at ease, to feel welcomed and embraced.

"Many people want to have a conversation with God, feel the spirit of the Almighty," said Dr. Roberts. "They want to have their souls quickened with that spirit—and coming into this kind of devotional allows them to feel that spirit."

Participants are welcomed with refreshments and invited to stay for lunch. In addition to drumming and singing, the Hush Harbor Devotional also features the chanting of prayers in a wide range of languages, including Arabic, Persian, Mandarin, and Spanish.

The Hush Harbor Devotional began about three years ago. The idea came from participation by New York City Bahá'ís in the Black Men's Gathering, which are regular events that were founded by Dr. Roberts in 1987 and have continued ever since.

The aim of that gathering, which has proved an ongoing success, is to change the conditions of men of African descent and help them to achieve spiritual transformation.

The use of the drumming combined with prayers began with the Black Men's Gathering and became the model for the Hush Harbor Devotional.

Organizers of the Hush Harbor devotional meetings: Lloyd Lawrence (left) and Kenneth Ray

"The purpose [of Hush Harbor] is not to perform, it's not to read perfectly, but to pray," said Dr. Roberts.

Kenneth Ray, who organizes the event with Mr. Lawrence, said he thought it had helped the community to understand its wonderful diversity.

"When we first started, Hush Harbor was mainly attracting the African American community, but now it is inclusive of people from all backgrounds, Bahá'ís and non-Bahá'ís alike," Mr. Ray said.

Mr. Ray said the question the organizers attempt to answer is this: "How many different ways can we present the [Bahá'í] Faith to as many different backgrounds?"

One of those attracted is P. J. Sanchez, a law student, who learned of the Bahá'í Faith initially from her mother and then read some Bahá'í material online. She came to realize the New York City Bahá'í Center was within walking distance from her apartment, and so she decided to attend a devotional gathering there.

"I was struck with the inclusive nature of the worship," Ms. Sanchez said.

"I felt as if everyone was actively participating, rather than just listening or responding by rote as I have felt in other forms of worship," she said.

"The lack of clergy and the lack of a script or plan—the lack of ritual, I suppose—for the devotional made the worship feel much more self-directed and organic, as if it was springing up naturally from the hearts and minds of the participants."

Ms. Sanchez said she was also struck by the diversity of the participants. "There seemed to be a much wider variety of race and class than I have usually found in various religions, and everyone mingled together without the formation of cliques," she said.

"Everyone participated in the devotional in a way that felt comfortable to them—shouting out or not, moving around or not, praying in English or in Spanish—and this was respected by all of the other participants.

"The musical nature of the Hush Harbor Devotional seemed very unique to me. Instead of music being an interlude from prayer, it was the mode of prayer itself. I found this to only enhance the words being said."

Ms. Sanchez attended a discussion about the Bahá'í Faith that followed the lunch and was able to ask about the various forms of worship in the Faith. She says she is interested in learning more.

One of the core activities of Bahá'ís around the world is to increase the efforts made to host devotional gatherings and to enhance their quality.

The Hush Harbor Devotional is now seen as an example of how to reflect on positive aspects of one's culture and to bring that to the rest of the Bahá'í community and the population at large.

"Really what's happened is we've witnessed men who have been marginalized in their community step forward," Dr. Roberts said.

"It allowed them to know that being a Bahá'í does not mean you have to put aside your culture, your way of doing things," he said.

Mr. Ray said that the devotional provides many with a different understanding of diversity and worship.

"It's a way for everyone to express his or her spirit—it's about the full participation of everyone in the room," he said.

"We seek to touch people's hearts. If people's hearts are affected, then Hush Harbor is serving its purpose."[3]

2006

May 20–21, 2006
[Savannah, Georgia]

Forty-three Black men were in attendance at the 1st Annual Savannah Black Men's Gathering, held May 20 and 21 at the Savannah, Georgia Bahá'í Unity Center. The Savannah Gathering started with the traditional joyous rumble of the brothers' sounding out rhythms on African djembes, which were fused into a jazz unison by

Participants of the 1st Annual Savannah Black Men's Gathering

the Phil Morrison Trio. The sound of the djembes led the Gathering's participants into a prayerful and meditative state. Soon afterward, the brothers began the traditional introductions. Auxiliary Board member Michael O'Neal formally opened the Gathering by encouraging the participants to think about the Gathering's purpose, their individual roles in the Bahá'í community, and their need for the Faith's institutions.

For the fourth year in a row, space at the annual Gathering in Maine had filled up months in advance. Because of the high level of participation, it became increasingly common for brothers to give Bruce Reynolds their registration payment for the next Gathering at the current one—virtually one year in advance! When space was no longer available, brothers would sometimes ask Bruce or Billy, with uneasy seriousness, whether they could just camp out on the lawn of Green Acre. Needless to say, this was not allowed. Some brothers, however, would push the envelope and attempt to have an exception made in their case. Nevertheless, those that were confirmed for attendance on Saturday, July 15 from all over the country (and some from other countries) made their way by car, train, plane, and bus to join their fellow brothers at the 20th Annual Black Men's Gathering.

July 16, 2006
[Green Acre Bahá'í School, Eliot, Maine]

After breakfast on the first full day of the Gathering (Sunday), if one was anywhere near (Manny) Reimer Hall, one could hear the joining together of musical instruments, particularly the drums. For some, this drumming and musical accompaniment of shakers, whistles, saxophones, and other instruments set the stage for the soon-to-follow prayers. The expression of these prayers and the style of praying that would follow were, for many, quite foreign. However, for each brother who found himself in the loving embrace and safe atmosphere of the prayer sessions at the Gathering, something incredible happened. He found that he was able to communicate with his Creator in a way he had never quite experienced, and he felt transformed.

This year was the first BMG for Dennis Davis of Little Rock, Arkansas. He recalls the following about his first BMG and prayer session:

I remember the first morning devotional and thinking to myself, we are going to pray for how long?! There must be a mistake in the scheduled program. Of course there was no scheduled program, but I was feeling a bit unsure about this marathon prayer session that I was about to embark upon. It was then that Billy Roberts called out, "O Lord, my God!" Around me over 100 other men echoed in unison, "O Lord, my God!" Dr. Roberts continued, "Open Thou the door" . . . The prayers continued on and on, with brothers offering prayers in a way that I had never witnessed . . . my breath was taken away. I immediately became lost in the ecstasy of communion with God in a way that moved my soul and touched my heart so deeply that I lost all sense of space and time. By the time I became aware of where I was, almost two hours had passed, and I was not ready to stop praying. I had never been in a space that felt as loving, safe, or spiritual in my entire life. I could feel the presence of something I had not felt until then. Even now, as I sit here writing this recollection, I am almost in tears just thinking about that special place of prayer with my dearly loved brothers.

July 18, 2006
[Green Acre Bahá'í School, Eliot, Maine]

Two days later, Carl Shorter from Buffalo, New York (another first-time participant of the Gathering) recalled his first time addressing the participants of the Gathering in his introduction:

This morning, like previous days, we're starting the day, after prayers, with introductions. So here I am, among a large group of maybe seventy-five to one hundred brothers. Over the past few days, since I was new to the Gathering and only twenty-five years old, I naturally settled in with the "younger" brothers. As the brothers started to introduce and share a little about themselves, the younger brothers would call out a nickname, usually either their first or last name in these lowpitched shouts. The elders of the gathering got up, one by one. A brother across the room stood up and said, "Alláh'u'abhá, my name is Bruce Reynolds." The young brothers would shout, "BRUUUUUUCE!" and he would continue with his introduction. The next person would come up. "My name is Phillipe Copeland." "PHIIIIILLIIIPE!" It went on like this, and I eventually found myself joining in even though I didn't know many people there. I finally stood up, deciding that I'm not going to use my last name since I didn't want everyone shouting, "SHORTER!" Instead, I say, "Carl . . . Buffalo." (That would become my new name for that Gathering—"Carl Buffalo," but it was always said with love.)

I began to bond very quickly with the young brothers in those opening sessions. This surprised me because, from my experience, it was preferable to remain guarded with other young Black men and to show no fear or vulnerability, but here at Green Acre, in this environment, I was able to let my guard down and be open to friendship and brotherhood. I will always remember the love and solidarity I feel here. I really wish that I had come here sooner because it feels like I am finding a part of myself that had been missing for a long time.

As mentioned in the previous chapter, each year Jihmye Collins of San Diego, California created a piece of artwork that was then made into a personal gift for the brothers at the annual gatherings. This year's artwork featured the image of Mr. Robert Turner, the first African American Bahá'í. In the latter years of the Gathering, Jihmye would donate the original piece of artwork that inspired the button gifts to the brothers, and the artwork would be auctioned as a fundraiser, usually for the National Fund.

Jihmye Collins describing his 2006 artwork that featured Robert Turner

Prior to the auctioning of the artwork this year, a type of moment occurred that did not happen very often—a tribute honoring Billy Roberts was read from a brother on behalf of the entire Gathering. Countless opportunities had presented themselves during past Gatherings for the brothers to make such a gesture, but Billy had always intentionally kept the focus of the Gathering on the spiritual transformation of the participants and their dedication to the service of the Faith. Even in this special moment, anyone in the room could sense that Billy was remembering something he heard years ago from member of the Universal House of Justice Amoz Gibson. Mr.

Gibson had relayed to Billy a saying that Louis Gregory had once recounted from 'Abdu'l-Bahá: Praise is wonderful as long as you don't inhale it. In various settings over the years, Billy would pass on those words to the brothers, encouraging constant self-reflection and a humble posture of learning.

Billy Roberts being honored

"Pile on" where Billy Roberts is being honored, encouraged, and thanked

July 21, 2006
[Green Acre Bahá'í School]

As usual, immediately following devotions on Friday morning, a time was reserved for reflections. However, just before reflections were to take place this year, a very special moment happened—a moment whose significance and power each of the brothers were quick to recognize.

Billy called out to the brothers who were present and who had met with him for the meeting in Greensboro, North Carolina in 1987 to join him in the center of the room. As these brothers made their way forward, everyone could feel and appreciate the love, devotion, and constancy of the efforts these eight men had demonstrated over the years. The four men who were absent—Jack Guillebeaux, Roy Jones, Ed Peace, and Len Smith—were certainly there in spirit. As plentiful applause filled the air, humility, joy, and thankfulness exuded from the hearts of these illumined brothers. Each of these men had been a source of inspiration for the participants, and the entire Gathering felt the dedication that each of them had to the Bahá'í Faith and to the Gathering.

Throughout the morning, brothers who felt moved to do so shared their reflections with the Gathering. Amidst the reflections, some brothers made personal pledges or promises that stemmed from having received encouragement and inspiration from other brothers.

One such example of a commitment came from the brothers from Los Angeles. After a week of hearing about the numerous examples of local Gatherings that were taking place all over the United States and abroad, the brothers from the Los Angeles area made a personal goal to initiate a Gathering in their city. Several other brothers in the room spontaneously shouted out to them that if the Los Angeles brothers planned a Gathering, they would support them and their Gathering and attend themselves, despite not living in the area. The sheer amount of inspiration and commitment expressed by all these brothers uplifted everyone.

*Eight of the original twelve attendees of the 1987 meeting in Greensboro.
Standing, left to right: Richard Thomas, William Roberts, John Mangum,
Van Gilmer. Seated, left to right: James Williams, Marvin Hughes, William
Varner, and Eugene Andrews.*

20th Annual Black Men's Gathering, Green Acre Bahá'í School, Eliot, Maine

November 17–19, 2006
[Roy, Washington]

The 2006 Black Men's Gathering Northwest was held at the Brighton Creek Bahá'í Conference Center in Roy, WA, from November 17 to 19, 2006. In attendance were twenty-two men of African descent—one from Idaho, one from Illinois, ten from Washington, and ten from Oregon. One participant was not a Bahá'í, although he was married to one. He had heard about the BMG and had decided to attend to know more. Clearly pleased with his experience over the weekend, he was very passionate and very eloquent about his thoughts throughout the Gathering. The unanimous consensus was that this was an inspirational event and would be a "must-attend" event for the next year.

The BMG continued travel-teaching to Africa in the winter of 2006. The journey began at the Bahá'í National Center on December 9th when thirty-two African American men from across the country assembled to prepare for service in Ghana through prayer and study of important guidance given to the Bahá'í world.

Participants of the 2006 Northwest Black Men's Gathering

December 9, 2006
[Bahá'í National Center, Evanston, IL]

To demonstrate their love and support of the participants en route to Ghana, the National Spiritual Assembly of the Bahá'ís of the United States honored the men with an invitation to have tea, where they greeted them and showered them with love and admiration. Billy had asked the brothers to bring photos of their families on the trip, and Burton Smith of Lansing, Michigan was prompted to share one with members of the National Assembly. He had brought a photo of his parents who, as one will recall, had attended the dedication of the Mother Temple in May of 1953.

William and Eva Smith (father and mother of Burton Smith, Julius Smith, Kenneth Smith and Marianne Smith Geula)

For Burton, the photo was a wonderful reminder of humility. Because his mother and father had become Bahá'ís in 1949 and 1950, respectively, and had married in 1951, Burton felt that the existence of his very essence was deeply connected and linked to the Faith.

During this significant and joyful gathering, which prepared them for their journey to Africa, the brothers received the rare privilege of being able to pray with the National Spiritual Assembly in its council chambers. They were escorted into the Assembly chamber, where they began to pray together with the institution. Their time together was highlighted by the song "God Is Sufficient Unto Me!"

After prayers were said by members of the National Assembly and the brothers prepared to depart, the members of the National Assembly burst into a spontaneous singing of "Alláh-u-Abhá" ("God is Most Glorious"). Each of the participants received a hug and kiss from the Secretary-General of the National Assembly, Dr. Robert Henderson, as they left. It was a magnificent, soul-stirring send-off for their trip to the motherland.

December 13, 2006
[Nkwanta, Ghana]

One group in Ghana traveled to the town of Nkwanta. Their host escorted them as they traveled about twelve hours through the Volta region. Along the way they picked up Auxiliary Board member F. C. Agama, who immediately captured the brothers' hearts. While making their way to Nkwanta, they stopped by many villages to see the Bahá'í friends. Many of them had not been visited in some time and had been feeling alone and isolated, and some were new Bahá'ís who were in need of encouragement.

What a joy it was for both the villagers and the brothers to be able to sit and discuss the Five Year Plan. The brothers reminded the villagers that they were like the Dawn-breakers in their villages—although they faced hardships and sometimes felt as if they would never have a large impact on their community, they should remember that Bahá'u'lláh was always assisting them and that through their steadfastness, they would achieve victory. This message not only seemed to lift their spirits but also helped the brothers in seeing how to deal with their own inevitable tests as African American men living in the United States.

While in Nkwanta, the brothers talked with many people, and they visited a school and spoke with the staff, with whom they had a meaningful dialogue. They also spoke with community leaders, as well as with people on the street. Every soul asked more questions than the brothers had anticipated; they were thirsty for spiritual truth. The brothers also visited the doctor of the community, and he told the group that all of the Nkwanta would benefit from hearing about the Faith. Alone, the doctor had helped bring down, in four years, the death toll from nine deaths per month to five deaths per year. He said he had accomplished this feat by offering medical assistance to the Nkwanta but more importantly by educating the mothers, since they were the initial teachers of the children. The doctor, of course, loved that the Faith emphasized the education of women, and he felt that the Nkwanta would embrace the Faith and offered to help organize a meeting with his staff so that they would be able to hear the message of the Bahá'ís. In addition, the group had many meetings with people of different faiths, all of whom expressed interest in the healing message of Bahá'u'lláh. The brothers thus were able to see firsthand the receptivity of the Nkwanta and why the NSA of Ghana had identified this particular community as a receptive teaching area.

Thirty-two brothers had spent nine packed days in different parts of Ghana, and prior to their return to the U.S., had scheduled a three-day stopover at the Bahá'í World Center. As it turned out, their schedule in Haifa was even more grueling than the one they had in Ghana. The brothers piled into five vans, which quickly brought them from one beautiful sight to another. On the second day, the brothers received a message to drop their current plans for the moment and go to the multipurpose room of the Seat of the Universal House of Justice to meet with two of its members.

As they sat there waiting for the members to arrive, the brothers noticed that they had not been this quiet since they received that special send-off from the chambers of the National Spiritual Assembly.

Soon, two members of the Universal House of Justice—Mr. Glenford Mitchell and Mr. Kiser Barnes—walked in. They both were full of joy and praise for the brothers and the work they were doing. Mr. Mitchell stated to the brothers, among other things, that "You have no idea the effect you are having on the Bahá'í world."

These words were very confirming and also humbling for the brothers. Mr. Mitchell had not mentioned that they were affecting the African American Bahá'í community or the American Bahá'í community. Rather, he had said the Bahá'í *world* community, and hearing this phrase was very humbling for the brothers.

Billy and other members of the BMG travel-teaching teams often received letters of appreciation from Bahá'ís in countries they had visited who expressed how much the BMG brothers had touched their lives. The following letter is from a white Bahá'í who grew up in Namibia but who was serving at the Bahá'í World Center. She made an interesting observation comparing the brothers to some of the Namibian believers: "I pray that the African believers there may attain the nobility I see in each of you—so many of them are still affected by what apartheid caused." The "nobility" she saw in the brothers was the transformative result of their participation in the BMG.

December 23, 2006
[Email from Brigitte Aiff to Billy Roberts]

Dear Billy,

Hope this finds you safe and sound back at home! . . .

Thank you again for everything. This visit of the BMG

group was very precious to me. Please convey my love to all the brothers when you send these photos on to them. In my reflections last night, after you left, I thought of virtues that stand out for me when I am with all of you: nobility, servitude, humility, reverence, and respect.

Nobility: having grown up in Namibia, I pray that the African believers there may attain to the nobility I see in each of you—so many of them are still affected by what apartheid caused.

Servitude: that came across so loud and clear for me this time, and it is a true example to me. Having served here for so long, I find myself looking at my service with fresh eyes.

Humility: this goes for me hand in hand with servitude—when you all shared about your experiences in Ghana, it never came across as "look what I have done" but always "how can I serve best?" and that shows such humility!

Reverence and respect: these also go together for me. Being in your midst, literally last night at one point (which was almost too overwhelming), and sharing in your devotions instantly connected me to the deepest part of my soul. One of my friends, who had pioneered in Africa for a few years, always speaks of the "joyful reverence" she encountered while in Africa, and that holds true for all of you as well.

And then of course there is love, which just shines out and can't help but affect everyone you come in contact with.

I feel blessed to have had these moments with you.

My prayers are with you.

Much love,

Brigitte

The members of the BMG trip to Ghana were Carroll Coley, Jihmye Collins, Raymond Collins, Phillipe Copeland, Nathan

BMG Ghana Travel Teachers, December 23, 2006

Davis, Brently Donaldson, Jonathan Ellis, Alfred Fox, Clarence Groves, Gordon Gullett, Jamey Heath, Travis Ivery, Shawheen James, Lloyd Lawrence, John McDay, Michael Paiya, Patrick Patillo, Edward Peace, Pierre Pickens, Marcus Potts, Lee Ratcliff, Shannon Reddy, Bruce Reynolds, William Roberts, Carl Shorter, Burton Smith, Neysan Sturdivant, Oluyemi Thomas, Fred White, Alton Williams, Aaron Yates, and Richard Yates.

2007

January 12–14, 2007
[Louhelen Bahá'í School, Davison, Michigan]

Over the weekend, the local Gathering held at the Louhelen Bahá'í School saw more than thirty men of African descent praying, singing, and studying the guidance. These brothers had come from all over the central states, from Illinois to Ohio, and the spiritual atmosphere they created became a spiritual and vibrant experience for all. And it should come as no surprise that over the course of the weekend, five participants of the Gathering formally declared their belief in the Bahá'í Faith.

As demonstrated in numerous instances over the years, the Gathering was a source of inspiration even to those who were onlookers and not actual participants. Louhelen Bahá'í School staff member Richard Hamrick, who had the blessing of attending the BMG at Green Acre, was able to observe this year's Gathering at Louhelen. Richard observed:

> The BMG gives Black men a chance to be together as brothers . . . as family. They get a chance to talk, to laugh, to cry,

Participants of the local Black Men's Gathering—Michigan, 2007

to sing, to be happy, to praise God, to play music, to ask questions, to enjoy the company of their brothers. These men represent the young and the old of the Black community. Knowledge and wisdom are passed on during this time, to ensure that the future is to be a blessed one. The love that has emanated from this weekend has been overwhelming and can barely be described in words. It is amazing to be greeted by total strangers as if you were a part of their family. The staff was allowed to join the men in prayer to end the weekend. The men played drums, prayed, and sang the praises of God. Now I will admit that I'm a crier, and this morning was no exception. I wept openly at the beauty, power, and sound that surrounded Unity Hall. I guess you just had to be there.

Over the weekend of March 30 through April 1, the BMG New England held its local Gathering. Counselor Gene Andrews and Billy had a chance to greet the brothers by telephone from a meeting they were both attending at the Bahá'í National Center. The brothers in attendance expressed their hope to see a resurgence of teaching activity in the region, and they reaffirmed their commitment to establish activities that would promote the teaching work.

Participants of the local Black Men's Gathering, New England, 2007

April 2, 2007
[Email from Billy Roberts to the Black Men's Gathering]

Sending at Jamey's request for your information.

Billy

My dear Brothers!

I am writing to inform you of our Local BMG here in Los Angeles. It will be held on the weekend of May 4th–6th. I of course am aware that it is many miles away for most of you, however we wanted to extend an invitation to those of you who may be able to join us.

If you find that this may be a possibility, please contact me as soon as you can. I, of course, will help you in any way I can in terms of a place to stay.

We are very excited about hosting a BMG here in L.A. and look forward to seeing some of you.

Alláh'u'abhá!

with my most deepest love,

Jamey Heath

April 5, 2007
[Email from Pierre Pickens to Andalib Khelghati and Frederick Landry]

Okay brothers,

I know you guys remember when we told Jamey we would go to L.A. and support him if they actually put together a local BMG so what do you guys think?

Let me know,

-p-

While one might think that such a long trip from the eastern side of the United States might be too long to take, the local BMG in Los Angeles would soon see three familiar faces from Chicago, Durham, and Nashville travel to California to support their dear brothers. It was yet another illustration of the love and commitment that had become a defining characteristic of so many aspects of the Gathering.

The Umoja Souljahs & Azania Junior Youth Empowerment programs were brother-sister Bahá'í Junior Youth Spiritual Empowerment Programs (JYSEP)—one for boys and the other for girls—held at the South DeKalb Bahá'í Unity Center located in Decatur, Georgia. These two JYSEPs sought to apply culturally responsive approaches to the lessons and activities of the junior youth empowerment program. Inspired by the spirit of the Black Men's Gathering, the creators of these two programs aimed to ensure that the

JYSEP's implementation was relevant to the cultural worldview and lived experiences of the Black youth it served.

Since 1996, the participating youth had gathered every Friday night. Most of the youth lived in the neighborhoods surrounding the center and would walk or ride their bikes to the center every week. The Bahá'í Center had a basketball gym, pool table, television and video game console, as well as other board games and activities the youth enjoyed. From these initial participants, the Umoja Souljahs was formed in 1998 (the Azania group was formed later), and they would meet each week after socializing and engaging in recreational activities. The youth would "circle up" in what they called their "Umoja (Unity) Circle" to delve into lessons, discussions, and activities designed to assist them in developing positive cultural identity and an understanding of their inherent spiritual nobility.

The youth learned about the contribution of African people to the world's development of language, literacy, reading, writing, science, mathematics, medicine, architecture, and much more. They learned about the experiences of enslavement and colonialism that occurred after the European invasion of America and its residual social, psychological, political, economic, and spiritual impact on Black people, as well as the entire nation. In addition, they learned how to read their daily social reality and respond to it in ways to help develop justice and unity more fully in their communities.

March 31, 2007 to April 1, 2007
[Birmingham, Alabama]

These lessons were supplemented with service projects and field trips designed to deepen the youths' understanding of the lessons they were learning. In March and April 2007, the youth visited the 16th Baptist Church and Civil Rights Museum in Birmingham, Alabama.

Participants of the Umoja Souljahs & Azania Junior Youth Empowerment Programs visiting Birmingham, Alabama. Group leaders pictured: Anthony Outler, Nasif Habeebullah, Von Habeebullah and Sundiata Spencer.

The Umoja Souljahs & Azania JYSEPs would go on to take other trips with the aim to educate and spiritually empower these young souls. One of these trips would come two years later when the groups would travel to Memphis, Tennessee to visit the National Civil Rights Museum and the historic Lorraine Motel.

These experiences were at once informative and moving for the youth. Many of them were deeply touched to visit the spot where Dr. Martin Luther King, Jr. was assassinated. Due to their socio-economic realities, most of the youth in the program had very few, if any, opportunities to visit places outside Georgia. The groups' leaders accompanied the youth in various fundraising efforts to raise money for the trips. In addition to the trips pictured, the groups also visited Nashville, TN as well as the Bahá'í National Center and

Participants of the Umoja Souljahs & Azania Junior Youth Empowerment programs visiting the Lorraine Motel and National Civil Rights Museum in Memphis, TN. Group leaders pictured: Von Habeebullah, Sundiata Spencer and Anthony Outler, May, 2009.

House of Worship in Wilmette, Illinois. They also attended the Million Family March in Washington, D.C., the Bahá'í Kingdom Conference in Milwaukee, Wisconsin and took a college tour to Florida where they visited historically Black institutions of higher learning (Florida A&M University, Bethune–Cookman University and Edward Waters College). These trips assisted in cementing the bonds of unity between the youth and strengthened their commitment to the JYSEP.

Decentralizing the Gathering was a focus over the past few years. The following message from Billy to the participants of the Gathering informed them of the emphasis and focus of holding the BMG on the local level. He explained that this change was based on the pattern established by the Universal House of Justice for the Bahá'í community worldwide. There were already thirty local BMGs in "far-flung places," and the BMG's "main stage" would now be the local Gatherings. There still would be the main annual Gathering but with this, there would also be a shift. The annual Gathering was now a place to learn how to support the local Gatherings. With a note of encouragement for this new stage, Billy told the brothers that they were now "ably assuming responsibility for establishing and leading" these local Gatherings.

May 29, 2007
[Email from Billy Roberts to the Participants of the Black Men's Gathering]

Dearest Brothers,

You are warmly invited to the Black Men's Gathering Leadership Forum. It will begin on 14 July through 21 July 2007 at Green Acre Bahá'í School in Eliot Maine. We ask that you plan your departure no earlier than 4:00 pm on Saturday 21 July so that you can fully participate in the closing ceremonies.

As you know we have decentralized the Gathering joining the pattern established by the Universal House of Justice for the Bahá'í Community worldwide. We have witnessed this year nearly 30 local BMG's in far-flung places. The main stage for the Gathering is now the local Gatherings that you are ably assuming responsibility for establishing and leading. Those not receiving this invitation are encouraged to participate in as many of the local BMGs as they like.

The BMG Central is now designed to support and reinforce the local Gatherings who are the focus of our efforts.

The recent messages from the Universal House of Justice celebrating progress made during this first year of the second Five Year Plan gives us much to discuss. And in true Gathering form I know we will pursue this with a sense of urgency and vigor unseen elsewhere in the Bahá'í community. During this past year we have learned a great deal and I anticipate we will have a full sharing expanding our understanding of the Plan and how the Gathering is supporting it.

We also anticipate brothers joining us from Barbados, Trinidad and Tobago, Jamaica, Ghana, South Africa, and Bermuda, along with others who have attended before.

We look forward to seeing you this summer.

With much love,

Your brother,

Billy

In total, four annual leadership forums were held from 2006 to 2009, and many elders of the Gathering and scores of brothers who were actively planning the local Gatherings attended them. While in the past, the centralized Gathering typically had an attendance of approximately 110–120 participants, only about sixty brothers attended the leadership forums. Although fewer in number, these brothers were dedicated to learning how to best support local Gatherings from their fellow brothers who hailed from the United States and several other countries.

BMG Leadership Forum, July 2007

Similar to the centralized Gatherings, the leadership forum included the major components of prayer and study of the messages from the Universal House of Justice. Also reminiscent of previous Gatherings, a small gift from the most recent travel teaching trip was presented to the brothers in attendance. This year, the gifts came from last year's trip to Ghana.

An African tribal brass trade bead—one of the gifts presented at this year's Gathering

July 19, 2007
[Green Acre Bahá'í School, Lucas Cottage]

After leaving the main grounds of Green Acre for the evening, five younger brothers joined Dennis Davis in Lucas Cottage to learn and rehearse a dance-line routine that Dennis had created. Except for Aaron Yates, none of these younger brothers were exactly accustomed to such expressions of the arts. However, these brothers knew that they were in a safe place, and what better place to learn a routine than at the Gathering!

For more than three hours, these young adults rehearsed a new dance routine while Aaron came up with additional lyrics to complement Dennis' chorus line. Learning the routine with an overlay of such powerful lyrics was stirring to each of these brothers. They were inspired with this new creative element that was wakened in them, and they were all thankful for Dennis' mentorship of them.

July 20, 2007
[Green Acre Bahá'í School]

Following the late afternoon break, the brothers who had gathered the previous evening in Lucas Cottage met in the southwestern corner of Reimer Hall. They lined up as Dennis gave a brief introduction and then quickly joined the group in the line formation. In order, the brothers in line were Philippe Copeland, Frederick Landry, Aaron Yates, Dennis Davis, Shawheen James, and Neysan Sturdivant. They stood in silence and were ready to offer what would be a spiritually uplifting and moving performance. Those gathered in the room watched as the brothers moved to the center of the room and began to dance and sing:

Introduction:
I know I've been changed.
I know I've been changed.
I know I've been changed.
Bahá'u'lláh has changed my name.
I know I've been changed.
I know I've been changed.
I know I've been changed.
Bahá'u'lláh has changed my name.

Verse 1:
Nobody knows me, brothers and I.
Nobody knows why we cry.
Nobody knows me, brothers and I.
Bahá'u'lláh says that we're the pupil of the eye.

Chorus:
All of my love (my love, my love), for peace and happiness.
I'm gonna give it to Bahá'u'lláh.
All of my love (my love, my love), for peace and happiness.
I'm gonna give it to Bahá'u'lláh.

Verse 2:
All the brothers are gonna work it out.
The House of Justice lifts all our doubts.
BMGs established all through the land.
To be aligned with the Five Year Plan.

Chorus

Verse 3:
Great injustices we have endured!
But it was fire that made us pure.
Imbued with vision from our suffering and pain.
Prepared us to serve the Greatest Name.

Chorus

At the conclusion, the brothers gathered showed their heartfelt agreement with the spirit and words uttered by the six brothers. Additionally, through their exuberant cheers and continued applause, the brothers showered the small group with love and encouragement.

Later that evening, as was the regular tradition on the evening of the last full day of the Gathering, the participants of the Gathering expressed their appreciation to the staff and youth volunteers.

The co-administrators of Green Acre, husband and wife Jim and Jeannine Sacco, along with most of the rest of the staff and

Green Acre Youth Volunteers

volunteers, were in attendance. Jim and Jeannine reflected on another wonderful week of having the Black Men's Gathering leadership forum at the school. They watched as the staff basked in the warmth of the joyful and loving spirit that the brothers brought with them (that evening and throughout the week). The brothers generously shared this spirit with the staff whenever they were all together—particularly during mealtimes. For the staff, seeing the brothers' love for the Faith was contagious and inspiring, and their warm gratitude for the services of the staff was evident throughout the week and then during the final evening of the Gathering. Jim and Jeannine were filled with happiness as the evening continued with the participants of the Gathering showing their appreciation to staff with drumming, music, prayers, loving testimonials, accolades, thoughtful gifts (often from Africa) and the famous group hugs, which left all of them feeling a strong soul-to-soul connection with these wonderful brothers whose presence they were going to miss terribly.

Jim had the privilege of being the recipient of the popular "pile on." Over one hundred brothers encircled him and chanted

"Yá-Bahá'u'l-Abhá," and Jim felt immensely loved and appreciated. The spiritual energy he received buoyed him well into the next year.

During the next morning's devotions and program, Jim was again transported to an incredibly spiritual place by the group singing of the brothers. The rich and deep resonance of over one hundred voices singing "Here Am I" made a deep spiritual impression that had a lifelong impact on him.

Jim and Jeannine Sacco, co-administrators of Green Acre Bahá'í School

Local BMGs throughout the United States and all over the world would continue to be held and would continue to make significant impacts on the participants and their communities. The following letter from Billy to Mokone Nakedi of South Africa reflected a milestone in the expansion of the BMG within the global Bahá'í community. It was the first BMG held in South Africa, and similar to the local BMGs being held throughout the United States, it attempted to align its program with the goals of the current Plan of the Faith.

October 3, 2007
[Email from Billy Roberts to Mokone Nakedi]

Dear Mokone,

It has been a long time since we corresponded, and I am hoping to hear about the Gathering you had last month. How did things go? I hope your efforts resulted in some successes.

Look forward to hearing from you soon.

With loving Bahá'í greetings,

Billy

October 3, 2007
[Email from Mokone Nakedi to Billy Roberts]

Dear Brother Billy,

Always good to hear from you. I thought I shared with you the outcome of the Gathering. It was awesome. Twenty-seven brothers attended and fully participated. As you always say, it was "wonderful," and it was the same here.

I have attached the message I sent to all the brothers who attended. We have shared the outcome of the meeting with all the brothers and plan to have regular (monthly) news snippets of what the brothers are doing.

Will send more info later.

Remember to greet my beloved Sister and all the brothers. Tell them the brotherhood is contagious and is infecting other members of the community. My community has CHANGED. This is wonderful.

Best regards,

Mokone

Dearly loved Brothers,

It was so wonderful to be in our first Black Men's Gathering meeting. This was a historic moment for the Black men, and indeed for South Africa's spiritual landscape. Please accept my sincere gratitude for participating in this Gathering. The stage is now set for us to exchange and support each other for the achievements of the goals of the Five Year Plan.

Our discussions were varied but inspiring. The sparks of light due to our expression of our various opinions lit the way forward to concrete conclusions. Here are the points we have agreed on:

1. Structure (or Organisation) - Black Men's Gathering.

2. Participants - Black Males or Males of African descent.

3. Purpose - To help each other to urgently arise, take ownership of the Faith and contribute to the Plan.

4. Added value - Develop unity, love, fellowship, and support.

5. Meeting Interval - Six months.

6. Date of Next Gathering - 28/29/30 March 2008.

7. Convenors for the next meeting - Siza Ziphethe, Malibongwe Fudu and Koketso Makola.

8. Hub of information flow - Mokone Nakedi.

9. Goal (To be achieved by the next meeting) - Tangible growth with regard to the Faith (e. g. move from Book 2 to 3 or be responsible for an additional core activity like devotional meetings, etc.).

Please share with the friends who have no access to e-mail.

Warmest greetings,

Mokone Nakedi

The BMGs that were occurring in various parts of the world were sometimes adjusted to take into consideration the particular needs and circumstances of the population in that country. The Bahá'í Encounter for Afro Descendants held in Brazil had adjusted their goals to serve the needs of both men and women of African descent. In Jamaica, the Gathering held was adjusted to include all men living in the country, regardless of race, age, and nationality. The following letter from the National Spiritual Assembly of the Bahá'ís of Jamaica described the Gathering and some of the societal conditions present there that resulted in the formation of the Gathering.

[Letter from the NSA of Jamaica to the BMG]

National Spiritual Assembly of the Bahá'ís of Jamaica
October 5, 2007
To the Wonderful Men Participating in Jamaica's Men's Gathering
Dear Friends,

Alláh'u'Abhá! As you assemble once again to deepen and offer praise and gratitude to God, your National Spiritual Assembly is filled with admiration for this wonderful effort that, we hope, will have a tremendous bearing on you and your various communities.

In a country, and indeed the world at large, that has seen so many of our men—including the young—estranged, lost, and dissipating their energies on idle pursuits, acts that are counterproductive to Bahá'u'lláh's teachings that "all men have been created to carry forward an ever-advancing civilization," such an action is naturally a welcome relief. The fruits yielded from your deliberations and the warmth radiating from your souls will, no doubt, send rippling vibrations in hearts devoid of this transcendence.

The Black Men's Gathering, founded in North America over twenty years ago, was created from the urgent need to rescue the fallen Black brothers, who through racial injustice, economic hardship and other factors have lost the resilience and the will, which they have been endowed with, to live life with pride and make a positive contribution. The BMG has helped to empower and direct them through spiritual connection to God. Without this connection, all humanity is lost. Today the Black Men's Gathering has grown to encompass men from African descent the world over and has been decentralized to other countries. The fact that you have embarked on your conclave bears eloquent testimony.

In Jamaica's case, it has made sense to open the meetings to all men regardless of age, race, or nationality, in order to address the general marginalization of males that exists in our society. For example, recent statistics show that 85% of students at the University of the West Indies are women, and only 15% are men. Given also the violence of our society, there is a clear need for empowerment, healing, and consecration.

The National Spiritual Assembly wishes you complete success and stands willing to assist you in any way possible, and will offer prayers on your behalf.

With warm and loving greetings,
National Spiritual Assembly of the Bahá'ís of Jamaica
Linda J. Roche, National Secretary

October 12–14, 2007
[Teaneck, New Jersey]

Over the weekend, thirty-two participants of the Fourth Annual New Jersey Black Men's Gathering came together in prayer, love, and fellowship. As the spiritually uplifting weekend drew to a close, the brothers gathered proceeded to commit themselves to creating plans for action to include continued participation in the institute process, specifically in target areas including Newark, Essex County, Trenton, and the Teaneck / Bergen County area. Additionally, the participants made plans to collaborate and focus on the spiritual empowerment of junior youth and youth in their communities. They also decided to encourage each other to become more visible in the field of service to both their fellow Bahá'ís as well as friends of the Faith.

Participants of the 4th Annual New Jersey Black Men's Gathering, 2007

November 2–4, 2007
Durham, North Carolina

The local Gathering that would be held over the weekend in Durham would differ in format from what had come to be known as a typical BMG. However, it proved to be monumental in the sense that it conceptualized the structure of the Gathering while allowing for a practical adaptation that was so important to the area. The Gathering began on Friday night with dinner at a local restaurant, which provided the brothers with time to meet and greet each other.

On Saturday morning, the brothers gathered at the meeting site and began devotions. Then they proceeded to explain the foundations of the Gathering to new participants. Personal introductions followed, which provided a segue into more discussion about the purpose of the BMG. Then the brothers turned to studying the guidance.

The local Gathering coincided with the Triangle's intensive program of growth. Although not a customary part of the Gathering, the brothers went out into McDougald Terrace, a local community in Durham. There they taught the Faith and visited the families of those children participating in the community's children's class. They ended up inviting a woman and her daughter to the Sunday program.

Auxilary Board member Betsy Ayankoya, who accompanied the visits in the neighborhood, recounted that:

Fifteen men from the BMG, three of them not yet Bahá'ís, joined forces with five believers from the community to make home visits to the families of children and junior youth in the community. The presence of the brothers lent confidence and credibility to the teaching activity. For a community that bears witness to the impact of longstanding racism and inequality, nothing could bring more hope than to be ministered by brothers who understand their plight on a personal level, and yet have overcome the impact of racial prejudice. For communities in desperation, the truest testimony and evidence of the revelation of the power of Bahá'u'lláh is to recognize Bahá'u'lláh's transformation on their own brethren. I felt that the biggest impact of teaching was on the brothers themselves. I saw them grow in confidence and joy with each visit! How amazing that everything we are told about teaching is true!

The conclusion of the Gathering and one of the highlights of the weekend was the devotional held at the end of the Gathering. In the words of one of the brothers who was attending Duke University:

Later that night the BMG, as the final event that day, came to Duke to participate in a planned devotional, which could not have happened without the BMG spirit, the support from the brothers, and the teaching that occurred (especially from my brotha James ;-) and many others). If I may say here that the devotion was a HUGE success and the people that we connected with are now thoroughly excited about what the Duke Bahá'í Club is trying to do. More people now know about the Faith as a result and it's the club's commitment to nourish the spirit that was so potent and inspiring during the devotion. In this sense the BMG helped inspire me to continue the teaching work at Duke, within the scope of the Five Year Plan, and showed me the potential and the power the Faith has to transform a campus!! The Duke [Bahá'í] Club is now wholeheartedly committed to monthly devotions for next semester, and, as a result of the devotions and the energy that it produced therefrom, the club has enough interest in the Faith, among the broader Duke community, to start two study circles in addition to the one that is currently going on. So you see, in just its infancy the local BMG is growing in its influence, and I must say that with future years, the local BMG will be a force to be reckoned with!!!"

2008

Over the weekend of the 25th through the 27th of January, long-standing participants of the BMG held another local Gathering—the first annual BMG of Texas in Dallas (with a few participants from Louisiana, Arkansas, Oklahoma, California, and Georgia). With twenty-two participants registered, the weekend began that Friday evening at a local food eatery in Dallas, which soon became filled with brothers seeing both familiar and new faces. Throughout the weekend, brothers from many clusters across the state participated in the Gathering, which was filled with powerful prayers, intense consultation, and study. As the weekend drew to a close, the brothers planned to diffuse the spirit of this new BMG across the state and began making plans on a cluster-wide basis. To that end, the following cluster-based commitments were made:

Dallas City (TX) Cluster: Teaching teams would reach out to specific populations (Latinos & African Americans); work on widening their circle of friends (community of interest); and maintain and increase devotionals.

Denton County (TX) Cluster: Teaching teams would initiate a monthly devotional with members of the Martin Luther King Committee of Flower Mound.

Douglas / Cobb County (GA) Cluster: Teaching teams would initiate Bahá'í children's classes and devotionals.

Galveston County (TX) Cluster: Teaching teams would start a Ruhi Institute (Study Circle) class.

Harris County (Houston, TX) Cluster: Teaching teams would sustain ongoing devotionals once a month, would begin a junior youth group, and would aim to have two home visits per month.

Little Rock (AK) Cluster: Teaching teams would begin a concerted effort to connect with Bahá'ís in Pine Bluff, AK and coordinate efforts with study circles.

Natchitoches Parish (LA) Cluster: Teaching teams would start a monthly fireside and a Book 1 study circle in February, 2008.

Northeast Texas (TX) Cluster: Teaching teams would begin neighborhood devotionals and would pass out flyers to invite neighbors.

Oakland (CA) Cluster: Teaching teams would sustain ongoing core activities.

Oklahoma City (OK) Cluster: Teaching teams would start a devotional and check with the Regional Training Institute (RTI) in Oklahoma for assistance with taking and completing study circles.

These commitments the brothers made at the conclusion of a powerful weekend were expected but still inspiring.

One of the consequences of the BMG and the action-oriented spirit it engendered was that it offered, over the years, special service opportunities for family members and friends of participants of the Gathering. Time and time again one became accustomed to seeing the power of the BMG to influence individuals and families who were not traditional participants of the Gathering. As mentioned previously, one area where this was true was in the arts. Be it in song and dance, or in physical artistic expressions, the BMG was transforming hearts in many ways, as shown by the e-mail below.

February 21, 2008
[Email from Tirzah Gregory to Billy Roberts]

Dear Mr. Roberts,

Louis Anderson told me that he spoke with you regarding the logo that I created for BMG Kansas City. I'm happy to offer it to the organization if they'd like to have it. Please take a look at the business card (front and back) I created for Louis and the flier that I made for his Kansas City annual BMG meeting. Let me know what you think—I'm happy to make changes for you as well. You can reach me . . . [on my cell phone]. I'm traveling to Michigan this weekend, but I should be reachable at that number. Thanks!

Much love and appreciation,

Tirzah Gregory (George Wilson's daughter)

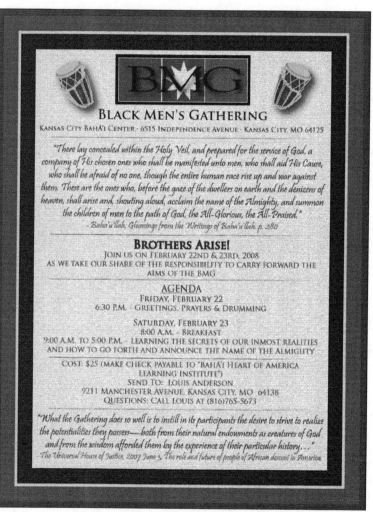

Artwork created for the local BMG in Kansas City

Artwork created for the local BMG in Kansas City

During the years the Black Men's Gathering was held in South Carolina, several brothers from the Middle Tennessee region attended. However, since the BMG had moved to Green Acre, some of these brothers had not been able to attend at the new location and relish that welcoming setting. Still other men of African descent in the region were interested in attending the Gathering but for one reason or another had not been able to attend. However, in the summer of 2007, a member of the BMG Coordinating Committee and elder of the Gathering moved to the Middle Tennessee area, and he was hopeful that together he and others could plan a local BMG.

In the months of November and December, 2007, a BMG planning meeting was initiated. The meeting was attended by Andre

Ballew, Gary Brown, Frederick Landry, George Minter, Zacheus Okediji, Jeff Rucker, Sutherland Seals, Corky Smothers, and Karen Streets-Anderson (representing the Nashville Local Spiritual Assembly). This meeting created the impetus to begin planning a local Gathering and also served as a way for those who would be planning the Gathering to get to know one another. Key to the overall process was the involvement and participation of George Minter of Murfreesboro and Corky Smothers of Nashville. Both of these men were previous participants of the Annual BMG in the mid-1990s at the Louis Gregory Bahá'í Institute. The planning committee would meet again in the early months of 2008 to finalize the plans for the Middle Tennessee local Gathering, and in March, they communicated their plans to the Local Spiritual Assembly.

March 3, 2008
[Letter from the Nashville BMG Planning Committee to Local Spiritual Assembly of Nashville, Tennessee]

Dear Loved Friends,

The Planning Committee of the 1st annual Nashville Black Men's Gathering sends you its warm and humble greetings!

For the past two decades, Bahá'í men of African descent have gathered in a spirit of unconditional love and fellowship, embracing and sharing experiences with others whom Bahá'u'lláh likened to "the pupil of the eye." These men gather in an atmosphere of safety and brotherhood, expressed by so many participants to be unlike any other atmosphere on the globe where they experience a unique opportunity to know and love God while also learning how to know and love themselves.

In recent years, the spirit and love from the National gathering has been decentralized to cities across the U.S. and widened to include those souls attracted to the message of Bahá'u'lláh.

We are pleased to announce that although such a gathering in the Nashville cluster is long overdue, as you are no doubt aware, this April from the 11th through the 13th, Nashville will be added to the growing list of cities across the U.S. to hold such a local BMG!

The gathering, founded and facilitated by member of the National Spiritual Assembly of the Bahá'ís of the United States, William H. Roberts, presents an environment that is always special and unique. Nashville's gathering will be no different and will include traditional African drumming, powerful prayers and song. We will continue the weekend's events by reading and consulting on the 3 June 2007 letter from the Universal House of Justice to an individual believer on the role and future of people of African descent in America. We will also include the sharing of learnings and successes that we have had in our own communities as well as the development of systematic plans and individual pledges for the year to come.

What may be of particular interest to the Spiritual Assembly is the style of devotionals that have developed at the annual and local gatherings and devotionals all over the United States. In these, a particular spirit continues to be captured where traditional African drumming, prayers, and songs are offered in a unique format where participants are encouraged to participate as they so feel moved. Nashville's local gathering this April wouldn't be complete without the sharing of such devotions. Therefore, the Nashville BMG will be holding a devotional to conclude its weekend gathering. These devotions will take place during the regularly held Sunday morning devotions at the Bahá'í Center at 11:00, and all members of the community and wider community are invited to attend and to participate!

We welcome your prayers for our success as the participants of the 1ˢᵗ Nashville Black Men's Gathering.

With love and greetings,

Frederick Landry

(On behalf of the Nashville BMG Planning Committee)

In 2006 and 2007, Savannah, Georgia had held its first and second local BMGs. Instrumental to the planning of these local Gatherings was Michael O'Neal of Savannah. Michael founded Parent University* in 1999 and was serving as an Auxiliary Board member, and he wrote to those who had assisted the two previous local Gatherings.

March 3, 2008
[Email from Michael O'Neal to various BMG participants]

Hello dear friends:

Again we are pleased to host this, the 3rd Black Men's Gathering of Savannah. Your support for the previous years' events has been phenomenal. Every time I am with someone who talks about the weekend of previous years, they mention what a wonderful and welcoming community we have. Many commented that they have never been received by a community like we received them. This year I would like to ask that we build on what we have learned in the past. Many people from around the center asked me about the BMG weekend for weeks after it happened last year.

---

* Michael O'Neal is the founder of Parent University. See "As Parent University grows and matures, it stays focused on core mission," April 23, 2018. https://www.bahai.us/as-parent-univerity-grows-and-matures-it-stays-focused-on-core-mission/.

So, please give me your suggestions on how we can use this event to further the Five Year plan. The scores of enrollments we have witnessed give us an invaluable gift to share with the brothers who are coming from near and far . . . Of course, it will be very inspiring for our newer friends to experience the BMG as well. My dear friends, the issue of race is still eating at the soul of our world community, and it is the Bahá'ís who need to demonstrate our mature and loving commitment to doing the things that will imbue healing and action in all of us. This event is one that is directed toward the healing of all by attending to the needs of a few. The healing happens when we are reminded of our purpose and our destiny as described by Bahá'u'lláh. And this healing surely affects us all. The June 3rd, 2007 letter from the UHJ gives us ample fodder for thought on this matter.

I am assured that we will rise yet again to the standards we have set for ourselves and make this year's event a memorable one. Once again tell me what your thoughts are . . . what is in your heart . . . I lean on you with confidence that we will not let each other fall. Please spread the word Savannah Area Cluster. Savannah BMG 3 is coming . . .

Love
Michael

For over twenty years, the vast majority of the planning of the BMG fell on the shoulders of Billy. However, similar to the emergence of the local Gatherings and the resulting ad hoc planning committees and groups that coordinated and led those Gatherings, the time had come when some of the coordination work of the Gathering could now benefit from a group of dedicated and experienced elders of the Gathering. In March 2008, Billy wrote the following e-mail to the elders of the Gathering.

March 10, 2008
[Email from Billy Roberts to the BMG Elders]

Dear Brothers,

Last July at the BMG Leadership Forum when the Elders consulted you urged me to identify a number of brothers who could serve to assist me in the ongoing coordinating work of the Gathering as it grows and develops in the future. I have done this and the team, chosen from among the Elders (listed below), will be meeting this weekend in Wilmette for its inaugural session. I ask each of you to bend your prayers in support of this important new stage in the development of the Black Men's Gathering and for the capacity of those called to serve in this way. Each has willingly made this a priority in his life, and we all are deeply appreciative for the services they will provide now and in the future.

Thank you in advance for your support and your prayers.

With love and heartfelt gratitude,

Your brother,

Billy

BMG Coordinating Group

Jamie Abercrombie, South Carolina / Southern Region; Jamey Heath, California / Southwest Region; Frederick Landry, Tennessee / Southern Region; Harvey McMurray, North Carolina / Southern Region; Michael O'Neal, Georgia / Southern Region; Mike Paiya, Oregon / Northwest Region; Pierre Pickens, North Carolina / Southern Region; Bruce Reynolds, Georgia / Southern Region; Morgan Spriggs, Oregon / Northwest

Region; Oliver Thomas, Michigan / Central Region; Richard Thomas, Michigan / Central Region; and Alton Williams, New Jersey / Northeast Region.

March 10, 2008
[Email from Billy Roberts to the BMG Coordinating Group]

BMG Coordinating Group, March 14 through 16 2008, Wilmette, Illinois

Dear Brothers,

The time is approaching when you will arrive in Chicago for the inaugural meeting of the BMG Coordinating Group. Attached are logistical details that will facilitate your visit. Please be aware that I have arranged for your housing at the Doubletree Hotel in Skokie. Each room will host two of you for the weekend. Breakfast is provided in the hotel restaurant "the Grill" each morning (opens at 6am) and can be enjoyed before the time for fasting begins (7am CST). I will be there to join you and assist in transporting you to the Temple for prayers on Saturday morning at 8:30am. From the Temple, following prayers, we will convene at the Bahá'í National Center in the large conference room.

Dinner will be provided at my home on Saturday evening and then you will be transported to the hotel. We will reconvene again on Sunday morning at 8:30am at the National Center concluding our meeting at noon.

Dress is business casual, and for those of you from warmer climates it is very cold in Chicago during this time of year, so come prepared. If you'd like to make contact to arrange a roommate in advance, the numbers of those attending are listed below.

I look forward to seeing you this weekend.

With warm embrace,
Your brother,
Billy

March 15, 2008
[Wilmette, Illinois]

To start the weekend, the coordinating group visited the Bahá'í House of Worship to pray and to spiritually focus themselves for the weekend that was ahead. Throughout their time together, the newly formed coordinating group consulted on various aspects of the Gathering including the program for the following summer.

BMG Coordinating Group, March 15, 2008

With many of the local Gatherings across the country, those participants who lived outside the area where the Gathering was being held—sometimes including attendees from various states across the country—offered a tremendous amount of love and support to the brothers who lived locally. In the same vein, members of the coordinating group or elders of the Gathering would support the efforts of the local brothers. The Nashville Gathering found support from brothers who lived in Pennsylvania, Wyoming, California, Georgia, Illinois, and New Jersey!

Although each local Gathering had components that were taken from the central gathering in Green Acre (such as prayer, songs, study of Bahá'í guidance, and personal introductions), each Gathering also had its own unique feel and moment (or moments) that stood out. For example, one of the highlights of the Nashville gathering was the participation and personal transformation of Robert Jordan.

Robert was a friend of the Faith and had been married to a Bahá'í for nearly twenty-five years. He had participated in various Bahá'í meetings during the years in which he had been married. Still, upon being invited to the Nashville Gathering, Robert displayed some hesitation and concern about attending. He told one of the Nashville Gathering's planners that he wasn't sure if attending was the right thing to do and that perhaps he shouldn't go. Although he didn't express this at the time, Robert was a bit apprehensive about organized religion. He was also uncertain about attending a gathering with other men, mostly because of his personal experiences with various groups of men over the years. While these past experiences weren't all bad or problematic, Robert couldn't imagine dedicating virtually his entire weekend to attending a single meeting. Still, he chose to attend the Gathering, mostly because he was asked by Frederick Landry—a Bahá'í whom he had known for the past fifteen years.

Robert's experience at the Gathering put his concerns to rest. In his own words, he felt as if his spirit had been awakened, and he wanted to experience more of what he felt during the weekend in Nashville. Robert was especially awestruck at seeing individuals coming together from different parts of the country to attend the Nashville Gathering.

Nashville's Black Men's Gathering, April 11–13, 2008

April 14, 2008
[Email from Frederick Landry to the Participants of the Nashville BMG]

Dearest brothers,

Here are the commitments made at the conclusion of our gathering! In addition to remaining committed to our own, we can also think of ways to assist each other in keeping their commitments (ex. encouragement, accompanying someone in their teaching efforts, etc.). I also remind everyone of the oath of confidentiality that we each agreed to at the beginning of the gathering and that such also applies to our commitments.

If for some reason your commitments were not recorded (or mis-recorded) or you were unable to attend the session on Sunday, please e-mail them to me, and I will amend the master list. Also, Garrison, thank you for taking down our commitments!

Many thanks,

Frederick

After attending the Nashville BMG, Robert committed to return next year and also to bringing others with him. His change of heart from his initial hesitation to attend the local BMG was certainly a testament to the spiritual forces present during the weekend as well as the various connections made. In fact, the very next weekend, Robert would make the drive south to attend the local Black Men's Gathering in Atlanta, Georgia!

In May of this year, Billy Roberts reached out to the coordinating committee and also to those brothers who were responsible for the planning of local Gatherings. These local BMGs would be held in the following areas: New York City; Western New York; New Jersey; Philadelphia; Washington, D.C.; Durham, NC; Roanoke, VA; Florida; Michigan; Western Michigan; Ohio; Kansas City; Chicago; Arkansas; Dallas / Houston; San Diego; Los Angeles; Bay Area / Oakland; Portland-Seattle; Nashville; Atlanta; Savannah; upstate South Carolina; and the Louis Gregory Institute.

Billy wrote to ask the committee to forward him the names and e-mail addresses of those who were directly involved in the planning of the local Gatherings so that he could invite them to this year's Leadership Forum. As usual, the Forum would be held in mid-July and would provide a loving environment for the brothers to dedicate themselves to serving their fellow communities. The brothers described the Forum to the Universal House of Justice:

July 19, 2008
[Letter from the Leadership Forum to the Universal House of Justice]

Universal House of Justice

Dearly loved Friends,

The brothers from this year's Black Men's Gathering Leadership Forum bring you our most heartfelt and warmest greet-

BMG Leadership Forum, July 2008

ings from the verdant grounds of Green Acre Bahá'í School in Eliot, Maine. This year's leadership forum was marked by an intensified effort to gain the skills and capacities required for advancing the process of entry by troops. This was done through focused consultation on the core components of the Five Year Plan. Furthermore, we gained insight and inspiration by reflecting on the encouraging accounts of the teaching work rendered by brothers across the country. To that end, our forum began with careful and intense study and consultation on this year's Riḍván Message, thus forming the foundational spirit and insight for the proceedings.

One of the highlights of this year's forum was our focus and training on Anna's Presentation from the Ruhi sequence. The brothers were given an opportunity to share their many joyful experiences as well as their challenges and difficulties in using this door-to-door teaching model as one approach to direct teaching. This was followed by each brother practicing giving Anna's Presentation. Such an activity was remarkably inspiring as many of the identified challenges and difficulties were alleviated when the brothers experienced firsthand the effectiveness and pure joy of teaching through use of the presentation. The spirit of commitment to direct teaching lifted our spirits and confirmed our pledge to employ this and other proven models of direct teaching to advance the Cause of God. To assist us in these efforts, each member of the forum received a color copy of Anna's Presentation with the expectation that it will be frequently used in our own home clusters.

A second highlight of the forum focused on reports from local Black Men's Gatherings. These gatherings, which took place in more than 35 locations across the United States—including new gatherings in the cities of Columbus, OH; Dallas, TX; Kalamazoo, MI; Little Rock, AR; Nashville, TN; Philadelphia, PA; and Springfield, IL—generated new and exciting learnings.

A particularly important highlight was the attention we spent on plans and programs for junior youth. Through the spark of consultation and shared vision, several participants are now preparing to launch new junior youth programs this August— with others anticipated in the coming year. In addition, several members of the local gatherings shared their learnings from their involvement in junior youth and youth activities, including programs in Chicago, IL; New York, NY; Los Angeles, CA; and Savannah, GA. Also inspiring were the learnings derived from the Animator training—a training that many of the participants have either undergone or pledge to complete.

As our days here drew to a close, the participants of the forum agreed that our aspiration to bring in scores of souls to the Faith is well within reach, and that we will bend our energies in an effort to bring the Message of Bahá'u'lláh to those souls "seeking the truth, and wishing to attain unto the knowledge of God." It is our ardent desire that we perceive the "honor and nobility in every human being" as we strive to make our mark in the remaining years of this Five Year Plan and bring the Word of God to those receptive souls in our communities.

Your ever-ready humble servants,

The Brothers of the 2008 Black Men's Gathering Leadership Forum

In the following report, the brothers of the 2008 BMG Leadership Forum shared with the National Spiritual Assembly its activities during its recent meeting, which included receiving reports from seven new local BMGs and junior youth activities. One of the highlights of this meeting was the contribution of ten thousand dollars that the forum provided for thirty-five junior youth to attend a workshop at Louhelen Bahá'í School.

July 19, 2008
[Letter from the Leadership Forum to the National Spiritual Assembly of the Bahá'ís of the United States]

National Spiritual Assembly of the Bahá'ís of the United States
Dearly Loved Friends,

We truly appreciate your letter of welcome to this year's BMG Leadership Forum. The walls of Reimer Hall vibrated with the fervor of our prayers as we beseeched God to guide our consultations and bless our plans.

Our hearts were expanded through our phrase-by-phrase perusal of the 2008 Riḍván message of the Universal House of Justice facilitated by Dr. William Roberts.

Auxiliary Board members Michael O'Neal and Oliver Thomas skillfully led an in-depth discussion of Anna's Presentation, including role play exercises and consultation on direct teaching. We are impatient to return to our communities to share our insights and participate in teaching plans.

We welcomed enthusiastic reports from 7 new local Gatherings held in Springfield, IL; Nashville, TN; Dallas, TX; Little Rock, AR; Kalamazoo, MI; Columbus / Cleveland, OH; and Philadelphia, PA; increasing the number of BMGs across the United States to over thirty-five.

We held a half-day panel discussion and report on jr. youth activities in Savannah, GA; Chicago, IL; Atlanta, GA; Los

Angeles, CA; and Brockton, MA; including the lessons learned and the ways youth activities can advance the process of entry by troops. We are eager to share this knowledge, implement activities, and encourage our BMG members to undertake such programs aimed at junior youth.

As a result of this consultation, we agreed to provide $10,000 in financial aid to allow thirty-five junior youth from Georgia, South Carolina, and Michigan to visit the Bahá'í House of Worship and to attend a junior youth workshop at Louhelen Bahá'í School. The participants in this program will be known as BMG Fellows.

Dr. William McMiller, board member of the Bahá'í-inspired social and economic development initiative Health for Humanity, presented a proposal entitled "BMG Reads." This collaboration between the Black Men's Gathering and Health for Humanity is designed to assist literacy-challenged youth to improve their reading skills. The forum decided to enthusiastically support this effort and to begin with pilot projects in Savannah, Georgia and Greenville, South Carolina.

We held consultations by region to reflect on the challenges and possibilities for further encouraging participants at local gatherings to more closely align their activities in support of the goals of the Five Year Plan.

In returning to your inspiring welcoming dispatch, the remarks during reflections ending this gathering consistently focused on spiritual transformation and actions to be pursued in our respective clusters.

With loving Bahá'í greetings,

Participants in the Black Men's Gathering Leadership Forum 2008

2009

Over the years, one of the marked achievements of the Black Men's Gathering was increasing the involvement and level of teaching work of young adults. Historically, the Gathering served as a place where young brothers who were serving the Faith in their communities could focus on their personal, spiritual, and social development, as well as gain and share inspiration and learnings from other young adults from across the country.

As the Gathering continued to decentralize, the elders observed that fewer young brothers were attending the Gathering at Green Acre. Billy began to reflect on why this pattern was occurring and to look for ways to re-include these young brothers in the Gathering. His reflection resulted in a realization that the Gathering was unintentionally being "dominated" by more mature voices. Also, many of the younger brothers could not relate to the struggles and challenges that the older brothers were facing. As a result, some of the younger brothers were beginning to question their place in the Gathering.

Billy concluded that the younger brothers deserved and needed a Gathering of their own, where they could share their challenges without having to struggle to have their voices heard. Therefore, to provide an opportunity for the young adults to gather in a style similar to the Gathering at Green Acre, a BMG dedicated to brothers ages 18 thru 35 was initiated in 2009. To increase the younger brothers' ability to attend, the duration as well as the financial cost was evaluated. To accommodate the schedules and life circumstances of the younger brothers, the Gathering was held for three days over a weekend and was in part subsidized by the BMG. Billy commented that ultimately, this Gathering was to be "a focused time for the young adults to address issues and concerns that [were] theirs." To that end, Billy asked longtime participant of the Gathering and elder Derik Smith to facilitate the first Young Adult Gathering.

At a glance, one might notice that visually, the format of the first Young Adult Black Men's Gathering was set up differently than other Gatherings. Whereas typically the brothers in attendance all gathered in one circle or concentric circles with no divisions between ages, the Young Adult Gathering had a slightly different (but purposeful) arrangement, with the non-young adult elders in attendance surrounding the young brothers as they held their own Gathering. For three days, the older brothers supported the younger brothers through their presence and unspoken acceptance. Of course, there were times when some of the elders felt compelled to contribute. Likewise, there were times when even the participants of the Gathering felt the need to solicit feedback from the older brothers. But through the gentle facilitation of Derik Smith, all were encouraged to allow the young adults to have *their* Gathering, with the older brothers just listening, which would prove to be very encouraging to the young brothers.

The twenty-four attendees of the first annual Young Adults Gathering were Bate Bate, Kafele Boothe, Nathan Davis, John Gullett, Shawheen James, Frederick Landry, Teddy Lawrence, Hassan Malouf, Emeric Mazibuko, Anis Mojgani, Trevor Nightingale, Isaac Oben, Anthony Outler, Juan Pacheco, Delvin Reynolds, Stephen Rice, Justin Stafford, Neysan Sturdivant, Kelsey Taylor, Henry Warren, Justin Williams, Kenya Williams, Raleigh Woods, and Renan Woods.

*Jihmye Collins, Bruce Reynolds, and Billy Roberts present Derik Smith with
the Gathering's yearly commemorative artwork, 2009*

The following letter from the Black Men's Gathering for Young
Adults to the Universal House of Justice marked one of several historical landmarks in the evolution of the BMG. Ever since its inception,
the BMG had rested on the shoulders of the elders. Now the new
purpose and focus shifted to young adult men charged with taking
ownership of their own empowerment. Their meeting was capped
off with the presence of former member of the Universal House of
Justice Glenford Mitchell and Counselor Eugene Andrews.

July 18, 2009
[Letter from the Young Adult BMG to the Universal House of Justice]

The Universal House of Justice

Dearly Beloved Supreme Body,

We, the members of the 23rd annual Black Men's Gathering, heartily greet you with gratitude and love. Assembling in
the arms of Green Acre, we have come together this year with

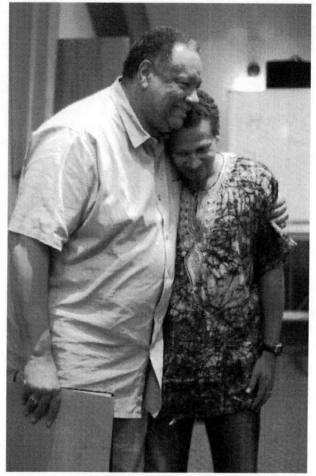

Billy Roberts and Derik Smith, 2009

a new purpose, one focusing on the action of the Gathering's young adult men. Much of the Gathering has been carried upon the shoulders of our elders, and in order for this legacy to continue the younger members of the Bahá'í African American Community must arise to more fully take ownership of both the Gathering and the paths its participants tread.

Though only a few days in length, this year's historic Gathering is one overflowing with blessings. We first had the ineffable bounty of greeting Mr. Glenford Mitchell, a retired member of the Universal House of Justice. Mr. Mitchell spoke to us about the innate potential of our spiritual powers. He shared with us that thought without action is useless, and reminded us that each and every one has the Image of God engraved upon them. Made from the Lord's beauty, we need only to remember this to remember who we are, and with that thought, we can only succeed. Mr. Mitchell gently guided our consultation as we studied your letter of June 3, 2007, responding to an individual brother's questions about the issue of our race's history of oppression. We discussed how it is exactly this sorrowful history that endows us with a larger capacity for love and justice.

In addition to the aforementioned letter, there was also deepening upon your Riḍván 2009 Message. We celebrate with you the victory of the recent 41 conferences held across the globe. The excitement felt by the Institution for these recent enterprises and the successes therein, were apparent, and filled us with hope and confidence. As we talked about the transformative power the plan has had on the worldwide community in such a short time, we joyously wonder what other transformations await.

Within the framework of the plan we are finding our place, planting trees and sowing seeds of service in both the African American community and our local communities back home. Through your continuous support, as revealed in your letter to the Black Men's Gathering dated August 20, 2008, we are emboldened to continue doing this work for Bahá'u'lláh. We cannot begin to express our gratitude for your loving encouragement. Throughout the history of the Black Men's Gathering, the House of Justice has wholeheartedly supported its endeavors, and as the younger members of the Gathering are being shaped to be its stewards, we recognize our responsibility to respect that legacy of selfless service and fidelity to the current plans of the Supreme Body, not only for our older brothers but in honor of the trust and reassurance we have always received from the Institutions.

The brothers attending the Young Adult BMG were further blessed by our brother Dr. Eugene Andrews, member of the Continental Board of Counselors. Dr. Andrews spoke on the importance of integrating the four core activities of the Five Year Plan, not just focusing on singular aspects of it. He pressed upon us the need to step forward in our communities, embracing the mantle of leadership—that today is a new reality, one not seen before, with a new set of hurdles and a new bar to attain and surmount.

With the world changing and shifting continuously, the technological age we live in is filled with unique opportunities. By implementing this technology for the institute process, we can find ways of keeping our spirits connected, regardless of the physical distances that separate us. We discussed the ways we can use this to further our support of one another when back in our home communities. Sharing with each other what has worked and offering advice in the areas we may need assistance in.

In later consultation, we reflected on the purpose of this year's assemblage, specifically for the young adult men of the Gathering. We are hungry to serve though at times not sure how. We wish to offer our hearts and hands up to the Cause though, in the presence of those brothers around us who have served the Faith as giants, at times we doubt our worth and wonder about our ability. We realize though there is no time for these thoughts. We must not sit in the past but embrace the future. Armed with the love of our elders, the love of the

Institutions, the love of the Divine Concourse—with the knowledge of this love, how can we fail! We need only to step forward. In this army of light, we have our marching orders; we need only to complete them.

Our prayers remain with you at the World Centre as you pursue your service to the world-wide community and as we visit and pray at the resting place of our beloved Hand of the Cause of God Louis Gregory and his wife Louisa, your work, sacrifice, and love is always remembered.

With the utmost love and gratitude, we humbly remain your servants,

The Participants of the Black Men's Gathering for Young Adults at Green Acre Bahá'í School, Eliot, Maine

The Young Adult Forum was a wonderful success, with a loving group of young adults across the country joining in a spirit of fellowship, love, and prayer. While few if any of the participants knew those in attendance when they first met, the forum concluded with strong bonds of kinship and connectedness between them all.

While the Black Men's Gathering was a continued opportunity for spiritual and social transformation, during a midweek break between the Young Adult and Leadership Forums, some of the brothers went recreational fishing, and Mr. Mitchell was able to join the fun.

Following the Young Adult Forum, the Leadership Forum took place. Just as he had done at the BMG for young adults, Mr. Mitchell shared many wise words of advice with the brothers at the Leadership Forum and encouraged them to press on in the teaching and work of the Faith. Embracing the universal spirit in all mankind was a central theme in Mr. Mitchell's encouragement to the brothers present as well as for them to find the courage and love to let go of racially driven resentments of the past.

Glenford Mitchell and Dan McCoy

Dennis Davis, Bill Davis, Mickey Ingram, Mike Paiya, Glenford Mitchell, Alton Williams, Dan McCoy at the 23rd Annual Black Men's Gathering, Eliot, Maine

[Letter from the Leadership Forum to the Universal House of Justice]

The Universal House of Justice
Bahá'í World Centre
Haifa, Israel

Dearly honored and deeply loved Friends,

Greetings from the participants of the 23rd Annual Black Men's Gathering. The Gathering continues to evolve. It now has two components, the Leadership Forum, to which are invited those individuals who are providing leadership for the more than 25 local Gatherings across the United States, and for the first time ever, a session for young men ages 18 to 35 to help encourage their participation in the Five Year Plan. Also, these young men will help replenish the ranks of the Gathering. We studied the 2008 and 2009 Riḍván Messages, your 23 June 2009 letter to the Bahá'ís of Iran, and the 20 August 2008 letter to the Black Men's Gathering. The transformative power of these documents thrusts open the doors to our hearts and minds in ways that cannot be adequately described.

We warmly welcomed our dear brother Glenford Mitchell to his first Black Men's Gathering. He gave poignant, inspiring presentations in which he shared highlights from a number of communications from the Universal House of Justice to the Gathering. He also read and provided insights to the 3 June 2007 letter. We were encouraged to let go of the resentments of the past and embrace our universal spirit in striving to become a new race of beings, and to become significant contributors to the Five Year Plan. He was at once a source of encouragement, insight, confidence, empowerment, and joy.

During consultation we shared experiences from our local gatherings with the intended purpose of being more responsive to the aims of the Five Year Plan. Additionally, and in response to your letter to us a year ago, we explored creative ways to engage communities of interest among African Americans. Each of us better understands the importance of our role participating and in furthering the framework for action consistent with the Tablets of the Divine Plan, and our birthright as members of the American Bahá'í community.

We leave the Leadership Forum grateful to the Universal House of Justice for its clarity and guidance to the community of Bahá, indeed the whole of humanity, to ascend to its spiritual destiny. We will forever be mindful of the urgency of the hour and have greater insights of our responsibility as spiritual descendants of the Dawn-breakers. We humbly ask for your continued prayers.

With loving gratitude,

Participants [of the] 23rd Black Men's Gathering Leadership Forum Green Acre Bahá'í School, Elliot, Maine

2010

As previously mentioned, an unintended consequence of the decentralization of the Gathering was the decrease in attendance of younger brothers. Additionally, another unintended consequence occurred as a result of these local Gatherings. Because the local Gatherings required a large amount of planning and coordination, brothers who would normally be serving the core activities in their clusters were now devoting their energies to organizing their local BMGs. As a result, there was a decrease in capable human resources who could facilitate core activities to support the Five Year Plans.

Therefore, in the appropriate spirit of learning, growth, and prioritization of the plans and directives of the Universal House of Justice, the coordinating group made an important decision—to replace the local Gatherings with regional ones. The strategy would be to allow the brothers to continue to have the experience of spiritual growth and empowerment at a BMG while allowing them to devote more time and energies to their respective clusters.

The BMG always strived to align its efforts with the current needs of the Faith, and in this message from Billy to the BMG of Michigan, the brothers were praised for their successful annual Gatherings. Billy informed them, however, that while these Gatherings had made great strides in empowering the brothers who attended, they also "drained capacity away from the development of cluster activities." Therefore, it was time for the BMG to move to a new level of operation. Local BMGs would be eliminated and replaced by a series of regionally based BMGs.

September 7, 2010
[Email from Billy Roberts to the BMG Michigan]

Dear Brothers,

Over several years you have responded to our request to initiate an annual Gathering for men of African descent in your area. Yours has been a highly successful enterprise! In this way you made the BMG experience available to a number of individuals, both members of the Bahá'í Community as well as those who are a part of the community of interest who might not have had that opportunity. We wish to express our gratitude to you for this effort.

Now we move forward to a new level of operation in response to the continuously evolving Plans of the Head of our Faith. While many of the "localized" Gatherings were extremely successful, we have found that the human resources necessary to carry them out were significant and drained capacity away from the development of cluster activities and the ongoing integration of effort applied to the core activities of the Five Year Plan in our local communities.

Since the principal aim of the Gathering is to empower men of African descent to find their way to full engagement in serving the Cause and thereby to free themselves from the structures society has imposed upon them, we feel a new strategy is best implemented at this point to better achieve this primary objective, namely to enthusiastically serve humankind.

With these thoughts in mind, the BMG Coordinating Group has called for the elimination of all local / area BMGs in the United States, to be replaced by a series of regionally based Black Men's Gatherings. Your Gathering will be transformed into a regionally based program. The following list outlines the sessions planned by the BMG Coordinating Group for the months ahead.

October 22–24, 2010 Wilhelm Property,
Teaneck, NJ—Northeast
October 29–31, 2010 Dallas Bahá'í Center
Dallas, TX—Southwest
January 7–9, 2011 Louhelen Bahá'í School
Davison, MI—Central
February 18–20, 2011 Bosch Bahá'í School
Santa Cruz, CA—West
April 8–10, 2011 New Hope Camp and Conf Center
Chapel Hill, NC—Southeast

While each of these sessions is open to everyone, we hope the brothers involved in your area will journey to the Louhelen Bahá'í School in January to participate with brothers from throughout the Midwest. We anticipate this to be an occasion that will serve to nurture relationships as well as learning beyond one's local experience.

Once again, I thank you for the efforts you have exerted, which have contributed mightily to the development of the BMG and in serving the interests of men of African descent as together we work to advance the revelation of Bahá'u'lláh. I look forward to seeing you there.

With loving Bahá'í greetings,
Billy

Central States Regional Black Men's Gathering, 2010

2011

Prior to this year's BMG Central States Regional Gathering, the coordinating group met to consult on various topics. One of those was that of homefront pioneering. To encourage the brothers to offer international service, the coordinating group consulted and decided to write to and personally encourage brothers who they thought might be in a position to offer such service to ultimately help fulfill the goal of the Five Year Plan. With this communication and other similar encouragements communicated in the past, several brothers who were inspired with the love of Bahá'u'lláh arose to serve the Cause.

January 9–11, 2011
[Louhelen Bahá'í School]

The BMG Central Gathering, held at Louhelen Bahá'í School, was the first regional Gathering of 2011, and it welcomed brothers from many states, including Kansas, Missouri, Illinois, Ohio, Massachusetts, Nevada, and of course Michigan. The sixty-five brothers gathered in the typical spirit of love and fellowship, with brothers seeing old and new faces, experiencing the power of trust, and creating bonds of fellowship. Veteran Bahá'ís, friends of the Faith, elders, and new brothers all made up the group of participants. Prayer and consultation on the guidance from the World Center were the hallmarks of the weekend's agenda, and the brothers studied the Riḍván 2010 message and the December 28, 2010 message to the Counselors.

BMG Central, January 7–9, 2011, Patrick Patillo, Richard Posey, Mario Meeks, Jamal Billingsley, Nelson Freeman, Al Daniels

Responding to the coordinating group's consultations on pioneering, Billy sent the following letter:

January 9, 2011
[Email from Billy Roberts to the Participants of the Black Men's Gathering]

Participants in the Black Men's Gathering
Dearly loved brothers,

The National Spiritual Assembly is calling for believers who have it in their possibilities to step into the field of International Pioneering for at least 6 months, thereby assisting to fulfill the goal of this Five Year Plan. Our community is now some 250 short of the 1500 pioneers to be sent to posts from the United States to serve in communities across the planet.

I write to you now to ask that you, the men of the Gathering, consider serving in this capacity in some post in the international arena. Many of us are retired and able to support ourselves for a period of time in one of these places. To serve in this way is truly meritorious and worth serious consideration. Please contact the Office of International Pioneering if you are interested in pursuing this service immediately.

I am attaching a listing of goals for your reference.

With deep affection and prayers for your enthusiastic response,

Your brother in service,

Billy

July 7, 2011
[Savannah, Georgia]

Continuing the mentorship of youth in his community, Michael O'Neal planned to drive several young adults to Green Acre for the Young Adult Forum. After he got off work, Michael drove to pick up Kizi Farmer, a youth from Savannah, Georgia. In addition to Kizi, another youth by the name of Dominique Bright was planning on attending but had to cancel at the last minute. Mike reached out to Jamair Wright, another youth who was also friends with Kizi and Dominique, to see if he was interested in making the long, 20-hour drive to Green Acre to attend the Gathering. Mike had been mentoring both Kizi and Jamair for the past few years and had been instrumental in their involvement in the Faith and the BMG. Jamair's recent personal circumstances—specifically, the arrest of a relative—caused him to reflect deeply on the invitation. After some thought, he decided to join Mike and Kizi, and the three of them headed north that Friday. But before they got too far toward their destination, they made a pre-planned stop in Buford, South Carolina to pick up a third youth—Lawrence Maldonado.

Mike had formed deep bonds of friendship with these youth, and he felt a personal connection to each. Years ago, they had engaged in service together. Together with Jamie Abercrombie, they had even rented three vans to travel to the Bahá'í House of Worship in Wilmette. Now today, they were traveling to Green Acre Bahá'í School to participate in the Black Men's Gathering.

Young Adult BMG, July 8–10, 2011

Lawrence would go on to do a period of service at Radio Bahá'í at the Louis Gregory Bahá'í Institute, and he would also be elected chair of his Local Spiritual Assembly. Kizi would continue to teach the Faith, and years later, his mother and grandfather would declare themselves to be Bahá'ís, with his grandfather being elected to the Local Spiritual Assembly. Dominique, who had planned on attending the Young Adult BMG with his fellow youth and Mike, would suffer a fate two years later that would unfortunately cut his earthly life short. He was the first junior youth in 2007 whom the Savannah community invited to register as a Bahá'í. Dominique's mother readily countersigned the card with virtually the same enthusiasm that Dominique had demonstrated when he had been given the invitation.

Soon after, Dominique would engage in the institute process as well as being part of a junior youth group. In fact, his declaration as a Bahá'í lit a frenzy in which other young people wanted to sign their declaration cards as well. In the Savannah area, one hundred twenty souls became Bahá'ís over the next year.

However, in 2013, as he was making plans to attend a Bahá'í youth conference and was inviting others to make the trip to Atlanta, Dominique was shot and killed as an innocent bystander during a crime. The bullet that killed him would likely have hit a young woman had he not been there. In the wake of the Atlanta conference, Michael O'Neal commented that Dominique had been a victim "of the very forces which the youth conferences helped to prepare the young people" to resist.

Over the years, a beautiful sight to see was when family members attended the BMG together. Whether it was a father-son, uncle-nephew or another family relationship, it created a special dynamic at the Gathering.

Father and Son: Jim and Neysan Sturdivant at the Southeast Black Men's Gathering, 2011

Son and Father: Aaron and Dick Yates at the 21ˢᵗ Annual Black Men's Gathering, 2007

Siblings: Andalib and Samandar Khelghati at the 19th Annual Black Men's Gathering, 2005

Siblings: Michael and Ormand O'Neal at the 19th Annual Black Men's Gathering, 2005

Father and Son: Dale and Brandan Mitchell at the 18th Annual Black Men's Gathering, 2004

Siblings: Kevin and Gene Andrews (Photo Courtesy of Kevin Andrews)

Throughout the years, there were various artists who made contributions so regularly that they became interwoven into the fabric of the Gathering. One of those artists, Cam Herth, designed many of the shirts and other items that had become familiar representations of the Gathering.

"Men of Action" T-shirt featured the BMG Gatherings that were happening through the U.S. and world

"Crying Towel." Inspired by Bruce Reynolds.

"BMG Devotional" T-shirt

In addition to these items created in years past, at the 2011 Gathering, Cam created a special gift that really represented one of the major goals of the BMG—service. The wristband pictured below was given to every brother in attendance as a reminder and constant source of encouragement of one of the hallmark features of the Bahá'í Faith and the Gathering. The wristband read "BMG—25 Years of Service."

Wristband given to all participants at the
2011 BMG

This year, the Gathering held at Green Acre Bahá'í School was fortunate to have several participants, including Billy, who lived in Bermuda. Billy and his wife Bette had arisen to serve as pioneers earlier that year. The Bermudians' contributions, both formal and informal, throughout the week were invaluable. In the Gathering's letter to the National Spiritual Assembly of Bermuda, the brothers shared that the believers of African descent in Bermuda had much to offer to the Bahá'í community "and to Bermudian society at large as well as to the world." Speaking of these believers, the Gathering also encouraged "that their capacity be pressed into service for the benefit of a country searching for ways to overcome difficulties both historical and recently emerging in nature."

Jamar Wheeler (the Roberts' son-in-law), Bette and Billy Roberts on the last day of the Gathering, 2011

July 16, 2011
[Email from the Participants of the 25th Annual Black Men's Gathering to the National Spiritual Assembly of the Bahá'ís of Bermuda]

Honored National Spiritual Assembly of the Bahá'ís of Bermuda

We send enthusiastic and loving greetings to you from the 25th Annual Black Men's Gathering held at the Green Acre Bahá'í School. Among the one hundred ten participants primarily from across the United States, this historic occasion was blessed by the presence of four members of the Bermuda Bahá'í community—Mr. Anthony Ball, Mr. Paget Wharton, Mr. Lloyd Williams (now resident in St. Kitts / Nevis), and Dr. William Roberts. How fortunate we were to have them in our midst! Their contributions, both formal and informal, continuously throughout the week were invaluable.

Our program included intensive study of messages of the Universal House of Justice intended to galvanize our understanding of the Five Year Plan. The momentum of the study and deep consultation was complimented by extended and ardent prayer, heartfelt calling out to God in song which makes the Black Men's Gathering so special. The strength and unison of sound and spirit projected by those many voices was truly extraordinary.

These believers of African descent and others like them resident in Bermuda have much to offer to your Bahá'í community, to Bermudian society at large, as well as to the world. Their unique vantage and personal experience in your society positions them well to offer insights and strategies invaluable to others in the African diaspora who seek to be community builders in the world utilizing the Revelation of Bahá'u'lláh. How important that their capacity be pressed into service for the benefit of a country searching for ways to overcome difficulties both historical and recently emerging in nature.

We pray for your success in promoting the Cause of God as you move forward establishing the community-building process called for by the Supreme Body in the beautiful islands called Bermuda.

We send to you our love and respect.

Participants of the 25th Annual Black Men's Gathering

July 16, 2011

The National Assembly of the Bahá'ís of Bermuda responded to the Gathering in the following e-mail:

11th August 2011

To the Participants of the 25th Black Men's Gathering

C/O Dr. William "Billy" Roberts

Beloved Friends,

We received your letter of love and respect with hearts filled to brimming with gratitude. Your encouraging and inspiring letter has [emboldened] us to move forward in our community-building process. It is clear and evident your program this year was truly extraordinary, and certain to leave imprints on the minds and souls of all participants for many years to come.

We are especially heartened because you made special time to communicate to us your most tender, warm, kind thoughts and observations concerning the Spiritual Development of our Island Home and trust we shall not falter in this great obligation.

Though hard to imagine and call to mind, the luminous, and harmonious sounds of those many voices in unison, we are stirred to the depths by the image it invokes to the window of our hearts. We are moved to quote our Beloved Guardian as he issued this plea: "I entreat you, dear friends, to continue, nay, to redouble your efforts, to keep your vision clear, your hopes undimmed, your determination unshaken, so that the power of God within us may fill the world with all its glory."

This is our longing, and dearest wish, both for ourselves and you, the participants of the 25th Annual Black Men's Gathering.

Deepest love, thanks, and gratitude,

The National Spiritual Assembly of the Bahá'ís of Bermuda

On the twenty-fifth anniversary of the Gathering, the BMG wrote a truly memorable letter to the Universal House of Justice and said that it began this year with a session for young adults and with a total of 108 brothers in attendance. Participants studied two Riḍván letters and three letters from the Universal House of Justice to African American believers. The Gathering went on to express its profound gratitude to the Universal House of Justice for its continued years of guidance and support.

July 16, 2011
[Letter from the Black Men's Gathering to the Universal House of Justice]

To Our Universal House of Justice

With joyous and humbled hearts, the 108 participants of the 2011 Black Men's Gathering greet you from the sweet-scented hallowed ground of Green Acre Bahá'í School. From here, where the presence of the Beloved Master is still felt, we are overjoyed to not only share news of our experience but more importantly to express our gratitude for your unwavering guidance. From the days when we met at the Louis Gregory Bahá'í Institute in South Carolina until now, we are inspired by your messages sent to the Bahá'ís of the world generally and to us specifically. These messages took us across the African continent and through the implementation of the current series of Five Year Plans. They have guided our actions and protected us in times of tests.

Over the past 25 years, the Black Men's Gathering has been vital in enabling its participants to respond to your calls, transforming their lives to become more visible in the Bahá'í community, provided tools equipping them to be active agents of the Institute process and able servants of our Faith. Without your warm and loving embrace, we dare say this would not have been possible. We are in awe of your precious and steadfast support.

Again, as in the past, Dr. William Roberts began this twenty-fifth Anniversary Black Men's Gathering with a session for young adult men of African descent. Twenty-five younger brothers came together and met for the weekend consulting about the recent messages guiding the Bahá'í world to gain insights about how they could define a place for their service so important at this time. Extensive discussion—on the idea of community building, reflecting on their relationships in the neighborhoods in which they live and about claiming ownership of these communities in order to play an active part in their development—was rich. Study of the guidance enabled them to gain a greater understanding of the infallibility of the House of Justice and its importance to us in our lives. Twenty of these men remained as participants of the Larger BMG for the rest of the week where they contributed ably to the consultation.

Always we study your Riḍván Letters, this year both the 2010 and 2011 messages. In addition, we deepened intensively on the 28 December message to the conference of Continental Counsellors. Also included in our study were the 1 January 2011 message and the 23 May 2011 message. Five members of the Auxiliary Board who were among us, along with Dr. Roberts, facilitated these study sessions with amazing acuity, offering extraordinary insight and ensuring those special conversations, so much a part of the BMG, were accessible to all.

Building on our understanding of the previous Plan, and in anticipation of the movement to come in the current Plan, our sense of urgency was ignited. An increased understanding of the role we must play and the capacity each has to offer will better prepare us for the opportunities ahead. The exigencies outlined by the Supreme Body in the 28 December letter reveal the urgency for each of us to arise and serve mankind. Your reminder of the statement of 'Abdu'l-Bahá, "ye must in this matter . . . lay down your very lives . . ." resonates within us. The possibility to contribute a share to the evolution of the Cause over the next five years is unlimited but also imperative for the transformation of ourselves, our society, and for all humanity.

We made time to have an in-depth study and consultation on three letters written by your Institution to individual African American believers over a fifteen year period. Those letters dated 1 April 1996; 3 June 2007; and 10 April 2011 provided a stream of guidance for us that could not be shaken. The Plan of God is our answer no matter the question!

Among stories and reminiscences of our twenty-five-year history of service, we paused to hear from Anthony Vance, Director of the Office of External Affairs for the United States National Assembly. His presentation provided valued insight into the painful circumstances of our fellow believers in Iran and the role we, as American Bahá'ís, can play in bringing attention to this situation.

The vibration in our spirits arising from intense prayer and song, ardent study and consultation on your guidance, intense love for the Bahá'í Institutions, for the communities we serve and for one another, uplift our vision and renew our determination. Our pledge is to, with prayerful hearts, take flight as active servants of the Plan and to demonstrate in deeds our devotion to the framework you have outlined.

The magnitude of gratitude the Gathering holds for the Supreme Body can in no way be adequately conveyed in words—your encouragement has been ever so gentle and vigilant inviting us to greater heights in service to our Faith.

Our experience this week at the Black Men's Gathering has been life-altering. May all people feel the power of this love! May it transform minds, hearts, and purpose. May it add beauty to this world! And may this same love cross the sea and earth, finding its way to Haifa, passing through the brilliance of the Holy Shrines, surround you and enter your hearts as you continue your service tirelessly.

Always, always, always your indebted servants,
Participants of the 25th Annual Black Men's Gathering
July 16, 2011

In their response to the letter from the participants of the twenty-fifth annual BMG, the Universal House of Justice reminded the brothers that even though the creation of the BMG was an exception to the principle of racial unity, the Universal House of Justice supported it. In the following letter, written on its behalf, the House of Justice mentioned the progress occurring in several African communities. These African communities were among those visited by members of the BMG during their travels to Africa during earlier plans. The letter explained that now was the time for the brothers to "raise their sights to new horizons" and to follow in the noble path of 'Abdu'l-Bahá.

August 28, 2011
[Letter written on behalf of the Universal House of Justice to the Black Men's Gathering]

Dear Bahá'í Friends,

The letter from the participants of 2011 Black Men's Gathering has been warmly received by the Universal House of Justice. It was pleased to note that a portion of the gathering was devoted to a study of the 28 December 2010 message concerning the new Five Year Plan, as well as the letters dated 1 April 1996, 3 June 2007, and 10 April 2011, which have particular relevance to African American believers.

A quarter century ago, the Black Men's Gathering was established with the aim of soothing hearts that had sustained slow-healing wounds and cultivating capacity for participation in a world-embracing mission. The approach involved drawing together a small number of participants from across the country with a capable facilitator. As you well know, in the Bahá'í Faith, the watchword of which is the oneness of humanity, it is no small exception to make arrangements for an assemblage that excludes others by race and gender.

Yet, acknowledging the uncommon circumstances, the House of Justice lent its support to your endeavor with high hopes and expectations. For these many years, the Gathering has served its members as a bulwark against the forces of racial prejudice afflicting your nation, and, indeed, attacking the Bahá'í community itself, creating an environment in which injuries could be tended, bonds of unity strengthened, sparks of spirituality fanned into flames, and the capacity for assuming the responsibility for the work of the Cause gradually developed through experience in the field of action. The House of Justice hopes that, from the various communications you have studied, you have perceived that the time has now come for the friends who have benefited from the Gathering to raise their sights to new horizons. The impact of the unfoldment of the Divine Plan is making itself felt in all continents of the world. The result is not only demonstrated in the growth in numbers and the invigoration of community life, but also in the stirrings of the society-building power of the Faith, as discussed in the 28 December message. During the last Plan, Africa particularly distinguished itself through its achievements. In the Democratic Republic of the Congo, more than 90 intensive programs of growth emerged. In the single cluster of Tiriki West in Kenya, more than 500 empowered individuals established a pattern of community life that embraced some 5,000 souls. Reports received from junior youth groups made it evident that thousands of young minds and spirits were galvanized and transformed as young people displayed a new attitude toward their communities, their families, and their education, determined to resist and cast aside the burdensome yoke of social ills such as tribalism. And in the establishment of hundreds of community schools across a dozen countries, the friends demonstrated their ability to apply Bahá'u'lláh's teachings to an embryonic educational network that made its mark on the spiritual, social, and material education of children, in many instances surpassing the performance of government schools.

The experience of the last five years and the recent guidance of the House of Justice should make it evident that in the instruments of the Plan you now have within your grasp everything that is necessary to raise up a new people and eliminate racial prejudice as a force within your society, though the path ahead remains long and arduous. The institute process is the primary vehicle by which you can transform and empower your people, indeed all the peoples of your nation. You have the capacity to serve as, and to prepare others to be, educators of children, animators of junior youth, teachers of the Faith, tutors of study circles, participants in elevated discourse, and initiators of social action. Let the well-prepared army you have assembled advance from its secure fortress to conquer the hearts of your fellow citizens. What is needed is concerted, persistent, sacrificial action, cycle after cycle, in cluster after cluster, by an ever-swelling number of consecrated individuals.

In the next year you will observe the centenary of the visit of ʻAbdu'l-Bahá to your shores and will recall His tireless and heroic exertions to quicken the peoples of America—in particular His fearless assault on racial barriers. Follow in His noble path, so that by the end of this new Plan and the one to follow, you will have an abundant harvest of victories to offer in His name by the centenary of His passing in 2021.

Rest assured of the supplications of the House of Justice at the Sacred Threshold that the Almighty will confirm and reinforce your devoted efforts to bring the light of Bahá'u'lláh's Message to an ever-increasing number of receptive souls.

With loving Bahá'í greetings,

Department of the Secretariat

The following letter, written on behalf of the Universal House of Justice to the participants of the Black Men's Gathering is yet another example of a long list of caring, encouraging, and loving messages from the Supreme Institution of the Faith to this faithful army of Black believers. This letter would have a significant impact on the future of the activities of the Black Men's Gathering.

4 December 2011

The participants of the Black Men's Gathering

c/o Dr. William Roberts

Dear Bahá'í Friends,

Recently, consultations were held at the Bahá'í World Centre with a few of the founders and long-standing participants of the Black Men's Gathering to reflect upon its quarter century of achievements and the future prospects for those who have benefited from the Gathering over the years. The Universal House of Justice was pleased to observe the distance that has been traversed since the first gathering in 1987, and to note the far reaching ramifications of the interactions of so many men who have fanned the flames of their devotion to Bahá'u'lláh and arisen to teach His Cause on the home front and in other lands. The sentiments expressed in your letter of 16 July 2011 from the most recent Gathering reflect the depth of understanding that animates your effort: "The Plan of God is our answer no matter the question." And, again:

> The vibration in our spirits arising from intense prayer and song, ardent study and consultation on your guidance, intense love for the Bahá'í Institutions, for the communities we serve and for one another, uplift our vision and renew our determination. Our pledge is to, with prayerful hearts, take flight as active servants of the Plan and to demonstrate in deeds our devotion to the framework you have outlined.

In assessing the range of your achievements, the House of Justice has concluded that the activities of the Black Men's Gathering, which were conceived as an initiative of limited duration, should now be brought to a close. This does not mean, of course, that all the challenges which brought about the initiation of the gathering are overcome or the concerns it addressed are completely allayed. It is, however, a recognition that new possibilities and new spaces for thought and action have been created in the Bahá'í community in the United States by the Divine Plan in these intervening years, and that your hopes and aspirations are best met in the future through possibilities discussed in the letter to you dated 28 August 2011, written on behalf of the House of Justice.

As you are aware, in early 2012, a series of regional Black Men's Gatherings will be held, and the House of Justice encourages your participation. There, together with Dr. William Roberts and others that have accompanied you in your journey over so many years, you can celebrate your achievements, reflect on the tasks ahead, and increase further your consecration to a Plan that opens the way to the fulfilment of the heartfelt longings of all peoples.

You are assured of the ardent prayers of the House of Justice in the Holy Shrines that you may be ever surrounded by the tender mercies and strengthening grace of the Blessed Beauty.

With loving Bahá'í greetings,

Department of the Secretariat

cc: National Assembly of the United States

The news of the Black Men's Gathering being brought to a close was, for many, unexpected. The Gathering was still a powerful force for the brothers, as well as for their friends and family all over the United States and the world. It was a source of love and fellowship where men of African descent were inspired by other men who had had similar life circumstances to which they could all relate. It was still a place where men could come to unburden themselves, to cry, and to share meaningful and inspirational exchanges with their fellow brothers. It was also a place to draw learnings and share experiences from fellow Bahá'ís involved in the plans given to the world from the Universal House of Justice.

The news of the Gathering's closing was for many not only unexpected but difficult to process. The Gathering had become for so many participants not only a safe space but perhaps their only perceived safe space. For some, the closure of the Black Men's Gathering brought on concerns and feelings of anxiety. For as the Universal House of Justice pointed out, "This does not mean, of course, that all the challenges which brought about the initiation of the gathering are overcome or the concerns it addressed are completely allayed." Now, the brothers had been called to recognize that "new possibilities and new spaces for thought and action [had] been created in the Bahá'í community" and that opportunities that had not existed in the past could now become a new platform for action. Any participant of the Gathering—as well as friends and families of the participants—could attest to the truth of these statements from the House of Justice. The participants of the Black Men's Gathering had exhibited great dedication to connecting the hearts of the brothers to their Creator through prayer and personal reflection as well as through studying, consulting, and acting in accordance with the plans and messages from the Supreme Institution, and the brothers were ready to obey the House of Justice without hesitation.

Still, the very thought of losing this space certainly brought on a range of mixed emotions for the brothers. To consult and reflect upon the December 4, 2011 message, the Coordinating Group came together in Northern Virginia—just outside of Washington, D.C., in late December—for what would be its last meeting.

After receiving the December 4, 2011 letter written on behalf of the Universal House of Justice, Billy prepared to study the letter with brothers in a series of Regional Gatherings encouraged by the Universal House of Justice. The focus of these Gatherings was to

BMG Coordinating Group Meeting at the Northern Virginia Bahá'í Center, December 23, 2011

"celebrate [the] achievements, reflect on the tasks ahead and increase further consecration to 'the Plan . . .'"

December 23, 2011
[Letter from the Billy Roberts to Participants in the Black Men's Gathering]

December 23, 2011

Men of the Gathering

Dearest Brothers,

This special letter is sent urgently, to share with you recent guidance received from the Universal House of Justice dated 4 December 2011, addressed to the participants of the Black Men's Gathering and entitled "Further to the letter dated 28 August 2011." The August letter was shared with you during the late summer in response to our letter dated 16 July 2011 to the House of Justice from the 25th Annual BMG at Green Acre.

In its December 4 letter, "the House of Justice encourages your participation" in the series of regional Gatherings where we will "celebrate our achievements, reflect on the tasks ahead and increase further consecration to (the) Plan) . . ." Together during this intimate exchange we will discuss prospects to raise our sights to new horizons and how to apply twenty-five years of experience from the Gathering into the future.

Since time is moving quickly it is important to alert you and to ensure you have the invitation to the schedule of upcoming Black Men's Gathering Regional Meetings. A list of these Gatherings is provided below so that you can arrange your time to attend one or more of them. You will note that the first of these Gatherings will be held in the Central States at the Louhelen Bahá'í School in Michigan in mid-January followed by the Gathering in the Northeastern States to be held in Danbury Bethel / Connecticut soon thereafter. Please look for the specific registration material for each of the 5 sessions emailed to you in the next week; however, you may wish to make travel plans immediately.

Please begin now to make your arrangements to attend.

I bring greetings and love to you from the vicinity of Washington, D.C. where the BMG Coordinating Group is concluding its two-day meeting, and together we look forward to greeting you in the next few weeks face-to-face.

With unbounded affection and admiration for each one of you,

Your brother,

Billy

The dates for the Regional Gatherings are:

Jan 13–15 Central States at Louhelen Bahá'í School
Jan 27–29 Northeastern States in Bethel / Danbury, CT

Feb 3–5 Southeastern States in Myrtle Beach, SC
Feb 17–19 Western States at Bosch Bahá'í School
Feb 24–26 Southwestern States in Dallas, TX

As the participants of the Gathering made plans to attend a regional Gathering, their ever-supporting National Spiritual Assembly addressed those that gathered. The NSA's words to the Gathering were, as always, filled with love, support, and encouragement.

2012

[Letter from the U.S. National Spiritual Assembly to the Black Men's Gathering]

January 13, 2012

To the participants in the regional Black Men's Gatherings

Dearly loved Friends,

As you convene your meetings in five distinct locales across the country, we greet you with immense pleasure. Many of you have traveled long distances to take part in these Gatherings, and we commend the faithful and purposeful spirit that has motivated you to undertake such journeys. We are confident, in each weekend's case, the proceedings will make your journey more than worthwhile.

From their "modest beginnings" in 1987, as the Supreme Institution of the Bahá'í world has observed, the Black Men's Gatherings, over the course of a quarter-century, developed into "a vibrant and spirited enterprise," fostering "a sense of fellowship" among African American men, helping them to deal effectively with the range of obstacles confronting them, rekindling their "faith and commitment to Bahá'u'lláh" and encouraging them to "find an effective part to play within the recent series of [Five Year] Plans."

Reflecting on the series of Gatherings that have been, for so many years, one of the brightest features of our national community's life, a floodtide of vivid memories is released: of impassioned voices upraised in fervent prayer and soul-stirring song; of eloquent speeches; of spontaneous and moving testimonies to the power of the King of Glory's word to inspire believers to surmount walls of discrimination; of unforgettable efforts to further disseminate the unifying Bahá'í teachings on the continent of Africa and in many places around the world where the dispersed peoples of African origin reside.

For all these reasons, the Gatherings have already found a permanent and shining place in the annals of the Faith's worldwide growth and development, adding luster to the golden legacy left behind by a legion of distinguished African American Bahá'ís for whose contributions we are all deeply indebted. Indeed, words cannot express the pride in your achievements we feel, nor can they adequately testify to the admiration that fills our hearts when we think of those who have labored so devotedly over the years to make these Gatherings possible.

As you wind down this phase of your activities, we eagerly look forward to your future efforts to make—within the current framework for action and in consonance with the House of Justice's hopes—"an unprecedented and systematic approach to reaching the African American population in the United States," including efforts in clusters especially designated for this purpose. As you take the necessary steps to realize this aspiration, be confident our warm and abiding affection and ardent prayers for great success will surround and support you.

With deepest love and gratitude,

Kenneth E. Bowers

Secretary

National Spiritual Assembly of the Bahá'ís of the US

Over the next two months, the announced five regional BMGs would be held across the United States. The Gatherings were bittersweet. There was, of course, the realization that something the men of the Gathering had grown to experience was coming to a close. But at the same time, there was the eagerness to advance from their secure fortress of the Gathering and continue to redouble their efforts to serve the Cause of Bahá'u'lláh. Each regional Gathering penned a final message to the Universal House of Justice, a body that over the past quarter of a century had provided guidance, love, and support.

[Letter from the Central States Gathering to the Universal House of Justice]

Bahá'í Black Men's Gathering

To our Beloved Universal House of Justice,

We send our humble greetings from the Central Region's Black Men's Gathering (BMG), the first in a series of regional celebrations to reflect, commemorate the achievements, and conclude the activities of the Black Men's Gathering. Fifty-two participants, including three Auxiliary Board members, and three of the original members of the 1987 gathering are assembled this weekend at Louhelen Bahá'í School.

We began our session in song and prayer before consulting on your letters dated 28 August, 4 December, and 12 December 2011. In particular, our focus was concentrated on "advancing from" our "secure fortress to conquer the hearts of" our "fellow citizens." As the Reverend Martin Luther King Jr. reminds us, "An individual has not started living until he can rise above the narrow confines of his individualistic concerns to the broader concerns of all humanity." Echoing this sentiment, the BMG has always encouraged us to be servants in the Faith, transcending complications, to serve our greater community. Through the Gathering, participants have been motivated to engage in the Institute Process and have remained steadfast to the Universal House of Justice and its Divine Plan.

Surrounded by your continuing love and support of this wonderful gathering, countless lives have been transformed and infused with the Spirit of Bahá over the years. As envisioned by Dr. William Roberts twenty-five years ago and championed by each brother since; song, prayer, and consultation became the foundation for the gathering. With the success of the BMG, participants became loyal stewards, and obedient servants of the Cause of God. Each man's nobility developed and emerged! Achievements were plentiful with none being more evident than the sincere fellowship among each member. Many brothers expressed their gratitude for this environment, one in which fathers strengthened relationships with their sons, strangers became life-long friends and love for the Cause of God blossomed.

Looking forward, we are elated to hear of five learning sites focused on the movement of the African American population toward Bahá'u'lláh to be developed in the United States. These clusters have a divine aim in educating Americans of African descent, especially children and junior youth through the Institute Process.

Though we will miss the BMG experience, we are excited to continue on our soul-stirring mission to further serve the Cause of the Blessed Perfection. As we reflect on the centenary of 'Abdu'l-Bahá's visit to America we hope to follow "His noble path . . . to quicken the peoples of America."

As one member stated, "We have matured and are ready for this next step" but humbly ask for your continued prayers for our success.

With sincere gratitude,

The Brothers of the Central Region's Black Men's Gathering

15 January 2012

[Letter from the Northeast Regional Gathering to the Universal House of Justice]

29 January, 2012

Dearly Beloved Universal House of Justice,

It is with great humility, joy and consecration that we write to you with greetings from the Northeast Region's Black Men's Gathering (BMG). Some thirty-nine of us have come together to celebrate the record of the BMG, to consider the tasks that await us, and to steel ourselves for future endeavors. In these consultations and in our devotions we have been joined by a member of the Auxiliary Board, by former Counselor Eugene Andrews, by Dr. Richard Thomas and by our cherished facilitator, Dr. William Roberts (the latter three—participants in the first BMG in 1987).

Following the pattern which has developed over a twenty-five-year history, we opened proceedings with prayer and song offered in that ardent, soulful style that is a recognized hallmark of the BMG, and one of its significant gifts to the Bahá'í World. These devotions led us into focused study of recent guidance received from the Supreme Body. Your letters of 28 August, 4 December, and 12 December 2011, informed a consultative conversation that carried us back to the first BMG of 1987, on through years of American and international victories won by the Gathering, and into an urgent appraisal of the needs of the current plan and the Institute Process.

In addition to this, we spent significant time considering the letter sent to you by the participants of the 2011 BMG. That communication presented a very solemn vow, a commitment of single-minded devotion to the Plan of God. We linked this promise of ours to your instruction that the "well prepared army" of the BMG "advance from its secure fortress to conquer the hearts of . . . fellow citizens." This instruction, both daunting and liberating, helped us to understand the seriousness of our own pledge and its relation to the raised level of expectation that you have for us.

Our vision is now trained upon "new horizons." We are prepared to make use of all that we have learned while nurtured in the stronghold of the BMG. Among our first steps will be to support the establishment of five learning sites throughout the country. We anticipate that the knowledge gained from these sites will quicken our efforts to bring greater and greater numbers of African Americans closer to Bahá'u'lláh, and that it will sharpen our focus on the needs of our clusters and neighborhoods, and on the spiritual empowerment of all children, junior youth, youth and adults.

As the final cycle of regional BMGs draws to a close in the coming weeks, we recognize the end of a precious era. However, as one among us remarked, Bahá'u'lláh has counseled His followers to see "beginning and end" as one in the same, indeed to "witness neither first nor last." So, as we send you this final message as members of the Black Men's Gathering, we ask only for your continued guidance and prayers, and again promise to you undying effort in this great, endless plan of God.

With all love and gratitude,

The Brothers of the Northeast Region's Black Men's Gathering

Northeastern States Regional Gathering, Danbury, Connecticut,
January 27–29, 2012

[Letter from the Southeast Regional Gathering to the Universal House of Justice]

Bahá'í Black Men's Gathering

Dearly Beloved Universal House of Justice,

We humbly send our greetings from Myrtle Beach, South Carolina, where the fifty-five participants of the 2012 third regional Black Men's Gathering have assembled.

With our hearts turned to the Blessed Beauty in thanksgiving, we began our session with fervent song and prayer.

To understand the directives to the Bahá'í world concerning the evolution of training institutes, we consulted on your 12 December 2011 message to National Spiritual Assemblies. Within the framework of your renewing guidance, we are committed to the training institute process, ready to strive for the resulting victories. The worldwide "sacred charge" to engage young people in their teens into the service of the Cause was taken to heart.

After consulting on the 28 August 2011 and 4 December 2011 messages to the participants of the Black Men's Gathering, our initial apprehensions were washed away by reflecting on the scope and magnitude of our achievements and acknowledging our readiness as a "well-prepared army" for the challenges that lie ahead in attracting our own people as well as all people to this Faith. We are humbled to recognize that the seeds of our labor have born fruits that have cast an indelible mark on global community life. Grateful to the Supreme Institution for allowing us to engage in a 25-year healing process, through which the power of the Revelation of Bahá'u'lláh and the love the House has showered on us over these years, we have evolved to a stage of consecration that will yield the "abundant harvest of victories" you have destined for us. The Brothers are excited by both the challenges ahead and opportunities associated with the three learning sites for African American outreach contained within our region.

As we look to the future, our dedication to the current and future Plans is unswerving even as we begin to "advance" from what has been our "secure fortress." We offer our sincere gratitude for your supplications to the Almighty on our behalf.

In His Service,

The Brothers of the South East Regional Black Men's Gathering

February 5, 2012

Southeastern States Regional Gathering, Myrtle Beach, South Carolina, February 3–5, 2012

[Letter from the Western States Regional Gathering to the Universal House of Justice]

Bahá'í Black Men's Gathering

February 19, 2012

To Our Supreme and Dearly Loved Universal House of Justice:

We the Black Men's Gathering (BMG) Western United States humbly extend greetings and love to you from the Bosch Bahá'í School.

Some 30 men of African descent from the western states of Washington, Oregon, California and other Brothers from around the country have again gathered to further our consecration to the Five Year Plan, and your specific guidance. It is with joy, faith, radiant acquiescence, and reliance in your unfailing guidance that we now focus on your central theme of transition into "new possibilities and new spaces for thought and action in the Bahá'í community in the United States."

Among those present in our session this weekend was an Auxiliary Board member for the Northern California coastal region and Regional Council members for both the Northwest and Southwest Regions. After our elevated initial prayer, chanting and singing we turned our full attention to your numerous messages. The weekend's focus was on your letter dated 12 December 2011 and how we, men of African descent, can increase our participation in the Five Year Plan. Part of the consultation was around reaching those African American souls "who are willing to engage in conversation about the world around them and participate in a collective effort to transform it."

We also reviewed the letter to you from the National BMG dated July 16, 2011, and your response dated 28 August 2011. During this consultation profound realization and gratitude of your 25 years of guidance was felt. Tears of humility flowed as we read and appreciated your love as you acknowledged the collective work of the BMG toward achieving the goals of the successive plans.

Dr. Billy Roberts and Dr. Harvey McMurray shared highlights of their meeting with representatives of the House of Justice in October, 2011. They recalled the significant memories of their journey as part of the BMG delegation accompanied by Counsellor Anita Williams. They told of love, hospitality and kindness extended by members of the House of Justice and their spouses. The Brothers were spellbound by the significance and specifics of the experience.

Finally, we studied your letter dated 4 December 2011 to the participants of the Black Men's Gathering. We recommitted to our 16 July 2011 message to you: "Our pledge is to, with prayerful hearts, take flight as active servants of the Plan and to demonstrate in deeds our devotion to the framework you have outlined." Of significance, we consulted on our relationship with the very young, particularly teenagers. We recognized this as being one opportunity area for further commitment and engagement.

With enhanced confidence and volition to act, we are prepared to advance from our secure fortress and conquer the hearts of our fellow citizens.

Our committed, enraptured hearts and comforted souls turn to the Blessed Beauty in gratitude, humility and thankfulness for his unfailing guidance expressed through our Universal House of Justice.

Participants for the 2012 Black Men's Gathering
Bosch Bahá'í School

[Letter from the Southwest States Regional Gathering to the Universal House of Justice]

February 26, 2012

Dearly Beloved Universal House of Justice,

It is with great joy, exhilaration and yet some sadness, that we, the 33 brothers greet you at the conclusion of the Southwest Regional Black Men's Gathering held in Dallas, Texas. Our joy and exhilaration emanate from the love and trust customarily generated from our bonding experience while immersed in the words of Bahá'u'lláh. Our sadness is rooted in the knowledge that this is not only the final Southwest BMG but the grand finale of the 25 years of this noble endeavor. We were blessed with the presence of Dr. William Roberts as well as Auxiliary Board member Oliver Thomas and James Williams, one of the original participants of the Gathering.

Our meeting began with joyous fellowship on Friday night where brothers re-kindled old friendships and established new ones. On Saturday we tearfully began communing with the Almighty, calling ourselves to prayer with the sound of drums, in the distinct style unique to the Black Men's Gathering.

Focused study of your letters dated 28 August 2011, 4 December 2011 and 12 December 2011 opened the way to new realizations. It became apparent in the midst of consultation, that the new paths of service available to the brothers are filled with great potential. Change for our people will occur through participation in the Institute process if only we recognize the new possibilities and spaces for thought and action you encourage us to pursue.

With great appreciation we listened to Dr. William Roberts and Dr. Harvey McMurray share moving recollections of the meeting with members of the Universal House of Justice in October 2011. The spirit of that meeting energized the hearts of everyone.

As the Gathering draws to a close, we pray that the Blessed Beauty accepts our service in His Name. We are forever grateful for the love and support of the Universal House of Justice.

With resolute hearts we are fully committed to further consecrate ourselves to the goals of the Plan.

With loving Bahá'í Greetings,

The Brothers of the Southwest Regional Black Men's Gathering

Southwestern States Regional Gathering, Dallas, Texas, February 24–26, 2012

After the five regional Gatherings held in 2012, the following message marked the final message written to the Black Men's Gathering from the Universal House of Justice. The contents of the message are, of course, touching and very poignant. For twenty-five years the BMG, which had blossomed out of an individual initiative, had exchanged affectionate and encouraging communications with the Universal House of Justice. And while that exchange was now coming to a close, reading the words from that beloved institution where it "recall[ed] with satisfaction the twenty-five years of [the Gathering's] endeavors in the path of service," any participant of the Gathering couldn't help but feel their spirits buoyed with such tender and supportive words.

15 April 2012
Transmitted by email
Participants of the Regional Black Men's Gatherings
c/o Dr. William Roberts
U.S.A.
Dear Bahá'í Friends,

We have received with deep appreciation five heartfelt messages from the participants attending the final series of regional Black Men's Gatherings across the United States. Each was a letter of love and affection sprung from the reservoirs of the spirit, pouring forth sentiments of devotion and dedication to the Cause of Bahá'u'lláh. Each reflected your determination to arise as champions of the Divine Plan. We recall with satisfaction the twenty-five years of your endeavors in the path of service, highlighted by innumerable devotions of distinctive style, growing courage in the teaching field, and determination to reach out to others in service to humanity. And we look to the promise of your future exertions with high expectations as each of you weaves his efforts into the fabric of community building in all corners of your nation.

A special word of appreciation is also offered for the dedicated individuals who created this initiative and, over the years, helped to kindle your flame and guide your footsteps. They were ever responsive and unswerving in adherence to the guidance of the institutions of the Faith.

You may be assured that you set forth upon your continuing services with our loving prayers in the Holy Shrines that you may be constantly surrounded by the tender mercies of the Blessed Beauty and strengthened by His sustaining grace.

With loving Bahá'í greetings,

The Universal House of Justice

cc: National Assembly of the United States

While the Universal House of Justice penned its last communication to the Gathering, a special communication was sent to Billy. This letter from the Universal House of Justice to Billy represented an intense and fitting tribute to one of most devoted servants of the Faith.

15 April 2012

Dr. William Roberts

U.S.A.

Dear Bahá'í Friend,

Further to the letter of today's date addressed to the participants of the Regional Black Men's Gatherings, we have been asked to convey the following.

Twenty-five years ago, you perceived a need among African American Bahá'í men for spiritual refreshment and empowerment and determined to take action to assuage their troubled hearts. The seeds that were planted in the ensuing small gathering at the Louis Gregory Institute have been lovingly nurtured by you, with the assistance of others, ever since. With wisdom, patience and sensitivity, and always carrying the guidance of the institutions of the Faith in your mind, you have supported the Black Men's Gathering as it grew in size and complexity, capably overseeing such developments as the creation of regional Gatherings within the United States. When certain of these initiatives needed to be redirected, you always responded with alacrity and consummate judgment. Perhaps your most challenging assignment has been bringing the organization which you have created, guided and inspired to a conclusion without any decline in spirit, even as you sent forth its participants to ever greater involvement in the activities of the current Plan. In all of these efforts, you have earned the satisfaction, admiration and abiding love of the Universal House of Justice for the manner in which you carried out your responsibilities. It will offer prayers in the Holy Shrines on your behalf that the Ancient Beauty may ever surround you with His manifold blessings and unfailing protection.

With loving Bahá'í greetings,

Department of the Secretariat

cc: National Assembly of the United States

Similar to the Universal House of Justice, the National Spiritual Assembly of the Bahá'ís of the U.S. had been a constant and loving supporter of the work of the BMG throughout its quarter-century history. The following is a moving and touching report from the National Spiritual Assembly of the Bahá'ís of the United States of the wonderful tributes to the BMG from the floor of the 104th Bahá'í National Convention.

June 18, 2012

To the American Bahá'í community

Dearly loved Friends,

Of the many comments and observations offered from the floor of this year's 104th Bahá'í National Convention, some of the most moving were the spontaneous and manifestly heartfelt tributes delegates paid to the power of the Black Men's Gatherings (BMG)—to the fresh insights, deeper understandings, strengthened bonds of unity, and greatly renewed consecration to the Cause of God that were the rewards of the friends' participation in them, fostering a legacy that will long endure.

These deserved accolades were framed by the delegates' awareness that, in guidance received from the Universal House of Justice in December of last year, both the National Spiritual Assembly and certain of the friends who over time have been most closely identified with their planning and execution were asked to bring the Gatherings to a close and to assist their regular participants in making the transition to a new phase in their activities.

You are no doubt familiar with the origins of the Gatherings and the highly commendable record of achievements they have compiled over the course of nearly a quarter century of existence. Designed to address the special needs of African American men, a distinct social group still recovering from the grievous and slow-healing wounds of several hundred years of oppression, discrimination, and injustice, the Gatherings, from their modest beginnings in 1987, soon gained impressive momentum. Year after year, they have continued to attract large numbers of believers from the far corners of the nation to attend the annual conclaves and to support activities, some of which have involved travels to Africa and to the Caribbean to bring the unifying teachings of Bahá'u'lláh to people of color—a mission the beloved Guardian, Shoghi Effendi, especially encouraged African American Bahá'ís to undertake.

At every stage in their evolution, the Gatherings have enjoyed the warm encouragement of this Assembly and have been recipients of the loving guidance of the Faith's Supreme Institution. In its December 4 letter to us, the House of Justice referred with pride to "the distinguished history" of the

Gatherings and characterized them as "a vibrant and spirited enterprise, which has assisted contingents of African American men to deal with certain obstacles confronting them, to foster a sense of fellowship and kindle their faith and commitment to Bahá'u'lláh, and to encourage them to find an effective part to play within the recent series of Plans."

Reminding us that at various times in the Faith's continuing unfoldment its Head has found it necessary to introduce "temporary measures to address particular challenges" and that these were "not expected to be permanent elements of the Faith," the House of Justice expresses its view "that it is now timely to bring the Black Men's Gathering to a close." In calling on the Gatherings' leadership to effect it—in a letter addressed to them, likewise, on December 4—the Supreme Institution notes that this change should lead none to assume that "the challenges which brought about the initiation of the [G]athering are overcome or the concerns it addressed are completely allayed." On the contrary, the House of Justice expresses its trust that the Gatherings' participants will now, as a logical outgrowth of the BMG experience, transfer—with a greater sense of purpose and with enriched understanding—their enthusiasm and energy to the work of the Five Year Plan taking place at the cluster level, counseling them that "your hopes and aspirations are best met in future" through efforts in that arena of service.

In concluding its guidance to the National Spiritual Assembly on the matter, the Supreme Body expresses its fond hope that the direction it is encouraging the Gatherings' participants to take will enable them to seek and discover new portals for "an unprecedented and systematic approach to reaching the African American population in the United States." Placing its hope in the context of this year's centennial of 'Abdu'l-Bahá's sojourn in North America, the House of Justice further elaborates:

> How fitting if an effort to embrace this [African American] population, which received the bounty of the Master's loving attention, could be significantly advanced within the context of the Plan during the centennial of His visit to America.

Dear friends, nothing would gladden our hearts more than to see you joyously come to the aid of your beloved African American brothers in such an endeavor—showing your complete and wholehearted support by working side-by-side with them as you together cultivate, as never before, this vitally important territory; praying for and celebrating with them every harvest you can together proudly bring in, fulfilling the high expectations of the Universal House of Justice for our incomparably blessed community. You may be confident our best wishes and ardent prayers for your great success will accompany your every step.

With loving Bahá'í greetings,

Kenneth E. Bowers

Secretary

From 1987 to the present, Billy had dedicated countless hours to the development of the Black Men's Gathering, and he had done so while simultaneously and devotedly serving the Bahá'í Faith, including in positions as an Auxiliary Board member, a member of the Continental Board of Counselors, and as a member of the National

Spiritual Assembly of the United States. Billy had taken on the weight of nurturing and lifting up the spirits of hundreds of African American Bahá'í men during a time when Black men in the United States were and still are being broken in spirit and body. He had also been motivated by the sad truth that some of these same broken bodies and spirits could be found within the Bahá'í community. He noticed their thinning ranks in the Faith he so dearly loved. If others noticed this reality, few knew how to bring them back into the warm embrace of the Faith and what it had to offer. Perhaps the Bahá'í community had not been "warm" enough to heal the spirits of these marginalized Black men or offer them protection from the everyday struggles they faced. So Billy took up this weighty challenge.

Looking back to 1987 and the twelve Black men who met in a motel room in Greensboro, where Billy first planted the seeds of the BMG, few among them realized that it would be a twenty-five-year journey of spiritual transformation. Even fewer realized how much love and understanding would be required to support it as it grew in size. Men with broken spirits needed safe spaces to vent their pain and anguish without judgement. And with Billy's gentle guidance and loving direction, the process of healing and transformation was possible.

Bringing the BMG to a close, and at the same time encouraging its participants to engage in even greater involvement in the series of plans of the Universal House of Justice, was yet another spiritual challenge for Billy. As expected, he faced it with the same resolve and firm commitment that had inspired him to create and support the BMG for a quarter century.

REFLECTIONS ON A JOURNEY OF SPIRITUAL TRANSFORMATION

The following are the reflections of participants of the Black Men's Gathering and their friends and relatives in the larger Bahá'í community who witnessed and shared the participants' journey of spiritual transformation. In the process of providing a safe and nurturing space for African American Bahá'í men to heal spiritual and emotional wounds, the BMG enabled many others to witness, understand, and even participate in BMG-inspired devotionals and related experiences. For twenty-five years, people of all backgrounds and ages played key roles in hosting and contributing to the BMG. Such sacrificial service will be remembered as a powerful example of Bahá'í multiracial community building.

The story of the Bahá'í Black Men's Gathering has always been about the journey of personal transformation. At the beginning of this collective spiritual journey, the participants did not know the extent to which it would transform the spiritual lives of individual members or what specific aspect or combination of aspects individual participants would consider to be the most transformative. Along the way, the evolving and culturally unique expressions of BMG service—the devotions, the fellowship, the focused study of the guidance from the Universal House of Justice, and the travel-teaching trips to Africa and other places around the world—exerted their influences on the personal lives of BMG members. After the close of the Black Men's Gathering, participants responded to the following question.

Question: "Personal transformation was at the heart of the Bahá'í Black Men's Gathering. Thinking about your experience in the Gathering, what specific aspect(s) would you consider most transformative?"

My first BMG at the Louis Gregory Institute was the beginning of my transformation. I continue to be transformed as I continue to serve and [be obedient to the institutions]. That first meeting I cried uncontrollably like a baby, and when I stopped crying I felt like all the weight of the world had been lifted from my shoulders. I felt that God was cradling me in his arms like a father does his child, and the child knows all is well and safe. I was no longer a Black man with low self-esteem but a man who happens to be Black and ready to accept his role and responsibility in [the] Bahá'í world and society at large. I could no longer be treated by anyone any other way. My family, friends, and Bahá'í community recognized my transformation without any awareness or effort on my part. So, since that time, I continue to serve and received the blessings that accompany service. I made my vows to the Lord, and I never will turn back. I will go and see what the end will be.

* * *

For me the heart of the BMG was service through personal transformation. Transformative aspects of the BMG were: 1) It was the only venue—including my local, regional or national Bahá'í community, seasonal schools, firesides, deepening, etc.—where I could share my condition of internalized racism and listen to the experience of the brothers! Sharing and listening help[ed] me to dislodge—without being judged—emotional issues among a crew who UNDERSTOOD. 2) Study of the writings, intense prayers recited or read from the heart with meaning (not just saying or reading them) or being seen or thought of as engaged[ed] in a performance. 3) Freedom to share one's own perspectives of [the writings] under consideration without being judged or "misunderstood." 4) Constant and regular encouragement from "elder" brothers to younger ones as well as age peers by sharing one's own experiences (foibles, etc.). This gave credibility to younger brothers and affirmed that they too could, and would, if focused on the Cause, move forward on their spiritual journey. 5) The music and songs affirmed [the] BMG's connection with Africa as well as our own cultural connections, e.g., coming from the North, South, Midwest, and West Coast—even Alaska, Central, and South America! 6) Various service projects also contributed to my sense of personal transformation. After one BMG session. . . . (My son) and I made a commitment to design a workshop on "What Men Can Do to Promote the Equality of Women and Men." With the help of my wife . . . we did design the workshop and held two sessions. Attendees were mostly women and a few men from the community at large. The average group size was eighteen members, of whom five were Bahá'ís—four women and one man. . . . The number of brothers the BMG experience reclaimed from anonymity insofar as their connection to Bahá'í community is concerned, was fantastic!

* * *

I found that the heartfelt devotions were transformative as well as the study sessions. There was something soul-stirring about so many African American men united in faith, spirit, and love that transported one to realms on high. The study sessions I found to be genuine, lacking in intellectualism (a positive thing), and always focused on action, rather than abstract principle[s]. My only regret is coming to know the Gathering in only its final years.

* * *

The most transforming aspect for me was learning to really believe in the power of prayer. Prior to then I always prayed, but I don't think I really believed prayer worked. My experience with the Gathering showed me just how powerful and effective prayers are. I've learned a lot over the years, but had it not been for the Gathering, I'd still be praying because that['s] what I was supposed to do, not because I believed prayer worked.

* * *

I learned to use prayer as refuge. Before the Gathering, I considered prayer a duty, but not as a way of dealing with problems or stress. The group prayer sessions with music and drumming were especially powerful. The drumming required a high level of group unity, and acting in unison with others immersed everyone in the same spiritual mind-set. The drumming and prayer sessions were very spiritually invigorating, and I had not experienced anything similar in any other situation, Bahá'í or non-Bahá'í.

* * *

1) Reading and deepening on the letters from the Universal House of Justice. 2) Participating in reading/singing prayers for what seemed like hours. 3) Socializing with brothers from all walks of life and experiences. 4) The "Pile On." What an intense moment of love and support of and for others. 5) Motivation and encouragement from the Gathering to return home and commit to some level of service. 6) Finally, but not least, the drumming. Oh yeah!

* * *

Transformation for me. Among these were the intensity of the act of worship, (praying, chanting and singing of the sacred verses) the level of love and fellowship generated when in the company of the spiritual brothers, the learning to accept oneself and other Black men as noble creations, the depth of the study of the holy writings and particularly the annual guidance from the Universal House of Justice in its annual Riḍván messages. Later, as the Gathering evolved, African drumming became an integral part of the weeklong fellowship and added a new sense of joy and reconnection with my ancestral roots, as most brothers would dress in exquisite African attire with increasing visits to Africa from 1997–2000. The expression of transformation from attending the Gathering was manifested in increasing levels of service and commitment to the Faith, and the 1996 Riḍván message motivated my wife and me to consider pioneering to Africa as was encouraged for people of African descent living in the USA. In the end, we were called to service at the Bahá'í World Center in Haifa, Israel and we were able to make two travel-teaching trips to Africa while serving at the World Center for five years. The BMG helped galvanize the spirit of service and obedience to the institutions in my heart.

* * *

Opportunities to serve the Faith both nationally and internationally that arose out of the Black Men's Gathering were, I swear, the most precious gifts that I have ever received in my whole life. Not only was this experience transformative, it engendered in me a "spiritual re-awakening." Personal transformation? Yes, indeed! Thanks to the Gathering, I really believe that I have become much more of a spiritually attuned creature and more understanding of the power of prayer than I was before. And what specifically caused this to happen? The manner and supreme reverence in which the Gathering held its devotions, and its importance was noticeably evident by the large amount of time and attention devoted to prayer each session, as well as the enthusiasm, joy, and fervor expressed by the brothers throughout the whole time the Gathering was held. Prayers were not just verbalized. Not at all. They were offered up with reverence, feeling, and commitment. I always felt energized both spiritually and physically! I remember so well a prayer being offered up by an elderly brother during my first Gathering. It was "the Long Healing Prayer." I have never been so moved by a recitation of that special prayer as I was by him. He wept the entire time. Every word spoken was presented with tremendous passion and feeling. I was swept up in the emotion of it all, and, as I hung on his every word, I was there with him! It is indelibly imprinted in my mind. I would be remiss if I didn't also mention how valuable to me was the considerable amount of time each Gathering devoted to studying in depth the correspondence from the Universal House of Justice and the National Spiritual Assembly —most notably the various plans. It was not just to read and discuss these documents. No! Our job was to understand, consult, reflect, and make a commitment—and when we departed, to act! Oh boy, what a learning experience in what I call the "BMG Spiritual laboratory!" This procedure is how I now personally address correspondence from the Supreme Body and the National Spiritual Assembly. The Gathering was such a great teacher! I still remain under its influence.

* * *

At the Black Men's Gathering, I was personally transformed through the *baptism of collective prayers.* The longing and tears could flow so easily, as I beseeched the Continuous Cause of God to strengthen me, so I might be worthy to serve. In such a virgin state, I was surrounded by a host of seasoned Baháʼí brothers of varying levels and from all walks of life, who accompanied my fledging prayers in a oneness that was indeed a palpable sacristy. Unity, being in love with the Almighty and with each other was the norm, and I had seldom experienced anything like it. I would have to add that the ethos of transformation was undoubtedly the *deepenings.* The teachings are, for sure, like diamonds, and one may need to go deeper to seek out and improve one's spiritual understanding of the gem found and through ardent dedication polish, so all may see the light therein. Dr. Roberts provided a meter that all may submerge and emerged through shared realization of not only what it means but also how we might each serve the Faith. Leaving these Gatherings with a renewed sense of purpose was, transformative.

* * *

I have and continue to experience the most affirming and transformative benefits of knowing and being linked to brothers of the Faith from all over the world. This aspect of the BMG has served to confirm and tangibly illustrate that our[s] is a worldwide religion open to all of humankind.

* * *

Attending the BMG for the first time in my Bahá'í life, I felt that this Faith, this Bahá'í Faith, was my Faith . . . it belonged to me and I was a part of it . . . This was also the first time that I experienced and felt the effect of continuous and intense prayer. I had never experienced this . . . The prayers that the brother[s] said at my first Gathering at the Louis Gregory Institute had a deep and profound impact on me. I was a relatively new Bahá'í at the time, so this was something new and different. I also liked the way this whole enterprise was focused on the Bahá'í writings; I later came to realize how important this focus would be.

* * *

I believe the BMG transformed how I felt about myself being Black. Even though I am light skinned, this issue never came up at the Gathering. Two other transformative items that happened while attending the BMG was the love I received from each participant. Never in my life have I received such joy from so many Black men. Finally, the amazing transforming item was the devotions. The spirit of prayer, song, drums, and music caused me to feel as though I was in the midst of my ancestors' village around a bonfire celebrating our heritage!

* * *

The Black Men's Gathering helped me realize my true identity as a Black man and a member of the Bahá'í Faith in such a way I do not believe any other space could have achieved. Through collective prayer, the sharing of my personal experiences, the loving physical embrace among Black men of various backgrounds, and the collective study of the guidance followed by plans of action, the Gathering allowed me to see and feel that I am just as important in this world as anyone else and that I not only have a great deal to contribute to it but a clear purpose and responsibility as a human being.

* * *

There were sixteen of us at the second Gathering, and I discovered that I, an African American man, was afraid of African American men. I realized this when I lost my fear of us during that Gathering. I'd heard so many times that I was not like the others that I believed it. It was the first time that I laughed with, sang with, and prayed with Black men. It was also the first time that [I] really laughed, really sang, and really prayed in my life. We even cried with each other, and I'd never seen us, nor have I ever cried in the presence of other men, especially Black men. When I returned home my wife notice[d] a change in me. I was much happier and not as quick-tempered. She urged me to attend the following year. The writings of Shoghi Effendi and the other letters from the Universal House of Justice became important and were for me to fulfill. . . . the Gathering made me look at myself and other Black men in ways that I'd never seen.

* * *

This was my first significant experience with a group of only Black men. It was my first realization that I was not the only Black man who carried around the weight of expectations, fear, and suspicions that others projected on me. I was allowed to unburden without confession just by being myself for the first time ever. As a result, my capacity as a husband, father, and servant of the Faith was enhanced in ways I had not even realized I needed. I became more congruent and coherent in all aspects of my life and no longer felt that I had to leave behind the collective experience of my community of origin. I also gained a new freedom to love and accept other Black men on their own terms. I feel all of this was made possible by the environment created by the Gathering, which was so centered in prayer and study of the word of God and which led to individual and collective acts of service based on the vision of the House of Justice.

* * *

The Gathering gave me solid examples of Black men tapping into their collective sense of nobility. I had examples to draw from my family and some men in the Conway, SC community, but never had I seen this nobility manifested by so many and in one location. Having these examples has aided me in my own life. I would draw strength from the stories of others. I could lean on their challenges and experiences for support.

I also learned how to be loving and supportive to other men outside of my family. The full embraces shared at the Gathering were unknown to me. I have also never seen grown men openly shed tears and weep without the least bit of shame, in public, around other men! Most importantly, the examples of these men has helped me to temper my anger and frustrations with the injustices still occurring in the U.S. and beyond. The Gathering has helped me to become a bit more patient, understanding, and forgiving not only with others, but with myself.

* * *

I had reservation[s] about the concept but decided to give it a try. My reservations were largely supplanted with a better understanding of the purposes, which I applaud. I think it served a useful purpose for the period in which it operated and in retrospect played a role in strengthening Black male involvement in the overall mission of the Faith.

* * *

Growing up as a Christian, I always felt less than Christian because I didn't feel the "Spirit" and speak in tongues. It has been my worship experience with the BMG that I have not felt "less than." I fully experienced a worship where there was a visual haze in the room. I heard one of the young brothers holler out, "Hallelujah!!!" Please understand, I felt a real Spirit of worship for the first time in my life at forty-five years old. That same spirit I took back to my community and "Yá Bahá'u'l-Abhá" is the Word on my lips along with "Hallelujah." My understanding of spiritual matters has been transformed. I'm having conversations [about Bahá'u'lláh] with my neighbors at home, my cousins at family gatherings, and brothers I grew up with. I feel a whole lot more courage in declaring my faith. Much to my surprise, people are saying: I know a little bit about that . . . tell me more.

* * *

What the Gathering did for me was to teach me how to pray and how to study the Guidance and then to align myself with the Guidance.

* * *

Prayer, I love the feeling of praying, but to pray in devotion with over one hundred Black men was and still is very awesome. The love of His Holiness Bahá'u'lláh and God with complete transformative power is something special to see and feel. I am clear that I was not the same brother before I had arrived at the Black Men's Gathering. Methinks, the local and central Gatherings brought me closer to hearkening to the Universal House of Justice['s] messages. This prepared me to want to act with improved vision in my home community and in my travels. "Prayer is the key," and currently the Universal House of justice messages are the unlocked lock source for me.

* * *

I had a very spiritual and emotional experience that I had not had since my churchgoing days, pre-1968. The calling out to God with heartfelt and intense fervor was overwhelming and inspiring; hearing the stories from the participants about their

Bahá'í life experiences and the depth of their longing to feel acceptance and serve the Faith was eye-opening. Studying the messages from the UHJ and learning from the brilliant and insightful points of views offered by everyone made me proud. Being at the forefront in the study and planning of putting those learnings into practice in my life [to] better serve my home community/cluster was enlightening, since I was never much of a planner. Realizing that my musical gifts could be powerful and useful tools in assisting in core activities, especially recording the verses of God and sharing them, has helped me find focus and purpose in service.

* * *

I learned to recognize, appreciate and love the breadth of the devotional expressions that were not confined to the "mainstream" Bahá'í Faith. At my first Gathering, I responded to the joyous expressions of worship internally with a "you cannot do that," but gradually I left behind my attachment to my expectations. Because of my experiences at the Gathering, I became capable of fully appreciating the beauty of different forms of worship and expressions of devotion. A specific example of my increased appreciation of [various devotional] approaches came at home where family members were engaged in traditional Catholic rosary service in Spanish. Listening with both heart and mind, I was able to engage the family in a discussion about the beauty of their worship and understanding of the affection held for Mary (I do not speak Spanish but understand some). The ability to truly love the different approaches and styles of worship has enabled me to connect to hearts in ways not possible before. Because of my increased understanding of the

range of devotion to God, I have become a more effective tutor
as well as more outwardly oriented.

* * *

My first and most memorable and transformative experience
occurred on the first day of the Gathering in Maine in 2005.
Shortly after leaving the dining hall the drumming was clear,
succinct, and live . . . The drumming, the rhythms, and the
music just took hold of me. Down to my very essence I felt the
spirit of the ancestors . . . spinning round in joyous embrace of
the proceeding . . . there was a sea of brothers of many hues and
shapes and sizes . . . and the expression of joy . . . emanated
from their beings . . . the room was pulsating with the spirits of
those present & those who have transitioned on . . . and they
were beaming with gladness!!!

* * *

I learned to listen to my Black brothers. For the first time in
my life, I participated in worship and prayers that took me to
a new realm of understanding the nonlinear meaning of my
Faith. I learned to have collective worship and follow that with
consultation with those around me to constructive thoughts of
doing God's will.

* * *

Before I was involved in the Gathering, I was largely inactive
in my community. Sure, I was on the Assembly and I came
to Feast, but I felt largely alienated from the teaching efforts.
When the House of Justice sent the Riḍván letters, they went

unread. I didn't feel they applied to me. Prayer didn't play an important role in my life in the Gathering, either; the writings were even less important. Each time I came together with the brothers, I learned why we prayed and read the writings. As I learned to be comfortable around men who shared my cultural roots and experiences, I healed spiritually. During the time of the Gathering, my parents departed from this earth, and I had issues with my immediate family and marriage. While I could have used these as excuses to not be active, I was active. I participated in my cluster agencies, served as institute coordinator, and started a couple of teaching projects where youth were posted as full-time coordinators. The most important thing I learned, though, was to read the guidance that the House of Justice gave each year. I also learned to pray, and I learned that Bahá'u'lláh cares that I am out there serving regardless of what people think. Lastly, I believe that the Gathering helped me transform where my service to the Faith came from. Before, I thought I served because others "let" me . . . but now my service comes from a love for the Blessed Beauty. When I get frustrated with the friends, I remind myself that the House of Justice gave us a challenge when it asked us to conclude the Gathering. How could I let down someone I love?

* * *

For me the love, support, and spirituality of the brothers showing fatherly light of love helped me, and so did spiritual education on how to help teach the Bahá'í Faith to mankind. Every year we studied the Five-Year Plan from the Universal House Justice, which helped me build my spiritual life to work hand-in-hand with my Local Spiritual Assembly, children, youth, and community. Enhancing the power, the quality of spiritual perception, and developing the capabilities and service to the community were transformative for me.

* * *

Although I was a Bahá'í for many years before I became engaged with the BMG, it was through this experience that I fully came to appreciate the importance of perusing the guidance from the Universal House of Justice and my personal responsibility for acting on such guidance. I learned to continually monitor my activity level in terms of "Am I doing the right things?" as opposed to "Am I doing things right?" Because of my involvement with the BMG, I learned how to really pray—without a time schedule or predetermined stopping point. I learned how to continue to pray until the Concourse on High descended and came to my assistance.

* * *

I thank God that we were able to have this experience. We have been able to share our innermost feelings without reservation. There was a special love and unity at the Gatherings, and I sincerely believe that when we returned to our communities, we shared this newfound love with everyone.

* * *

For the first time I recognized and felt deeply how a Faith that inspired me to accept all human beings as equal could deliver me from a profound sense of injustice towards people of color and the poor that made me arrogant, defensive, and riddled with anger. Being "moral and righteous" could be a refuge from truly being vulnerable, humble, and loving. One particular time sequence was quite instructive. At the first Gathering I attended, during the devotionals, some brothers began hitting soda bottles, shrieking, and stomping loudly. As much as I had sung and listened to music from the Black Diaspora, I felt these guys were just being too crude and out-of-control. I sat there assuming they were acting out, as I had seen some people do getting "happy" in church and seeming to fake it. Then as I glanced around the room packed with sweating Black men, I began to feel too removed, too judgmental, alien. Why not join these others and celebrate and pay homage to Bahá'u'lláh just as they are? I let myself go and persisted in not monitoring as much as entering the spirit of the moment, really taking in what was being shouted and sung and moaned and beat upon and thudded. I began weeping and felt pain drain from me. Forget the necessity to be an example, to not be "down home," to observe what propriety was in a religious sanctuary—because others were looking, could take tales back after the service, and too much emotionalism could be an indication that it was performance more than piety. I felt at one with God in ways I never had before, and I rarely analyze that or even repeat what I revealed above. But I KNEW what happiness had been found, for many others in many centuries and cultures when, perhaps, the mysterious, omnipresent soul soars.

* * *

BMG'S Influence on Members' Involvement in Local Bahá'í Community Building

To be clear, some BMG participants did not need the BMG to influence or initiate their involvement in their local Bahá'í community. Many were already active members of their local communities, and many served in various capacities on local, regional and national committees, agencies, and other institutions of Bahá'í service. However, regardless of their prior levels of service and involvement in their community, as a result of their experiences at the Gathering, these men played a key role in the development of their communities. To that end, the following is another question to which the participants were asked to respond.

Question: "To what extent did the BMG influence participants' involvement in their local Bahá'í community?"

I think after attending the BMG . . . and realizing that this is actually "my" Faith, I became more confident and involved. We started having firesides, which were more common then, in our home once a week. I got involved in the "Institute for the Healing of Racism" sessions that we held in Pullen Park in Raleigh, NC once a week. I served on the DTC (District Teaching Committee). Our local community had the city of Wilson, NC as a teaching goal, and as part of the DTC, I regularly visited various communities in our district in Eastern North Carolina.

* * *

My involvement in the Bahá'í community now is a labor of love. I am an Assembly member, a Ruhi tutor, and I conduct devotions and other activities that promote the Faith. I also volunteer for special programs held at the House of worship in Wilmette.

* * *

It reinforced my service to the Bahá'í Faith and gave me a clearer vision through [the] study of the messages of the Universal House of Justice. It renewed my enthusiasm for sharing the teachings of the Faith with friends, family members, and co-workers. I was appointed to serve as the Auxiliary Board for Protection during the last few years of the Gathering.

* * *

I had always been active in the [local Bahá'í] community, but what the Gathering did was help me be aligned with the messages from the UHJ. In addition, it made it OK for me to bring my culture to the community. Thus, it impacted the core activities that we were hosting, as well as Feast and holy days.

* * *

[G]etting a heads-up with the intense study and discussion undertaken by the BMG on the messages from the UHJ and their agencies helped me in my consultations with institutions and individuals locally, to plan and participate in these core activities.

* * *

Finding one's voice in the local Bahá'í community and developing the confidence to express it with frankness and honesty was among the many "gifts" the BMG bestowed upon its participants.

* * *

The BMG experience taught me how valuable my voice is to the conversations taking place at various levels in the Bahá'í community. It also helped me to embrace the soulfulness of African American music within the context of Bahá'í devotions and taught me that this contribution enriches community life.

* * *

In community gatherings / events / etc. the BMG helped me learn how to speak with candor and truthfulness in a loving manner. Everyone's voice and contribution was important.

* * *

It helped me pray openly, encourage my sister and fellow believers more; and gave me the administrative skills to both locate / read / understand the writings and to actively apply and teach as I never did before.

* * *

The BMG's focus on music, devotions, and the arts provided a channel through which Black male Bahá'í artists could express their talents in their local community with confidence. In one sense, the BMG legitimized their cultural and artistic expressions within the larger Bahá'í community.

* * *

I serve in any area of the Faith because of the BMG, especially in the performing Arts.

* * *

I became more active in my [Bahá'í] community and brought music and our method of sincere prayer to it. I was already on the Local Spiritual Assembly and an assistant to the Auxiliary Board, but I used the understanding gained at the Gathering to better fulfill my job in both.

* * *

I am still growing but being at the BMG gave me the confidence to teach the Cause. Now I teach the Faith through music, which I played and learned at the BMG as a form of worship.

* * *

I interacted with other Black male Bahá'ís who were involved with the Faith, and many of them were more active than I was. It was enlightening to learn how others were putting their faith into action with various activities and events. Studying the writings with other Black friends allowed a new and different perspective on those writings that I would not have gotten in an environment that included white friends (as well-meaning as they might be). In view of the society we live in today, to believe that the Bahá'í experience of Blacks and whites being exactly the same is pure denial. The BMG permitted a full expression of the Black experience in a safe environment, unfettered by having to accommodate others or being concerned about appearing to be a Black radical or racist.

* * *

Simply put, the Gathering gave me strength and recharged my batteries. I felt that my participation in the activities in my community helped me "earn" my way back to the Gathering, so I had something to share. I knew the brothers loved me unconditionally, so I didn't have to earn anything, but I wanted to aspire for something higher. Specifically, when called, I served within my cluster and helped it become an active "A" cluster. The confidence I found in the Gathering allowed me to do large campaigns where we coordinated the outreach to hundreds of apartments and homes. But key to my journey was my growing confidence to be able to share the Faith with Black men whom I encountered. I learned not to be afraid of doing that.

* * *

Through collective study of the Guidance and consultation on plans of action throughout the years attending the Gathering, not only have I developed a better appreciation for the messages from the House of Justice and a better understanding of the overall vision of the Plan, I feel my relationship with members of the Bahá'í community and involvement in activities have strengthened tremendously (teaching, attending devotions on a regular basis, and regularly participating in the core activities), and I am better able to articulate and deal with the challenges Bahá'í communities face with regard to racism and other forms of prejudice as we try to move forward.

* * *

My experience in the BMG literally propelled my most ardent desire to serve the Cause of God. I just had a "hard hat" longing to build and assist. Devotions were a natural fit, and I made a commitment to go through all the Ruhi books so that I could begin facilitating them.

* * *

[My son] attributed his "opportunity of becoming part of the [Area Teaching Committee] as well as the courage needed for going door-to-door . . ." to the BMG. All these activities, he wrote, were "Seeded by the gifts one received through the hallowed stays at Green Acre as well as Louhelen."

* * *

I am the chair of my LSA, am very active with JYSEP, and am a study circle tutor. I am learning, now, not to rush the consultative process. I'm learning to enrich the study circle experience so that the participants come away feeling that they truly learned something. I have plans to visit the learning site in NC to learn more strategies to enhance our JYSEP during the first week in April.

* * *

Many of the things I learned from my BMG experience and shared with Manchester Bahá'ís have been very enthusiastically and positively received. Much credit for this is given to our community members themselves. They were quite familiar with the mission of the BMG, were supportive of it, and, by being so close in proximity to Green Acre, they repeatedly took part in the festivities on the last day of the Gathering. As a result, my community established and enjoyed their own special relationship with the BMG—in particular, the BMG-style devotions. At the Nineteen Day Feasts, we now have more prayers set to music and much more singing. At the children's and junior youth classes, I have been called to teach a number of songs from the BMG. These songs were enthusiastically received; their favorite song, which they sing with great exuberance, is "Come on in the Room."

* * *

The influence of the BMG experience on participants' involvement in their Bahá'í local community was not limited to the individual BMG members themselves. Their wives also felt the stimulating influence of the BMG and joined their husbands in joint efforts to serve their local Bahá'í community. Below are just a few thoughts from various participants and their wives.

> The one thing I can say is that the Gathering motivated me to start a weekly devotional, which my wife and I have now been doing for close to ten years. We hold it every Wednesday, except on Feast and holy days. We had to cancel only five devotionals—three for weather and two for pilgrimage.

* * *

In fact, on Sundays . . . the local Gatherings were opened to all. We enjoyed the support of many, many people throughout the cluster. Our Bahá'í friends invited their friends, prepared food, and came to worship in the style of the Gathering (drums, etc.). Many of these participants are still active and asking when we are going to do it again.

* * *

Hosting an artful devotional at our home once a month has plunged me deeper into the reflective spirit world, side by side with others. This devotional has resulted in several enrollments in the Faith. I am happy that the Gathering urged us to take all the Ruhi books and do the practices. I have done so and now I am co-animating a junior youth class in the Oakland, California community. To continue to learn and serve with the splendid young people is good indeed. Within the structure of our junior youth class, we have a solid musical devotion on percussion instruments . . . We explore unique tonal vibrations that connect with our daily lives with more familiarity.

* * *

I definitely became far more involved with my wife in hosting regular devotionals.

* * *

Before his journey of transformation, my husband's engagement in Bahá'í community life . . . was limited to occasionally attending Feast, holy days, and LSA meetings. As a result of the relevant accompaniment of the BMG, he has studied several of the Ruhi courses and is now directly inspiring his sons, his daughter, his grandson, his household, and his community.

* * *

Contributions that the BMG made to the community-building process of the Faith.

Although the following question was asked of spouses, friends, and family members of former BMG participants, some of the responses were from the BMG participants themselves. This mix of responses offers rich insights into the BMG's contributions to the community building process of the Faith. For example, many BMG members mention how the BMG influenced their spiritual and emotional well-being, which in turn contributed to community building. Some participants listed a range of important contributions that assisted community building.

Question: "Now that the Black Men's Gathering has formally ended, what would you say were the most important contributions it made to the process of community building within the Faith?"

Personal spiritual enrichment; greater degree of focus; awareness of purpose; greater involvement in all Bahá'í activities; personal growth and development; greater insights into core activities; greater attentiveness, commitment, and contribution to all aspects of Bahá'í life.

* * *

Getting more involved in community activities and teaching the Faith.

* * *

Teaching the Cause to the Black community.

* * *

Deepening the brothers in the Faith gave us a sense of community, brought us together, made us bond together as a group, and increased our respect and trust in each other. In my community, we are the strongest group, and our belief in each other almost knows no bounds. Other "Blacks" have recognized this bond we share and have "joined" us in learning about the Faith and being a part of the group.

* * *

The BMG gave Black men a new status within the Bahá'í community. The profound implications of Bahá'u'lláh's pupil of the eye metaphor began to manifest itself within the community. The obvious presence of Black men in the forefront of the teaching work made the community more attractive to all seekers.

* * *

It created lifelong bonds between the brothers. With that engendered love, the brothers were more able to share their love with the Bahá'í community and with the community at large. There was more participation at Bahá'í events, Feasts, Assembly meetings, committee meeting, and meeting with other agencies of the Faith. The Faith has been strengthened by the active participation of Black men, and the American Bahá'í community's vision has been enhanced by utilization of the "Pupil of the Eye."

* * *

It provided us a safe place to go get reinvented and recharged. The transformation I experienced at each Gathering was a pillar in my life as a Bahá'í and is sorely missed. We live in an area where we are unmistakably the minority—Black Bahá'í men—and the BMG really helped to keep racism at bay, to minimize its impact. I miss the BMG.

* * *

I think the BMG empowered African American males to participate more fully in their communities, and it released an energy into the Bahá'í community that was missing. Every individual in the community should be empowered to fully participate in all activities of the Faith. In the words of the Guardian, Shoghi Effendi: "I hope, and indeed pray, that such a participation may not only redound to the glory, the power, and the prestige of the Faith, but may also react so powerfully on the spiritual lives, and galvanize to such an extent the energies of the youthful members of the Bahá'í community, as to empower them to display, in a fuller measure, their inherent capacities, and to unfold a further stage in their spiritual evolution under the shadow of the Faith of Baha'u'llah."*

* * *

Changing the nature of worship in the community; really refocusing on teaching in the community; reemphasizing bringing the Faith to people of color ("Love the Brothers"); sharpening the focus of the community on studying the messages of the

---

* Shoghi Effendi, *The Advent of Divine Justice,* ¶102.

402

House of Justice; and providing the inspiration for several outreach activities that have affected the nature of the Bahá'í community to this date all shaped community building. When it came to teaching the Faith, the BMG taught us to not let imaginary blockers get in the way of who and how we teach, so that we could "Be as unrestrained as the wind."

* * *

The Gathering taught me not to give up and that when the swords flash, go forward. It taught me that this is my Faith and that given the thinking toward Black men, we may sometimes want to give up and quit. From what I learned at the Gathering, I continued to participate in community-building projects. I joined a men's group, began creating relationships in my neighborhood with the young brothers, and began addressing the Feast in a constructive manner. I have had devotional gatherings at my home and still am, for that matter. I let the friends know that Black men are like the Bábís; we don't quit.

* * *

It increased the capacity of the Bahá'í community to accept greater diversity in its events and activities.

* * *

It empowered my community to believe in unity among the races and unity of the different ways of worshiping God in a devotional attitude.

* * *

It let all of us know we were all one, regardless of color. After our stay at Brighton Creek, we would come back to Tacoma and go out in teaching teams together in the community and share our faith!

* * *

I believe the veil was lifted and allowed the community to feel comfortable and welcoming.

* * *

Bringing the community together as a whole was the main contribution. Most saw the Gathering as very positive and an encouragement to everyone. They saw the empowerment that came to the brothers.

* * *

The BMG gave Black men a new status within the Bahá'í community. The profound implications of Bahá'u'lláh's pupil of the eye metaphor began to manifest itself within the community. The obvious presence of Black men in the forefront of the teaching work made community more attractive to all seekers.

* * *

If there was any doubt before, I think Black men are now confirmed in their contributions to the Faith.

* * *

The BMG built confidence and deepened the faith of those who participated. It enabled participants to see ways in which they could go back into their communities to serve, and it provided a long-lasting, caring support system. It brought new energy and new resources into the community by unlocking the potential of the participants. It gave the Bahá'í community another way of worshipping that expanded the diversity of the Faith and that resonates with so many of the populations the Faith seeks to serve.

* * *

It shined a light on the potential for healing and community that could be realized around the Revelation of Bahá'u'lláh when a group comes together. It helped these men become stronger and more engaged in their home communities.

* * *

It transformed the face of participation in the U.S. administrative order at several levels, including the National Convention and Local Spiritual Assemblies. It helped many Black men "own" the Faith in new ways.

* * *

The BMG, during its twenty-five years, gave African American men a safe place to be. It helped them develop spiritual strength and capacities that allowed them to face the daily attacks—which they all have received—with courage, faith, and love. It showed them their true nobility and gave them knowledge that no one can take from them. The BMG was the ark, the stronghold from which the brothers have now emerged ready and spiritually armed.

* * *

Diversity in worship! The identification of supporters (non-people-of-color)! The foundation and support of gentleness and patience, which enabled the brothers to share their experiences while living within dominant cultures.

* * *

The BMG gave the men a place where they could get together, be real, and encourage each other to be true to themselves, and therefore true to their Faith. They took ownership of their beliefs and gave each other permission to stand and be counted. The American Bahá'í community was in desperate need of the contributions of the African American Bahá'í community but instead of following the Guardian's instructions about the most challenging issue, there had been a serious lack of communications on both sides for decades. Everyone believed in Bahá'u'lláh, of course, but community gatherings were often a bit awkward, with people trying to fit in where they didn't always feel welcome or comfortable. Once the men at the BMG gave each other all that love, and they sang all those prayers together, and cried all those rivers, they went back to their communities and shared that love and sincerity, and it was irresistible! At first there were some people and some communities who were suspicious, but thank God for the Universal House of Justice's encouragement and sanctioning of the BMG, because then we as a community just had to accept it and learn from the whole process. Unity through diversity is so important, but before the BMG, we didn't have that . . . people were . . . just tolerating each other. We can't build community if everyone's not at the table, or if everyone's voice isn't heard, respected, and believed. Even if we don't always understand each other, we must still listen and believe another person when he or she shares his or her feelings. That's when we can begin to build community.

* * *

I think the devotionals left a lasting impression . . . the BMG caused a lot of Black men to get more involved than they had been in the past, which is a wonderful thing because they are an important part of the Bahá'í community and their voices needed to be heard.

* * *

The BMG's contributions to community building involved letting Black people know they are accepted and can belong to the Faith. It healed and transformed many individual Black men and women, and it lit a spark in the devotional style of Bahá'í communities across the globe. It raised awareness among white and other non-Black people of the spiritual needs of the Black community, and it showed them what role they can have to help feed those needs.

* * *

The BMG's role in community building was crucial and historical. The most oppressed and marginalized population in the US were chosen to become quickened and standard-bearers of this Cause. We won't fully understand, until some time has passed, how important the BMG has been for the transformation of the brothers of African descent, and through them the whole community. Clearly, the gift of the devotional gatherings, and the acute awareness of the primacy of authentic and nurturing relationships, are contributions. I think this movement is an integral part, maybe even the kernel, of how America is going to achieve its spiritual destiny.

* * *

I think the BMG galvanized thousands of Black males in our community who never felt they really had a role or a place in the community. . . . or they were confused about their role. I understand that Black males in America face a myriad of challenges that are unique and with which most white Bahá'í men or women, no matter how compassionate or open minded, can never hope to understand. These challenges needed to be addressed in a safe environment (frank, candid, honest, private). I was sorry to see the BMG end, but I trusted that the Universal House of Justice had its finger on the pulse of humanity and knew that it was time to move forward into a different format. I would like to see the graduates of the BMG continue its functions on a smaller scale in smaller venues, perhaps, while also keeping the spirit and energy flowing throughout the country. The BMG was a unique contribution to the American Bahá'í community, and I think only the African American Bahá'ís have that spirit and energy. It is a gift they bring to the world, and I am so grateful to be a recipient of this great bounty. They say in order to make an omelette, you have to break some eggs. Sometimes people have to be knocked out of their comfort zones to make changes. The BMG met with some resistance in the beginning (I heard the rumors), but obviously it was an essential need that had to be met, and it was met well. Somehow, we need to continue the progress that has been made. We can't lose the momentum. There are no laurels to rest upon. It brings joy to 'Abdu'l-Bahá whenever we are all gathered in love and unity.

* * *

Influence of the "BMG Devotional Style" on Community Devotions

The transformative influence of the BMG was not limited to only the participants, their friends, and their relatives. Over the years, when the brothers of the BMG returned to their respective Bahá'í communities, they brought with them a refreshing, energetic, and culturally unique devotional style, complete with drumming, new songs, and hourlong prayer sessions, along with a newfound courage to express them. Many local Bahá'í communities incorporated BMG devotional styles into their regular community devotions, and as a result, a significant cultural shift occurred in many local Bahá'í communities. The following comments speak to the BMG influence on community devotions.

Question: Did the "BMG Devotional Style" have any influence on your community devotions?

Yes, there was a significant change in the devotions in the Rochester and Buffalo area after a number of the brothers came back from the BMG. The devotions in this area were always blessed with lots of singing, but it was mostly saying a few prayers.

* * *

Yes, it gave the courage to introduce African American spiritu-als into the spiritual life of the community.

* * *

Oh my, yes! No more rushed prayers. BMG-style devotions allowed other friends to participate differently. Devotions were joyful celebrations. The local brothers became more galvanized and met (and continue to meet) at least once a week just to fortify themselves and to support local efforts in the commu-nity at large. They studied, prayed, sang, ate, and drummed together . . . and of course grew in love for one another as brothers.

* * *

Yes, most definitely, these authentic, spontaneous, heartfelt outpourings are so valued, especially in a community where the controlled formal ... tradition has been the norm.

* * *

It has changed the way the brothers who have been to the BMG hold a devotional. It always brings back memories of the BMG whenever I attend any devotional.

* * *

Yes, we routinely have BMG style devotionals that feature singing prayers, drumming . . . and requests from the community for this influence. The community members at least want those who attended the BMG to . . . add that unique character to the event.

* * *

It radically affected our community devotions, and they have never been the same since I introduced worship in the style of the Gathering many years ago. Worship is much freer than in the past and on a much more personal and meaningful level.

* * *

It added spirit, communal singing at regular frequency, and the learning of new songs . . . it also featured longer times for prayer during the devotional portions.

* * *

Yes, our community devotions are still held in BMG style with drums and the songs that were sung during the BMG. My father is definitely still a very strong participant in these devotions.

* * *

Nowadays, it seems that the word *devotional* means *the BMG devotional style.* So pervasive is this style of worship that everybody wants to hear the vibrancy of the drums. Whenever I hear "God is sufficient unto me," other versions of this chant pale in comparison to the style in which the Gathering rendered it. Even those not yet Bahá'ís are attracted to the drumming, the chanting, and the singing, all in BMG-style invocation.

* * *

They completely transformed the devotions and added such a deep and powerful dimension. I am addicted to their style of devotional gatherings. The first time I approached the cabin in Teaneck, N.J. from the parking lot, I could hear and feel the drumming, and it felt like the heartbeat of the world. I love the songs, I love how their simplicity allows for all of us to participate, and I love how they are based on the Word of God.

* * *

The influence has been enormous. The BMG devotional style brought an enormous energy to our community. It truly jump-started the activities in the early days of our cluster development several years ago. It brought in large, very diverse populations, and several people declared. Others, though they did not declare, have become part of the cluster activities—supporting other devotionals and other activities. Today, the BMG-style devotional is still very much in demand and is frequently incorporated into devotionals, holy day celebrations, meetings, unit conventions, workshops, and other activities. What was once perhaps considered a novelty is now the norm in our cluster.

* * *

When the members of the Oakland, CA community . . . brought the BMG devotional style to our Feast and other gatherings, it was greeted with open hearts and minds by most of the community. I think, because music and song have been a part of Oakland for some time and because of the presence of a number of African Americans on the LSA and in other communities, there was a platform to accept these beautiful members of our community and the gift of the BMG.

* * *

We white folk are still trapped in the tendency to sit still and be quiet in "church"—a holdover from Puritan Protestant ethics perhaps?—and we desperately need the energy and powerful voices the BMG brings to devotional worship. We NEED the contributions of these voices. There is a place for silence and stillness, but there is also the need to "Make a joyful noise unto the Lord!" Since the influence of the BMG, we have begged to include drumming in all our devotional programs and always encourage people of all other cultures to express their culture in whatever style is comfortable to them.

* * *

I think the community tries to feel the spirit of the BMG style of worship because it took them to feelings they normally would not feel or witness at Feasts and other functions.

* * *

The singing of prayers had an influence on soulful elevation. In my world travels, I noticed and had been told that the sacred intonations had a similar effect on people of diverse backgrounds. I never tried to intone anything, but through the experience of the BMG, I feel comfortable singing alone. While pioneering and living in Germany, I was asked to join the National Bahá'í Choir and had the honor of singing with the choir at the 100-year celebration of the Bahá'í Faith in

Germany. If it had not been for the BMG, this would have never happened, and for that I will be forever grateful.

* * *

Absolutely! When I returned to Bermuda, whenever the Black men hosted the Sunday morning spiritual gatherings at the Bahá'í Center, we always did it BMG style—lots of prayers and lots of drumming. Initially we hosted a BMG-style fireside every Thursday night at the Bahá'í Center. Now we still host a fireside every Thursday night at the Center, but we just don't refer to it as the BMG Fireside—rather, just a Bahá'í fireside. Participating in the BMG gave us a presence back in Bermuda. Whenever we did things, there was this expectation of ourselves and the rest of the community that there was going to be a great spirit and energy to the activity being hosted.

* * *

The wives of the BMG members were among the first to support their husbands' involvement in the BMG and to appreciate how the Gathering influenced their husbands' spiritual and emotional well-being. As explained by one BMG member: "When I finally decided to ask Billy for permission to attend the Gathering the first year it took place at Green Acre, and was accepted, my wife was ecstatic. She declared, 'You need this!' She even paid for my plane fare. I came back a changed man; my name had been changed."

Seeing the influence of the BMG on their husbands explains why some wives expressed regret when the BMG ended. As one wife wrote,

Since the privilege and protection of the gathering of these BMG souls was officially ended, I have worn the Black BMG bracelet as a symbol of hope for its reinstatement and return. I share the following observation derived from my personal and professional perspective . . . The USA is in dire need of the "pupil of the eye" to reach the next level of growth. We will not only not make "entry by troops" without it, we will not sustain any meager progress toward it.

Another wife shared how her husband was adjusting to the transition:

It's as if now the plant (an organic being that requires purposeful sun, rain, and nutrient soil) struggles to withstand the wind, snow and erosion of soil alone. This weekend he assisted me by serving as a shuttle driver for a large gathering of Bahá'ís (related to my work), and his soul was revived by the chance presence and stalwart love of four BMG souls who happened to be on his bus. His spirit came alive again, and for another rare and precious moment, his spirit was lifted and the radiance of that spirit directly impacted the event as he literally led a call-response prayer at one of my event devotionals. It was completely spontaneous and illuminating.

Other brothers shared the following reactions:

I really love sharing my evolving music on my bass clarinet, saxophone and percussion instruments in the Bahá'í and general community. I have become an improved person and artist through practicing, serving artistically, and connecting with the inner reality of many people over the decades. I credit much of the clear focus of my learnings from being a participant of the Black Men's Gathering, which has humbled my heart and soul more. Smiles . . .

* * *

From my first BMG in South Carolina, I felt that the creation of the Gathering was one of those foreordained movements that was necessary to address the humiliation of the spirit of men and people of African descent in America and the West in general. The BMG taught me that "My calamity is My Providence." This means that out of the blood, sweat, tears, and broken spirits of slavery, imprisonment, and exile, a new "race" of men can be born. In America, there is no Black tribe, but a Black people or race—a "race" no longer constrained by tribal ties, language, and other limitations, but immersed, freed and resilient, with the revelation of oneness proclaimed by Bahá'u'lláh, so that we can truly "overcome" and be a beacon of light for all of humanity. "Thy kingdom come; thy will be done on earth as it is in heaven."

* * *

I do not think of nor did I experience the BMG as being primarily like a cocoon. The BMG did provide a "safe" place to grow one's spiritual understanding and service. The large number of teaching trips to various localities in sub-Saharan Africa, travel teaching and visiting in Brazil, and in the Arctic—the land of the Inuit / Eskimo in Nunuvat—are evidence that belie the notion of "cocoon-ness." There were the brothers who, upon returning to their home communities, set up drumming sessions in devotional gatherings, held firesides, spoke at public meetings, worked with children and youth in their communities, and were inspired to go on pilgrimage! Outside my immediate family and a few white friends, there continues to be no place else to share my experience with others who can and do understand—from the heart of their own experience, not solely intellectually—what it means to be a Black man. I would not be surprised if some of the brothers feel isolated and alone, and why not? I have found it impossible to deeply share my heartfelt experiences as a Black man within the community. Why! Because the so-called "friends" tend to listen from the perspective of their own experience—which is radically different from mine. There are no forums for such careful conversations with Bahá'ís in general where I live—whether it concerns new immigrants, First Nations, Metis, Inuit people, or Blacks who are descendants of settlers from the U.S. in the late 1800s. Anything with which our white brethren feel discomfort is avoided. So, we "live," we pray, and we serve the Faith under the guise of unity—but it is the unity of the majority community members that is predicated on their comfort level. I pray that this situation will change soon.

* * *

I believe with all my heart that the BMG was a necessary space that not only has improved the ability of Black men to realize their true identity as servants of the Cause but has improved the overall "culture" of the American Bahá'í community as a whole due to its undeniable effect and influence.

* * *

I cannot help but miss the warm camaraderie, friendship and wonderful times we had at the BMG.

* * *

One of the songs that we sang was "[I know I've] been changed," and I was changed. It made me a better man, a better artist, and a better Bahá'í.

* * *

I thank God for having been allowed the unique and wonderful privilege of attending the Gathering. There was no place before or since where I could raise my voice in praise of God with such freedom in the company of others. The challenge now is to foster communities everywhere that can create such an environment for the present and future generations of Black boys and men so that they can be allowed to contribute their share to building a better world.

* * *

I am actively working to meet others who want to participate in the core activities. I know the brothers are only a phone call away, but I miss the fellowship of the Gathering. With my eyes on the future, I have resolved to meet Black folks when I can and introduce them to the Faith. . . . I remember what Dr. Roberts told Ted Jefferson when he had a similar issue with his community . . . "You have to love the Bahá'ís, Ted." I've interpreted that to mean go and serve and don't get distracted.

* * *

The Black Men's Gathering has played a critical role in bringing me closer to Bahá'u'lláh. It was at the Gathering that I first engaged in intense prayer and study of the messages from the Universal House of Justice. I had never been in any environment that was more conducive to assisting me in becoming closer to the Words of God. I developed a deeper appreciation for the Universal House of Justice through the hearts of my dear brothers, who demonstrated a burning desire to be in service to this most glorious Cause. I am forever in debt to the Universal House of Justice for allowing the Black Men's Gathering to be a vessel through which I found a deeper and more meaningful path of service to Bahá'u'lláh.

* * *

An African / American woman asked me a question. She knew of the BMG. She was not a Bahá'í. She asked me, "If all of you brothers were having such a good time and a good experience bonding together for so many years, how is it that someone or some other group of people from outside of the country can tell you all that you all cannot get together anymore?" She was making a reference to someone other than ourselves determining our fate. Is not that what we have struggled for, for so many centuries—self-determination? My own perspective is that the BMG is too powerful of a concept to just go away quietly. The ideals of brothers sitting and bonding in prayer, in spirit—with a little bit of tomfoolery in good taste—will continue to live on. There are too many brothers here and abroad who already have the concept in their mind of a BMG, whether they have heard of it or not. I rarely have had a conversation with any brother who did not get a sparkle in his eye when the idea of Black men coming together for the betterment of themselves and families and mankind was mentioned. Charity begins at home and spreads abroad. Yes, it is the spirit of the African man / woman that causes the spirit of another African man / woman to be quickened—not just here but across the entire planet. But before we can spread the spirit of unity abroad, much work is needed here among the youth of African ancestry. The consciousness of the BMG is still present, and it can be likened to a caterpillar now, evolving in the quiet places of our minds. The earth has been impregnated with the concept of the BMG, and it will return in perhaps another form or venue, but it will return! The concept, if we really think on it, is one of the most powerful concepts on the planet at this time.

* * *

In the beginning, I didn't understand why the Gatherings had to end. They seemed so greatly needed. However, I never questioned the House of Justice. After prayer, it's easy to see that we are all needed in the current teaching effort.

* * *

When the Universal House of Justice called for the BMG to draw to a close, it explained that it was now time for the men of the Gathering to take the wonderful body of learning they had acquired over the twenty-five-year period out to share with the larger community. I understood completely. The House is divinely guided and inspired. Hence, this definitely was the right thing to do. Still, I was sad for quite a while. I missed the BMG terribly. But now, whenever I reflect, I am at peace and filled with gratitude and appreciation for what I experienced at the many Gatherings I attended. I felt the joy of traveling to the African continent in obedience to the House of Justice during the Four Year Plan, and the warm love and camaraderie of the brothers. I know this feeling of euphoria will be with me forever because I realize that even though the BMG has come to a close, it is not dead. It definitely is alive, well and kicking inside all of the brothers as a source of inspiration. So now, my focus is on my community, and full speed ahead!

* * *

I am just so very grateful to have had the opportunity to meet so many wonderful Bahá'í brothers who were so committed to the advancement of the Faith in their respective communities. Being around these enthusiastic souls was contagious and made me want to do even more in my own community. To be honest, I was most disappointed to see the BMG, as we knew and experienced it, come to an end. However, I do fully understand and accept the will and directive of the Universal House of Justice spurring us on to higher challenges and horizons. The BMG will always occupy a very special place in my heart. It was a very special experience.

* * *

After supporting and encouraging the BMG for twenty-five years, in 2011 the Universal House of Justice asked the organization to draw to a close. Most of the BMG participants accepted this guidance, but not without some understandable sorrow. While they missed the annual BMG, they knew it was time to move on and were more than prepared to help other brothers do so gracefully. Others, no less faithful and obedient to the guidance, struggled emotionally as they made the transition. Fortunately, they had been prepared for this transition by the well-established BMG practice of studying the guidance and encouraging brothers to return to their local Bahá'í communities and participate in and support the core activities. There are countless examples of participants of the Gathering that heeded the call of the Supreme Body to "Let the well-prepared army you have assembled advance from its secure fortress to conquer the hearts of your fellow citizens."

The following question was designed to allow former BMG members and their spouses, friends, or family member, to share comments and thoughts that might still linger in their minds. The responses reflected a range of emotions. Some participants offered much gratitude to the BMG and to Billy and the institutions of the Faith for supporting the BMG for over twenty-five years, while others expressed regret that the BMG has ended. As with other responses, the participants' wives, other family members, and friends also shared their final comments about the BMG. Several wives of BMG members simply said, "Thank you!"

* * *

Question: Are there any other comments / thoughts that you would like to share?

Thank God for that process! Thank God that Counselor William Roberts took the initiative to bring those men together to pray and encourage each other. It was truly historical and heaven-sent.

* * *

I would like to send much love and appreciation to Billy Roberts and to the many other brothers who worked so long and hard to bring this idea to fruition, by the grace of God!!

* * *

I'd really like to thank the Bahá'í Faith for saving my life and Dr. Billy Roberts and the BMG for giving me a chance to feel spiritual love and fellowship again with a group of seekers, for the grace and strength of God's love, and for the holiness of God's Messengers for this age. I would also like to thank Bahá'u'lláh, the Báb, 'Abdu'l-Bahá, Shoghi Effendi, and the Universal House of Justice.

* * *

To me the BMG was a fantastic learning experience.

* * *

The safety of the environment provided the ONE place on this planet—dramatic statement, I know—where he could achieve a comfort, understanding, and healing that was critical for his advancement on this earthly place. His soul was impacted on the FIRST visit and continued with every visit with other souls. The BMG souls did for him what his very family, and wife, could not.

* * *

One of the great pleasures of the BMG for me was how much I laughed.

* * *

The Black Men's Gatherings have served a wonderful purpose by giving all of us, I think, a deeper understanding of the meaning of what Bahá'u'lláh meant by "the pupil of the eye." The Gatherings were brilliantly conceived, spiritually charged, and meaningful. Yet, I concur with the wisdom of the Universal House of Justice as to their completion. The purpose is served and has been particularly relevant to those of us who grew up in the abasement of a segregated South and a demeaning America. As a result, God willing, we are now more healed and more ready for a new day of service.

* * *

The BMG has taught me how to love unconditionally. I am thankful from the bottom of my heart that God has blessed me to be part of the wonderful experience I received from the BMG. Priceless.

* * *

I'm very blessed for having the BMG experiences, and I treasure it almost as much as going on pilgrimage. Both were transforming, confirming, and edifying.

* * *

The BMG has surely been a life-changing experience, and I will be eternally grateful for the blessings bestowed upon me. I am often uncomfortable talking about things I have done for the Faith. My service to the Faith is a blessing to me and my family. It's about what the Faith has done for me, and not the other way around.

* * *

I am an eternal member of the BMG.

* * *

My best most lasting and trustful friends were forged through the several travel-teaching trips I was fortunate enough to participate in. Additionally, the Gatherings, both state / regional and national-based, served to create and reintroduce the concept of "trust" in me. This trust is a type of longed-for humanity that everyone needs but that we as people of color are taught to hide to survive. I will forever be grateful to those who were led to formulate and perpetuate the BMG.

NOTES

1987

1. Colin McCord and Harold P. Freeman, "Excess Mortality in Harlem," *New England Journal of Medicine* 322 (1990):173–77, DOI: 10.1056/NEJM199001183220306.

2. Fox, James Alan, and Marianne W. Zawitz, "Homicide Trends in the United States," Bureau of Justice Statistics, https://bjs.ojp.gov/content/pub/pdf/htius.pdf.

3. Cooper, Alexia, and Erica L. Smith, "Homicide Trends in the United States, 1980–2008," U.S. Department of Justice, Bureau of Justice Statistics, https://bjs.ojp.gov/content/pub/pdf/htus8008.pdf.

4. Bonczar, Thomas P, "Prevalence of Imprisonment in the U.S. Population, 1974–2001," Bureau of Justice Statistics Special Report, August 2003, NCJ 197976, Table 5, In 1986, 9.9% of Black adult males were incarcerated in a state or federal prison, https://bjs.ojp.gov/content/pub/pdf/piusp01.pdf.

5. U.S. Census Bureau, Statistical Abstract of the United States: 1999. In 1985, 11.2% Black males had completed a 4-year degree or more. https://www2.census.gov/library/publications/1999/compendia/statab/119ed/tables/sec04.pdf.

6. Venters, "Hand in Hand. Race, Identity, and Community Development among South Carolina's Bahá'ís, 1973–1979," in Bramson, *The Bahá'í Faith and African American History,* pp. 143, 147.

1990
1. Luke 2:49.

1996
1. Universal House of Justice, *Turning Point: Selected Messages of the Universal House of Justice and Supplementary Materials, 1996–2006*, p. 59.

2. 'Abdu'l-Bahá, *Selections from the Writings of 'Abdu'l-Bahá*, no. 76.1.

3. *The Four Year Plan and the Twelve Month Plan, 1996–2001: Summary and Achievements*, p. 40.

4. "The Year in Review," *The Bahá'í World, 1996–97*, p. 58.

5. Ibid.

1997
1. 'Abdu'l-Bahá, *Will and Testament of 'Abdu'l-Bahá*, p. 14.

1998
1. Letter from Dr. William Roberts "to the fifteen Men of African Descent who are responding to the Universal House of Justice from the BMG," January 4, 1998.

2. Letter dated 8 August 1996 from the Universal House of Justice to the National Spiritual Assembly of the Bahá'ís of the United States.

1999
1. "The Year in Review," *The Bahá'í World, 1998–99*, p. 92.

2. Riḍván Letter "To the followers of Bahá'u'lláh in North America, in Alaska, Canada, Greenland and the United States," in *Turning Point: Selected Messages of the Universal House of Justice and Supplementary Materials, 1996–2006*, p. 59.

2000
1. *The Four Year Plan and the Twelve Month Plan, 1996–2001: Summary and Achievements*, p. 40.

2001

1. *The Independent*, distributed by AllAfrica Global Media, https://allafrica.com/stories/200101150049.html. Subscription required.

2. Email dated August 18, 2000 from the Universal House of Justice to Members of the 14th Annual Black Men's Gathering.

3. Report from Billy Roberts to the Universal House of Justice dated December 22, 2001 of the travel-teaching visit to Liberia by the BMG.

4. Ibid.

5. Ibid.

6. Ibid.

7. Ibid.

8. Ibid.

9. Letter dated January 1, 2011 from the Universal House of Justice to the Bahá'ís of the World.

2003

1. E-mail dated August 7, 2003 from the Universal House of Justice to the Participants in the Black Men' Gathering.

2. E-mail dated August 7, 2003 from Billy Roberts to the International Teaching Center, Haifa, Israel.

3. Report dated February 10, 2004, from the Black Men's Gathering to the Universal House of Justice.

2005

1. Letter dated April 21, 1996 from the Universal House of Justice to the Bahá'ís of the World.

2. Bahá'u'lláh, in *Bahá'í Prayers: A Selection of Prayers Revealed by Bahá'u'lláh, the Báb and 'Abdu'l-Bahá*, p. 19.

3. Report by Stephanie Vaccaro. Photographs by Mike Relph, https://news.bahai.org/story/409/?storyid=409.

SELECTED LETTERS

1990

- Letter from the Black Men's Gathering to the Universal House of Justice, July 29, 1990.

1991

- Letter from Billy Roberts to the Participants of the Gathering, May 21, 1991.

- Letter from Black Men's Gathering to the Universal House of Justice, July 28, 1991.

- Letter from the Universal House of Justice to Billy Roberts and the Black Men's Gathering, August 6, 1991.

1992

- Letter from the Universal House of Justice to Billy Roberts, August 3, 1992.

1993

- Letter from Billy Roberts to the Participants of the Black Men's Gathering, April 18, 1993.

1995

- Letter from the Black Men's Gathering (West) to the Universal House of Justice, February 19, 1995.

- Letter from the Black Men's Gathering (West) to the National Spiritual Assembly of the Bahá'ís of the United States, February 19, 1995.

- Letter from the Universal House of Justice to Billy Roberts, March 7, 1995.

- Letter from Billy Roberts to the Participants of the Black Men's Gathering (West), March 8, 1995.

- Letter from Billy Roberts to the Universal House of Justice, March 8, 1995.

- Letter from the Black Men's Gathering to the National Spiritual Assembly of the Bahá'ís of the United States, July 30, 1995.

- Letter from the National Spiritual Assembly of the Bahá'ís of the United States to the Black Men's Gathering, August 2, 1995.

- Letter from Billy Roberts to the Participants of the 9th Annual Black Men's Gathering, August 19, 1995.

1996

- Letter written on behalf of the Universal House of Justice to Billy Roberts, August 8, 1996.

- Letter from the Universal House of Justice to the National Spiritual Assembly of the Bahá'ís of the United States, August 8, 1996.

- Letter from Billy Roberts to the Participants of the Black Men's Gathering, December 2, 1996.

1997

- Letter from the National Spiritual Assembly of the Bahá'ís of the United States to the Black Men's Gathering, August 9, 1997.

1999

- Letter from the Spiritual Assembly of the Bahá'ís of City of New York to the Black Men's Gathering, July 15, 1999.

2000

- Letter from the National Spiritual Assembly of the Bahá'ís of the Nigeria to the Black Men's Gathering, February 14, 2000.

- Letter from the National Spiritual Assembly of the Bahá'ís of the Zambia to the Representatives of the Black Men's Gathering, February 15, 2000.

2001

- Letter from the Black Men's Gathering to the National Spiritual Assembly of the Bahá'ís of the United States, July 20, 2001.

- Letter from Billy Roberts to the Participants of the Black Men's Gathering, December 14, 2001.

2002

- Letter from Billy Roberts to the Universal House of Justice, January 11, 2002.

- Letter written on behalf of the Universal House of Justice to Billy Roberts, January 15, 2002.

- Letter from Black Men's Gathering to the Universal House of Justice, July 19, 2002.

- Letter from the Universal House of Justice to the Black Men's Gathering, July 25, 2002.

2003

- Letter from Black Men's Gathering to the Universal House of Justice, July 19, 2003.

- Letter from Black Men's Gathering to the Continental Board of Counselors for the Americas, July 19, 2003.

- Letter from the Universal House of Justice to the Black Men's Gathering, July 28, 2003.

- Letter from Counselor Gene Andrews to the Black Men's Gathering, July 31, 2003.

- Letter from Billy Roberts to the National Spiritual Assembly of the Bahá'ís of Trinidad and Tobago, August 7, 2003.

- Letter from the International Teaching Centre to Billy Roberts, August 12, 2003.

- Letter from the National Spiritual Assembly of the Bahá'ís of Trinidad and Tobago to Billy Roberts, August 19, 2003.

- Letter from the Regional Bahá'í Council of the Southern States to the Black Men's Gathering, August 29, 2003.

- Letter from Billy Roberts to the Regional Bahá'í Council of the Western States, September 24, 2003.

- Report dated February 10, 2004, to the Universal House of Justice from the Black Men's Gathering.

2004
- Letter from Counselor Stephen Birkland to the Black Men's Gathering, January 31, 2004.

2005
- Letter from the Spiritual Assembly of the Bahá'ís of San Diego to the Black Men's Gathering, May 26, 2005.

- Letter from the Black Men's Gathering to the National Spiritual Assembly of the Bahá'ís of Australia, July 16, 2005.

- Letter from the Black Men's Gathering to the National Spiritual Assembly of the Bahá'ís of France, July 16, 2005.

- Letter from the Universal House of Justice to the Black Men's Gathering, August 3, 2005.

- Letter from Counselor Gene Andrews to the Black Men's Gathering, August 3, 2005.

2007
- Letter from Billy Roberts to the Participants of the Black Men's Gathering, May 29, 2007.

- Letter from the National Spiritual Assembly of the Bahá'ís of Jamaica to the Jamaican Men's Gathering, October 5, 2007.

2008
- Letter from the Black Men's Gathering Leadership Forum to the Universal House of Justice, July 19, 2008.

- Letter from the Black Men's Gathering to the National Spiritual Assembly of the Bahá'ís of the United States, July 19, 2008.

2009

- Letter from Black Men's Gathering Young Adult's Forum to the Universal House of Justice, July 18, 2009.

2011

- Letter from the Black Men's Gathering to the National Spiritual Assembly of the Bahá'ís of Bermuda, July 16, 2011.

- Letter from the National Spiritual Assembly of the Bahá'ís of Bermuda to the Black Men's Gathering, August 11, 2011.

- Letter from the Black Men's Gathering to the Universal House of Justice, July 16, 2011.

- Letter from the Universal House of Justice to the Black Men's Gathering, August 28, 2011.

- Letter written on behalf of the Universal House of Justice to the Black Men's Gathering, December 4, 2011.

- Letter from Billy Roberts to the Participants of the Black Men's Gathering, December 23, 2011.

2012

- Letter from the National Spiritual Assembly of the Bahá'ís of the United States to the Black Men's Gathering, January 13, 2012.

- Letter from the Central States Regional Black Men's Gathering to the Universal House of Justice, January 15, 2012.

- Letter from the Northeastern Regional Black Men's Gathering to the Universal House of Justice, January 29, 2012.

- Letter from the Southeastern Regional Black Men's Gathering to the Universal House of Justice, February 5, 2012.

- Letter from the Western States Regional Black Men's Gathering to the Universal House of Justice, February 19, 2012.

- Letter from the Southwestern States Regional Black Men's Gathering to the Universal House of Justice, February 26, 2012.

- Letter written on behalf of the Universal House of Justice to the Regional Black Men's Gatherings, April 15, 2012.

- Letter written on behalf of the Universal House of Justice to Billy Roberts, April 15, 2012.

- Letter from the National Spiritual Assembly of the Bahá'ís of the United States to the American Bahá'í Community, June 18, 2012.

BIBLIOGRAPHY

Works of 'Abdu'l-Bahá
Selections from the Writings of 'Abdu'l-Bahá. Wilmette, IL: Bahá'í
    Publishing, 2010.
The Will and Testament of 'Abdu'l-Bahá. Wilmette, IL: Bahá'í Pub-
    lishing Trust, 1990.

Works of the Universal House of Justice
*Turning Point: Selected Messages of the Universal House of Justice and
    Supplementary Materials, 1996–2006.* West Palm Beach, FL:
    Palabra Publications, 2006.

Compilations
Bahá'u'lláh, the Báb, 'Abdu'l-Bahá. *Bahá'í Prayers.* Wilmette, IL:
    Bahá'í Publishing Trust, 2002.

Other Works
Bramson, Loni, ed. *The Bahá'í Faith and African American History.*
    New York: Lexington Books, 2019.
Landry, Frederick, McMurray, Harvey, and Richard W. Thom-
    as. *The Story of the Bahá'í Black Men's Gathering: Celebrating
    Twenty-Five Years, 1987–2011.* Wilmette, IL: Bahá'í Publish-
    ing Trust, 2011.
Momen, Wendi. *A Basic Bahá'í Dictionary.* Oxford: George Ronald,
    1989.
The Bahá'í World, 1996–97. Haifa, Israel: Bahá'í World Center,
    1998.

The Bahá'í World, 1998–99. Haifa, Israel: Bahá'í World Center, 2000.

The Four Year Plan and the Twelve Month Plan, 1996–2001: Summary and Achievements. Haifa, Israel: Bahá'í World Center, 2002.

Venters, Louis. *A History of the Bahá'í Faith in South Carolina.* Charleston, SC: The History Press, 2019.